SAVING
OUR STUDENTS
SAVING
OUR SCHOOLS

SECOND EDITION

This work is dedicated to the memory of
America A., Angie P., Ben S., and Jacey Jo B., kids no longer with us . . .
to Marian Pritchett and to everyone who helps children at risk.

How many effective schools would you have to see to be persuaded of the educability
of poor children? If your answer is more than one, then I submit that you have
reasons of your own for preferring to believe that basic pupil performance derives from
family background instead of school response to family background. . . . We can, whenever
and wherever we choose, successfully teach all children whose schooling is of interest to us.

—Ron Edmonds

SAVING
OUR STUDENTS
SAVING
OUR SCHOOLS

50 Proven Strategies for Helping
Underachieving Students
and Improving Schools

Robert D. Barr
William H. Parrett

SECOND EDITION

CORWIN PRESS
A SAGE Publications Company
Thousand Oaks, CA 91320

For information:

Corwin Press
A Sage Publications Company
2455 Teller Road
Thousand Oaks, California 91320
www.corwinpress.com

Sage Publications Ltd.
1 Oliver's Yard
55 City Road
London EC1Y 1SP
United Kingdom

Sage Publications India Pvt. Ltd.
B 1/I 1 Mohan Cooperative
   Industrial Area
Mathura Road, New Delhi 110 044
India

Sage Publications Asia-Pacific Pte. Ltd.
33 Pekin Street #02–01
Far East Square
Singapore 048763

Printed in the United States of America.

Library of Congress Cataloging-in-Publication Data

Barr, Robert D.
Saving our students, saving our schools: 50 proven strategies for helping underachieving students and improving schools/Robert D. Barr, William H. Parrett.—2nd ed.
      p. cm.
Includes bibliographical references and index.
ISBN 978-1-4129-5792-2 (cloth)
ISBN 978-1-4129-5793-9 (pbk.)

   1. Children with social disabilities—Education—United States. 2. Teenagers with social disabilities—Education—United States. 3. Problem children—Education—United States. 4. Problem youth—Education—United States. 5. School improvement programs—United States. I. Parrett, William. II. Title.

LC4091.B37 2008
371′9—dc22   2007029946

This book is printed on acid-free paper.

07   08   09   10   11   10   9   8   7   6   5   4   3   2   1

Acquisitions Editor:	Hudson Perigo
Editorial Assistant:	Jordan Barbakow
Production Editor:	Veronica Stapleton
Copy Editor:	Carla Freeman
Typesetter:	C&M Digitals (P) Ltd.
Proofreader:	Kristin Bergstad
Indexer:	Molly Hall
Cover Designer:	Michael Dubowe
Graphic Designer:	Lisa Riley

Contents

Preface

The most urgent need in public education today is to help teachers, administrators, and policymakers become more effective in the education of underachieving students. Until a decade ago, the task of teaching all of these students was considered virtually impossible. Previously, a number of major research studies concluded that schools could have little or no positive impact on these students. Now, of course, that has all changed. Research over the past fifteen years has completely reversed the earlier flawed conclusions, and we now know that all students can and will learn and that an effective school can overcome the debilitating effects of poverty and dysfunctional families. This research led a number of states and finally the federal government to establish policy requiring annual progress toward closing achievement gaps, high academic standards for all students, testing designed to assess student achievement, highly qualified teachers for all students, and the monitoring of school performance through mandated disaggregation of data. Recently, studies of high-poverty/high-performing schools have identified thousands of elementary, middle, and high schools where all students now are achieving high academic standards. As of early 2007, while the achievement gaps persist nationally at the high school and middle school levels, gaps have been significantly closed at the elementary school level.

Still, there is so much yet to be accomplished before all students are learning effectively and achieving proficiency. There remain legions of low-performing and failing classrooms, schools, and school districts. Facing an escalating series of increasingly challenging federal and state sanctions, educational leaders and policymakers are scrambling to identify interventions and research-based strategies that can be successfully implemented by teachers, parents, and administrators.

The good news in all of this is that a growing body of high-quality research is quickly moving the field of education toward a science of teaching and learning. This book represents a comprehensive effort at collecting, analyzing, and summarizing what we know about the effective education of low-performing students. Fifty strategies have been identified that relate directly to improved achievement for the most needy, demanding, and challenged of our students. We know that these students will learn effectively, and we understand more and more about how to achieve the demanding goal of effectively teaching every one of them.

Research has also continued to emerge concerning "what we know," "what works," "best practices," and how many low-performing schools have "turned around" to become models of high achievement. Research summaries have been published regarding best instructional practices and programs for poor and culturally diverse students. Digesting and interpreting this material has been a challenge—yet the authors believe that the fifty strategies presented in this book represent a unique and timely contribution to educators working to improve the performance of underachieving, low-performing students.

As part of a final set of external reviews by a number of practitioners and researchers for the original edition, our good friend Joe Nathan, of the Hubert Humphrey Institute at the University of Minnesota, provided an invaluable critique, which in turn led to a number of improvements and a better, more comprehensive product. Our work on both editions of this book has represented the proverbial "changing a flat tire while the car was moving" enterprise.

The authors wish to thank a number of nationally recognized scholars and educational leaders for significant contributions to this book. The work of these individuals and their colleagues is so important to the focus of this book that we have chosen in several cases to use "their words." We wish to express our appreciation to these individuals and their publishers for permission to share this important work. Teachers and administrators are encouraged to explore their complete publications in great detail. Collectively, their landmark works are as important in this era to the improvement of schools and the lives of children as any currently available. These works include Rick Stiggins, *Student-Involved Classroom Assessment*; Robert Marzano, Debra Pickering, and Jane Pollock, *Classroom Instruction That Works: Research-Based Strategies for Increasing Student Achievement*; Mike Schmoker, *Results: The Key to Continuous School Improvement*, 2nd Edition; Kati Haycock, *Dispelling the Myth: High-Poverty Schools Exceeding Expectations*; Craig Jerald, *Dispelling the Myth Revisited: Preliminary Findings From a Nationwide Analysis of "High-Flying" Schools* and *Dispelling the Myth Over Time*.

We must also recognize the legions of students, teachers, administrators, parents, school board members, and state legislators whom we worked with and interviewed during the preparation of this book. During the writing of this book, we have worked with educators in more than thirty states, which has provided us with occasion to try out sections of our book, test out ideas, and gain firsthand experience from students, teachers, and administrators. So rich was the content of our interviews, they quickly became a significant part of the book. We have also included the voices of students, teachers, and administrators, which we believe provide a complement to the research. We have organized these collected interviews into sections titled "Unconventional Wisdom: What Works for Experienced Teachers." These sections have been quite meaningful to collect and assemble and actually could have emerged as a separate publication. Our only hope is that we have adequately captured the passion, frustration, commitment, and creativity of all whom we have interviewed. We feel an unusual obligation to continue to present these powerful voices and ideas to the education profession through a second edition.

Acknowledgments

In addition to the work of nationally and internationally recognized scholars and all of the remarkable educators whose interviews became the centerpiece of this book, we have so many others to acknowledge for their assistance. Our thanks to all of the people at Pearson/Skylight who originally edited, published, and marketed the first edition of this book in 2003.

Almost immediately, educators across the country found this work highly useful. It has been used for a wide array of national, state, and local conferences, policy summits, professional development sessions, and study groups. State organizations in Arkansas, Idaho, Kentucky, New Jersey, Oklahoma, and Oregon have distributed the book widely. An increasing number of teacher educators, educational leadership, and other graduate programs are using this work. In 2005, Corwin Press purchased the first edition from Pearson/Skylight and engaged their comprehensive marketing strategies to broaden its "reach." We are deeply grateful to the leadership at Corwin Press who made this transition possible, and for the wonderful assistance we have had in the production of this second edition. Our thanks to Douglas Rife, Robb Clouse, Hudson Perigo, Jean Ward, Megan Thorpe, Jordan Barbakow, Carla Freeman, and Veronica Stapleton.

Special thanks go out (in no particular order) to a number of colleagues and friends who have guided and contributed to one or both editions of this book: Wayne Jennings, Executive Director of the International Association of Learning Alternatives; Cheryl Amos, Director of FIND School in Richmond, Indiana; Dixie Robinson, a teacher at the FIND School in Richmond, Indiana; Jeff Chandler, Georgia Department of Education in Atlanta; Sylvia Hooker, Principal of Fairmount Alternative School in Newnan, Georgia; Al Tony Gilmore of the Civil Rights Department of NEA; Barbara Kennedy and Connie Lester of the Kentucky Department of Education; Bill Scott of the Kentucky School Board Association; Clemmye Jackson, Accelerated Learning Program

Director, Ames Community Schools, Iowa; Graduate Dean George Jackson of Iowa State University; Ray Morley, Iowa Department of Education; John Erickson, Superintendent of the Vancouver, Washington, Public Schools; Dona Bolt and Pat Burk, Deputy Superintendent of Schools of the Oregon Department of Education; Nancy Golden, Superintendent, Springfield, Oregon; John Metcalf, Director of Curriculum for the Lander Public Schools in Lander, Wyoming; Joe Nathan, Director of the Hubert Humphrey Institute for School Change, University of Minnesota; Marybeth Flachbart, Margo Healy, and Rose Rettig, of the Idaho State Department of Education; Tom Martin, Wyoming State Department of Education; Jay Smink and Linda Shirley of the National Dropout Prevention Network; Sybil Fickle, former Dean of Continuing Education, and Dan Rea of Georgia Southern University; Lori Fisher, Executive Director, and her former colleagues Sally Anderson, Bob Haley, and Sharron Jarvis, of the J. A. and Kathryn Albertson Foundation in Boise.

A number of our students, graduate research assistants, professional staff, and faculty colleagues at the Center for School Improvement & Policy Studies at Boise State University provided vital contributions to the completion of this book. Our sincere appreciation goes out to Claire Anderson, Cathy Beals, Jonathan Brendefur, Kathleen Budge, Andrea Daigle, Becca Dickinson, Diana Esbensen, Marybeth Flachbart, Molly Jo Fuentealba, Margo Healy, Kerri Hoffman, Julie Hutchinson, Phil Kelly, Lisa Kinnaman, Mark Lewis, Greg Martinez, Jenny Newhouse, Valerie Orman, Brad Peachy, Rosie Santana, Craig Sheehy, Roger Stewart, Jane Walther, Sarita Whitmore, Scott Willison, and Deb Yates.

Finally, for their day-in and day-out tireless contributions, we are indebted to Beverly Moss, our world-class, word processing wizard and text editor; to Jenny Newhouse and Becca Dickinson, for their tireless detail work on this second edition; and also to our graduate assistant, Tera Luce, who did so much of the online research and was indispensable to the earlier work.

Finally, we give our heartfelt thanks to our spouses, Beryl Barr and Ann Dehner, for their patience, support, and editorial help. Even our kids, Bonny, Brady, Jerry, Meilin, Mia, and Jonathan, once again patiently tolerated missing dads and encouraged us both in their own special ways. Also thanks to the Barr grandkids: Sam, Sadie, and little Isabella.

Our thanks and heartfelt appreciation to all of you!

Corwin Press would like to thank the following individuals for their contributions to the work:

Bruce Haddix
Principal
Center Grove Elementary School
Greenwood, IN

Donna Adair Breault
Assistant Professor, Educational Leadership
Georgia State University
Atlanta, GA

Erika Hunt
Project Director
Center for the Study of Education Policy
Illinois State University
Normal, IL

Kim E. Vogel
Principal
Parkdale Elementary School
Parkdale, OR

Theodore J. Kowalski
Kuntz Family Chair in Educational Administration
University of Dayton
Dayton, OH

About the Authors

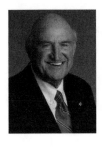**Robert D. Barr** has gained national and international recognition for his research on at-risk children and youth, teacher education, and alternative schools. He is a nationally recognized speaker, consultant, and scholar in the areas of at-risk youth, school improvement, and alternative education. He has appeared twice on PBS's *Firing Line*, featuring William F. Buckley, and has been interviewed on *ABC Evening News*, with Peter Jennings, and on the Fox News Channel's *The O'Reilly Factor*. He has been quoted in *The New York Times, USA Today,* and *The Wall Street Journal,* served as an expert witness at many state and federal trials, and presented testimony to subcommittees of the U.S. Congress.

Previously, Dr. Barr was Professor and Director of Teacher Education at Indiana University (1970–1981), Dean of the Oregon State University College of Education (1981–1990), Dean of the Boise State University College of Education (1991–1998), served for two years as a board member of the Northwest Regional Educational Laboratory, and was appointed by five governors in three states to various commissions. He served as an Idaho delegate to the Education Commissions of the States. He has received three national awards for excellence in teacher education: AACTE, Distinguished Achievement Award; AASA Showcase of Excellence Award; and the Theodore Mitou Award. He is currently a Senior Analyst with the Boise State University Center for School Improvement & Policy Studies. Barr has had extensive international experience in Indonesia, China, Japan, and Chile and was a visiting professor at the University of Innsbruck, in Austria.

Dr. Barr has worked as a consultant in school districts and Departments of Education in more than forty states. Since 1995, he has keynoted more than a dozen national conferences and been a featured presenter at the American Association of School Administrators and the Association for Supervision and Curriculum Development almost every year during the past decade. The National School Board Association has selected Barr with coauthor William Parrett four times since 1996 for their prestigious *Meet the Expert* sessions.

Barr has been widely published in almost every educational journal and is the author or coauthor of eight books. Barr and Parrett have coauthored four books: *The Kids Left Behind: Teaching the Underachieving Children of Poverty*; *Saving Our Students, Saving Our Schools: 50 Proven Strategies for Revitalizing At-Risk Students and Low-Performing Schools*; *Hope Fulfilled for At-Risk and Violent Youth*; *How to Create Alternative, Magnet, and Charter Schools That Work*; and *Hope at Last for At-Risk Youth*. Barr's editorial "Who Is This Child?" was reprinted in French for distribution internationally and was nominated for a national award by the Educational Press Association. Other books authored by Dr. Barr include *Alternatives in Education*; *Values and Youth*; *The Nature of the Social Studies*; and *Defining the Social Studies*. *Defining the Social Studies* has been identified as the single most influential book in the field of social studies.

 **William H. Parrett** is the Director of the Center for School Improvement & Policy Studies and Professor of Education at Boise State University. He has received international recognition for his work in school improvement, small schools, and alternative education and for his efforts to help youth at risk. His professional experiences include public school and university teaching, curriculum design, principalships and college leadership, media production, research, and publication.

Parrett holds a PhD in Secondary Education from Indiana University. He has served on the faculties of Indiana University, the University of Alaska, and Boise State University. As Director of the Boise State University Center for School Improvement & Policy Studies (1996 to present), Parrett coordinates funded projects and improvement initiatives, which exceed $1.5 million annually. His research on reducing achievement gaps and effective schooling practices for youth at risk and low-performing schools has gained widespread national recognition.

Parrett is the coauthor of *The Kids Left Behind: Teaching the Underachieving Children of Poverty*; *Saving Our Students, Saving Our Schools: 50 Proven Strategies for Revitalizing At-Risk Students and Low-Performing Schools*; *Hope Fulfilled for At-Risk & Violent Youth*; *How to Create Alternative,*

Magnet, and Charter Schools That Work; *Hope at Last for At-Risk Youth*; *Inventive Teaching: Heart of the Small School*; *The Inventive Mind: Portraits of Effective Teaching*, and numerous contributions to national journals and international and national conferences.

Parrett's media production, *Heart of the Country*, is a documentary of an extraordinary principal of a village elementary school in Hokkaido, Japan, and the collective passion of the community to educate the heart as well as the mind. Since its release, the production was nominated for the Pare Lorentz Award at the 1999 International Documentary Awards (Los Angeles, CA) and has won the Award of Commendation from the American Anthropological Association; a Gold Apple Award for best of category at the National Education Media Network Festival (Oakland, CA); a National CINE Golden Eagle Award (Washington, DC); and a Judges' Award at the 24th Northwest Film Festival (Portland, OR). In addition, *Heart of the Country* was an invited feature and screened at the Cinema du Reel (1998) festival in Paris and the Margaret Mead Film Festival (1998) in New York City. This work has received critical acclaim for its cinematography and insight into the universal correlates of effective teaching and learning and the power of community participation in public schools.

Parrett has also served as visiting faculty at Indiana University, the University of Manitoba, Oregon State University, Hokkaido University of Education (Japan), Nagoya Gakiun (Japan), Gifu University (Japan), and Heilongjiang University (People's Republic of China). His consultancies include state departments, boards of education, state and regional service providers, and school districts in thirty-nine states and ten nations.

Throughout his career, Parrett has worked to improve the educational achievement of all children and youth, particularly those less advantaged. Toward this goal, he has garnered more than $12 million in external funding to create programs and interventions designed to help educators, schools, communities, and universities benefit from research and best practices. These efforts have positively impacted the lives of thousands of young people.

PART I

Accept the Challenge to Teach All Students

The convergence of a number of powerful developments has combined to present American public schools with an enormous challenge: teach all students to acceptable levels of achievement and leave no child behind. The federal No Child Left Behind (NCLB) Act of 2001 demands that all students achieve mandated levels of achievement proficiency, an expectation to which public schools have never been held. Undoubtedly, public education can and will continue to educate a large percentage of the nation's students who will one day graduate from college. The critical issue today is whether or not schools can and will successfully educate all of the nation's students.

This book is dedicated to helping educators address the needs of this vast, neglected majority of public school students and providing detailed assistance to those committed to helping all students learn effectively and achieve acceptable academic standards. It is also dedicated to improving achievement of low-achieving students and turning around the low-performing schools they attend.

Throughout this book, the term *at risk* is used to describe the broadest possible range of students. And while it is difficult to find any single term to adequately describe the vast complexity of students struggling in inadequate schools, the term *at risk* seems to best capture their situation. These students include all of those who are underachieving and as a result are at risk of failing, dropping out, and living out their lives unemployed,

underemployed, and with the possibility of other tragic social consequences. This challenging group of underachievers may include the poor,
the culturally diverse, the mainstreamed, and the unmotivated. It may
include teenage parents, the bored, the disengaged, and the disinterested
affluent students. At any one time, it may include students experiencing
family upheavals that disrupt and distract their interest in learning, as
well as the students struggling to learn English. It also includes any
students whose risky behavior and lifestyles place their futures in jeopardy, both in school and without. These are our students, and this is our
challenge. These are our students at risk.

In the past, this underachieving population of students has too often
been ignored, neglected, and even impaired by school programs. These
students have been left behind, with little opportunity to catch up. The
contemporary technological marketplace has further proven that these
students are no more successful outside of school than they were in
school. The demographics of this group are sobering:

- One-fourth of all American youth drops out of high school; few of
  these students ever achieve middle-class status during their lifetimes, thus perpetuating the tragic cycle of poverty. Most of these
  students face lives of unemployment or, at best, underemployment.
- There is a direct relationship between students who are illiterate
  and those who drop out of school. More than 50 percent of the
  1.8 million men and women in prison in the United States today
  are illiterate high school dropouts.
- One-fourth of all high school graduates who progress to higher
  education drop out of college.
- One-third of all college freshmen take remedial classes (National
  Commission on the High School Senior Year 2001).

LEAVE NO CHILD BEHIND

As more and more schools address the challenges of NCLB to teach all
students, there is a growing body of evidence that documents how low-
performing schools are becoming high-performing schools and how these
schools, often with the most challenging, at-risk students are succeeding.

Recognizing the opportunity for the federal government to critically
influence the school success of low-performing and other at-risk
students, Congress passed landmark legislation during the 2001–2002
session. The NCLB legislation, for the first time ever in the United States,
requires that all students be tested for adequate yearly progress toward
academic proficiency levels established by each state. For the first time

nationally, the phrase "All means all" has been backed up by policy that requires every school district to devote serious attention and intervention toward the academic needs of the many types of students at risk. While this policy mandate is still relatively new, its intention is clear: to redirect every school district's attention to the needs of this population of students, to make schools account-

LEARN MORE ABOUT THE NO CHILD
LEFT BEHIND LEGISLATION
ON THESE WEB SITES

- <www.ed.gov/nclb/landing.jhtml>
- <www.ascd.org/portal/site/ascd/ menuitem.44cb9f9033aaf17cbfb3ffdb6210 8a0c/>

able for every student's achievement, and to close achievement gaps between various student populations. Figure 0.1 (page 4) outlines how the particular components of NCLB impact low-performing and other at-risk students.

In addition to the other aspects of NCLB discussed in Figure 0.1, the education policy provides support for research in teaching and learning, teacher preparation, teacher quality, community learning centers, and faith-based efforts. As of 2007, most aspects of NCLB are working as intended. Every state has an accountability plan in place, measuring student performance annually in Grades 3–8 and once more in high school. According to the U.S. Department of Education, more reading progress has been made in the last five years than in the previous twenty-eight years combined, with achievement gaps between Hispanic and African American students and their white peers at historic lows.

Despite the initial successes of NCLB, much work remains if the goal of 90 percent proficiency in reading and mathematics is to be accomplished by 2014. A variety of improvements related to funding, support, and accountability will undoubtedly characterize the reauthorization of this policy in 2008.

This book provides a comprehensive collection of the best available research that documents the effectiveness of fifty strategies for improving student learning and schoolwide performance (see Figure 0.2 on page 5). While these strategies work well with all types of students, they have been proven to be unusually effective with the most challenging, low-performing, and other at-risk children and youth. Suggestions and recommendations that reflect best practice also have been included from highly effective, experienced teachers. As a result, this book provides a comprehensive collection of effective strategies that are supported both by research and the long-term classroom experiences of many of the nation's finest teachers.

Saving Our Students, Saving Our Schools has been organized so that parents, teachers, administrators, and educational policymakers can identify specific strategies that relate to the challenges and issues confronting schools and communities today. The goal of this effort is solely to provide educators, service providers, parents, and families with access to

The new educational policy of No Child Left Behind (NCLB) involves several major initiatives.

Required State Standards

Each state is required to establish its own standards of what students should know and be able to do in the core subject areas: reading, writing, and math.

Adequate Student Progress

Local school districts are required to document "adequate yearly progress" in achieving a new level of academic standards. Adequate yearly progress refers to the growth rate in the percentage of students who achieve the state's definition of academic proficiency. Each state is challenged to establish high criteria for improving academic achievement.

Measuring Progress

The educational achievement of every child in Grades 3 through 8 will be tested, and each school will receive report cards highlighting its successes its and/or failures. Schools will be held responsible for making sure that every student learns. By testing every child in every school, parents and teachers can work to close the achievement gap and ensure that all students learn what is being taught.

Reading First

A comprehensive initiative called "Reading First" is designed to make sure that all children learn to read well by the end of third grade.

Math Achievement

The Math and Science Partnership plan seeks to increase the number of well-qualified math and science teachers by increasing teacher salaries and incorporating research about how to best teach math and science to every student.

Getting Students Help

For the first time, Title I funds are tied directly to educating of the most needy children rather than maintaining the status quo. When schools fail to meet state standards three years in a row, children are eligible to obtain supplementary services, including tutoring, remedial education, extra classes, summer school, afterschool programs, and other academic services designed to help boost achievement.

Figure 0.1   No Child Left Behind: A New Direction for Public Education

TOPIC STRATEGY NUMBERS*

Topic	Strategy Numbers
Basic Education	5, 8, 26, 27, 31–37, 39, 40
Best Practices (Pedagogy)	4–5, 8, 10, 11, 17, 21, 22, 25, 26–28, 30, 32, 33, 36, 37, 39–43, 47, 48
Brain-Compatible Learning	3–5, 22, 25, 26, 31–34, 36, 37, 39
Caring and Understanding	3–6, 14–16, 28, 29, 37, 44–47
Collaboration	1, 2, 5, 12, 14–16, 28, 48–50
Communities of Support	14–20, 29, 37, 44–50
Diversity	3–8, 14–16, 37
Gender	3, 4, 37, 44
Leadership	6, 9, 10–14, 18, 21, 27, 28, 31, 35, 44, 47
Parents/Families/Communities	1, 4–6, 14–17, 18, 37, 45, 48–50
Poverty	5–8, 21, 28, 37, 44, 47, 49, 50
Reading	25, 30–37, 39, 40–44, 50
Respect, Social/Emotional Growth	3–8, 25, 37, 44–47, 49
Safety, Violence	22–24, 46–47
School/Classroom Environments	4–6, 14, 16–20, 26, 28, 37, 43, 48–50
Schoolwide Improvement	5, 9–13, 17–20, 25, 28–30, 35, 36, 37–39, 42, 43, 48–50
Standards, Assessments	9–13, 28, 30, 36, 38, 39, 41, 43

Figure 0.2   Visual Index of Strategies

NOTE: These strategies will be discussed in Part II of this book.

the compelling evidence for embracing the absolute reality of education today—a reality in which all children, particularly low-performing and other at-risk students, will improve their achievement and school success to acceptable standards and beyond.

1
Confront the Challenges

I just don't know what I'm going to do. Every year, my first-grade class has more and more of these kids. They don't seem to care about right or wrong, they don't care about adult approval, they are disruptive, they can't read, and they arrive at school absolutely unprepared to learn. Who are these kids? Where do they come from? Why are there more and more of them? I used to think that I was a good teacher. I really prided myself on doing an outstanding job. But I find I'm working harder and harder, and being less and less effective. A good teacher? Today, I really don't know. I do know that my classroom is being overwhelmed by society's problems, and I don't understand it. What's happening to our schools? What's happening to society? I don't understand all of this, and I sure don't know what we're going to do about it.

—Elementary Teacher, Georgia

OUR SCHOOLS HAVE CHANGED

Choose any part of the United States; drop into any community and ask any teacher about his or her professional life today. At the start of the twenty-first century, the response is almost universally the same:

Teaching is not as easy as it once was. Today there are just so many students at risk.

Teachers are not only talking about the challenging students who come from poor or dysfunctional families, many of whom arrive at school unprepared to read and keep up with their more advantaged peers. Teachers are also talking about so many of today's students from advantaged homes and families who are not interested in learning or are not motivated to achieve. Teachers will freely talk about the intense and ever-increasing pressures on them to succeed with all students effectively, even the most difficult kids. Indeed, the challenges, pressures, and frustrations are unprecedented. These challenges, generated by a number of relatively new forces in society, are creating a dramatically different environment for today's educators and schools. (See Figure 1.1, as well as the discussion that follows.)

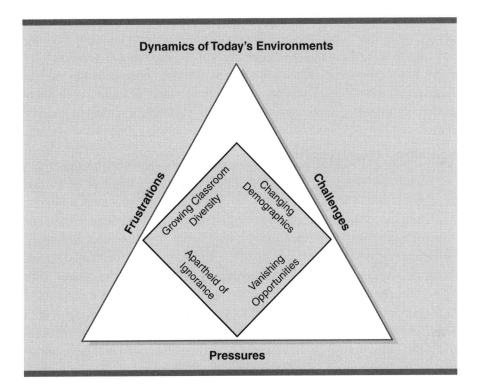

Figure 1.1

Growing Classroom Diversity

Each year, the nation's public school classrooms contain increasing numbers of at-risk students who are poor, non-English-speaking, mainstream disabled, culturally different, or come from dysfunctional and/or single-parent families. Increased family mobility further adds to a constantly changing student population. Today's typical classroom often ranges from the highly gifted and talented to the disabled, from the wealthy and advantaged to the poor, from different backgrounds to a cultural mosaic. Indeed, the typical classroom of today may be simply and best characterized as *diverse.* Data accumulated in the 2000 census report that the number of Hispanics in the United States now equals the number of African Americans in seven states and that Hispanics will soon become the nation's largest ethnic minority group. Many school districts today enroll students who represent forty or more different language groups. Students enrolled in special education have more than doubled in the last fifteen years. This is not your parent's public school classroom.

Changing Demographics

In the United States today, people over sixty-five years of age outnumber teenagers, and the fastest-growing category of households is the childless one. Almost half of all households consist of a single person living alone. In the year 2000, more and more wealth was centered in the top 1 to 2 percent of the nation. There are increasing numbers of millionaires today as well as a growing underclass of individuals and families living in poverty.

Vanishing Opportunities

There may have been a time, a generation or so ago, when dropping out of school posed little barrier to success and prosperity and carried little or no stigma. At the beginning of the twentieth century, more than 90 percent of school-age youth dropped out of school but found almost unlimited opportunities to work in the forests, fields, and factories of the United States. According to the National Commission on the High School Senior Year (2001), as recently as the 1950s, when the national dropout rate hovered at 50 percent, there were still good jobs available for those leaving school early. Unfortunately, those opportunities are rapidly disappearing, and today they exist for only a very small percentage of our youth. The majority of jobs that are available for our undereducated youth pay minimum wage with few benefits and are insufficient to support a family or household.

Following welfare reform, most adults in the United States now work, even though many are employed at only the minimum-wage level. Most students in the United States come home from school to an empty house and spend between two and four hours or more alone each day. As a result of these demographic changes, public school classrooms are characterized by

- diminishing parental involvement,
- increased student mobility, and
- a growing percentage of students who are at risk of failing in school, dropping out, and further disconnecting from society.

Apartheid of Ignorance

To achieve the good life in the technological marketplace that has grown to characterize today's world requires a high-quality education. Between those whose wealth has soared to unparalleled levels and the underclass of the "other" America who have suffered declining economic prosperity, a growing apartheid of ignorance has emerged. Those who are well educated can access and participate in the richest economic system in earth's history. For those who lack education, the door of opportunity is slammed shut, locking too many out of any real likelihood of economic opportunity and success.

WHO ARE THE AT-RISK STUDENTS?

Over the years, a number of organizations have carefully documented the annual conditions of children and families as well as the behavior of youth that places them at risk. Three such groups, Children's Defense Fund, Federal Interagency on Child Family Statistics, and National Centers for Disease Control, taken together, provide a vivid longitudinal portrait of the underclass of poor, disadvantaged children in the United States, as well as the types and degrees of risky behavior of the nation's teenagers:

- One in five children lives in poverty.
- The number of children living in poverty has remained at around 20 percent for more than twenty years.
- More than three million children each year are abused or neglected.
- A nonparental relative is raising more than two million children each year.
- Two-thirds of the mothers of young children work outside the home.
- Every day, more than thirteen million children, including six million infants and toddlers, are in child care outside the home.

Recent research has helped parents and educators understand that not just poor and abused children are at risk. Major surveys and research studies have begun to document the behaviors of youth that may place students at risk.

In 1987, the National Centers for Disease Control began coordinating a National Youth Surveillance Program through which they survey thousands of teenagers every two years. This survey gathers data on student participation in a variety of risky behaviors involving drugs and alcohol, sexual activity, safety/violence, tobacco use, nutrition, suicide, and other indicators of adolescent risk. This ongoing research effort not only documents the behaviors that place students at risk but also allows schools and communities to follow trends in youth behavior.

Teachers, parents, and administrators can also use relatively simple approaches to identify and anticipate which students are likely to fail in school and/or drop out. (A number of research-based profiles and checklists to help identify these students are provided throughout this book.)

An abundance of research over the last decade both presents and confronts our nation's schools with a growing number of important conclusions. This research has further provided a substantial knowledge base for educational redesign and improvement (see Figure 1.2).

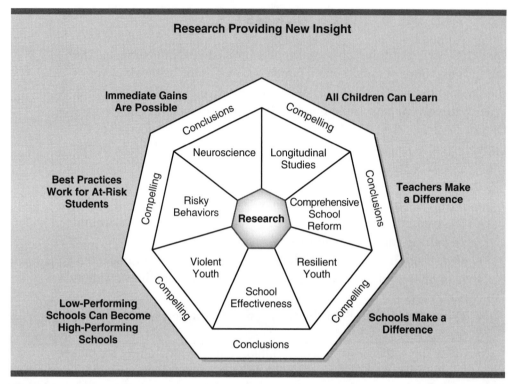

Figure 1.2

Neuroscience Research

Research on the human brain has and continues to yield dramatic new insights into teaching and learning. In 1969, there were only approximately 500 neuroscientists studying the brain; today there are more than 300,000. This research, even while in its earliest stages, is yielding a dramatic, new understanding of how the brain works to process information (Jensen 1998; Sylwester 1998; Wolfe 2001).

Longitudinal Studies

A number of ongoing longitudinal studies today are providing a rich resource of information that permits long-term predictions to be made concerning low-performing and other at-risk youth. Two of the most revealing include a thirty-year study at Yale University regarding learning disabilities and an equally important twenty-year study of High/Scope Perry Preschool students in Ypsilanti, Michigan. Both studies have yielded invaluable predictive conclusions in support of early intervention for youth at risk (Barnett 1996; Shaywitz and Shaywitz 1990).

Research on Resilient Youth

Since the 1980s, researchers have focused their attention on successful students who have all or many of the characteristics of the at-risk failing student. This research has led to an identification of factors that appear to influence the successful development of children and youth (Benard 1991; Krovetz 1999).

Research on Violent Youth

As the nation's attention has increasingly focused on youth violence, research from diverse fields has contributed to a growing understanding of the profiles and warning signs that alert teachers, parents, and educators to violence-prone and bullying behavior (Benard 1991).

Research on School Effectiveness

A number of important studies (including the Louisiana School Effectiveness Study and studies by the Education Trust of low-performing schools that have become high-performing schools) have helped identify a number of crucial factors that are essential to teaching all students effectively. In addition, other effective school research has documented best practices, effective strategies, and other essential components of successful schools (Barth et al. 1999; Jerald 2001; Teddlie and Stringfield 1993).

Research on Comprehensive School Reform

Since the early 1990s, a number of comprehensive school reform models have been assembling data to evaluate and document their effectiveness. These studies, conducted by a number of independent researchers, have led to conclusions regarding schoolwide reform and improvement efforts, as well as a large number of more-specific, targeted classroom interventions (Herman 1999; Slavin and Fashola 1998).

Research on Risky Behavior

The National Centers for Disease Control coordinate a biennial study of adolescent risk behaviors (see Strategies #1 and #22 in Part II). High school students are sampled from throughout the nation regarding various behaviors that correlate with health risks. These data provide sobering insights into an alarming scenario of youth at risk.

COMPELLING CONCLUSIONS

As a result of the unprecedented educational research of the last decade, a number of major conclusions have emerged:

- **All children can learn.** Today, we know with absolute certainty that all children can learn, even the poor, language challenged, and learning disabled. A growing knowledge base of data makes it clear that all children and youth can learn and achieve acceptable standards of academic excellence and school success.

- **Schools make a difference.** Recent research has completely rewritten previous conclusions about low-performing and other at-risk students and effective schools. During the 1960s, the most eminent scholars concluded that poverty had such a negative, pervasive impact on children and youth that schools could have little or no positive effect on these students' education. Recent research has dramatically challenged these earlier conclusions. Today, thousands of schools serving poor, at-risk students report academic levels similar to those of middle-class and upper-class students. It is now evident that a good school can overcome the debilitating effects of poverty and dysfunctional families.

- **Teachers make a difference.** Teacher quality is the single most influential factor in student achievement. Working in the same school with similar children and youth, certain teachers can significantly raise student achievement and school success, while other teachers may have little or no positive impact on student achievement. Students in too many classrooms actually show a decline in achievement over the course of the school year. It takes two years for a student with an ineffective teacher to regain the resulting loss in achievement. If a student has an ineffective teacher for two years in a row, he or she is unlikely ever to catch up (Sanders and Rivers 1996).

- **Immediate gains are possible.** Research has clearly identified instructional strategies, educational programs and interventions, and exemplary models that ensure not only that all students learn and achieve but also that schools and classrooms can expect immediate, dramatic results if proven approaches are implemented appropriately.

- **Low-performing schools can become high-performing schools.** Throughout the United States, a growing number of low-performing schools have become high-performing schools. By employing research on effective schools, applying research on best practices for low-performing and other at-risk students, and monitoring student performance, these schools have transformed student learning in a dramatic manner. Many of these schools report that they have accomplished this remarkable transformation with the same students, the same families, and the same educators.

- **Best practices work for at-risk students.** Research from a wide variety of sources has identified and documented a large number of strategies for schools and classrooms that can ensure the success of at-risk students. Some of the best practices represent essential factors in school and classroom design; others identify specific classroom instructional strategies. Taken together, the effectiveness of these strategies is magnified and can be used to ensure successful student performance for even the most difficult and challenging students.

- **High-Poverty/High-Performing Schools**. In recent years, a number of studies have focused on high-poverty schools that also have high student achievement. These studies have focused on what these schools have done to become successful and how they have done it (Barr and Parrett 2007).

2
How Schools Fail Students and Manufacture Low Performance

You can't believe what they did to me. In the second grade, I was retained. In the third grade, they diagnosed me as attention deficit, placed me in special education, and put me on Ritalin. They put me in an educational "slow track," and I never got out. No one ever really tried to teach me anything. Believe it or not, I am now in college. It took me three semesters taking noncredit makeup work, but now I am really making progress. I am on track to graduate with a business degree in two more years.

—Student, Washington

Research over the past decade has identified the essential characteristics of effective schools and the best practices and strategies for successfully educating all students. It has also documented public school policies, programs, and practices that have a tragic, negative effect on low-performing and other at-risk students. Many of these policies, programs, and practices can be found in almost every school in the United States. Taken together, these practices do not support at-risk students; rather, they represent an insidious effort that brutalizes, stigmatizes, isolates, and abandons the very students who are most desperately in need of help.

DESTRUCTIVE SCHOOL POLICIES, PROGRAMS, AND PRACTICES

Almost a dozen public school policies, programs, and practices with regard to poor, minority, and other at-risk students have unfortunate, long-term negative effects on these challenging children and young people. Rather than assist at-risk students, some school approaches exacerbate and complicate the problems these students are facing and collectively have disastrous effects on their ability to learn effectively and succeed in school. Despite the mass of research documenting the negative effects on students, these approaches continue to be widely used in public schools throughout the United States. Teachers everywhere should familiarize themselves with this research and the successful efforts to combat these negative school policies, programs, and practices.

Assignment to Schools and Programs

At-risk students and their parents are denied choice in the vast majority of public schools. Most students are assigned to schools, programs, and educational tracks. Affluent parents seek residence based on good schools or choose private schools. Poor families are often trapped in failing schools.

Inequitable School Funding

Distressed neighborhoods or communities are usually served by schools with significantly fewer financial resources. More experienced, better-trained teachers with higher salaries and graduate degrees are too often found in the more affluent schools. Funding public education with property tax revenue creates a tragic economic divide that continues to dramatically separate our public schools into rich and poor.

Schools Fail to Teach Basics

Students from poverty-level homes and/or dysfunctional families often arrive at school unprepared for the achievement expectations of public schools. Subsequently, far too many schools fail to effectively teach these children during their first years. If students do not learn to read by the end of the third grade, certain unfortunate consequences await them as they continue through school (Karoly et al. 1998). (See Figure 2.1 on page 16.)

Retention and Assignment to Tracks

In too many schools, students who do not quickly master basic skills are retained and required to simply repeat everything again, or they are tracked into "basic" classes with low expectations. Students who are retained and tracked almost never catch up to their age group peers, and many fail to advance from the slow-learning track (Fager and Richen 1999; Loveless 1998; Roderick 1995). (See Figure 2.2.)

Consequences of Not Reading at Grade Level by Grade 3

- Students cannot successfully do homework or schoolwork.

- Students' self-concepts suffer, behavior deteriorates.

- Students face a 90 percent probability of dropping out of school.

- During their lifetimes, students are very likely to be unemployed, underemployed, or, even worse, unemployable.

Figure 2.1

SOURCE: From Karoly et al. (1998).

Consequences of Retention and Tracking

- Teenage students report that being retained is like "going blind" or "having your family killed in an automobile accident."

- Retention is one of the primary causes of dropping out.

- No educational practice has been studied so thoroughly and so well as retention. The overwhelming conclusion: retention has destructive effects on students, particularly those at risk.

- Tracked classes are often camouflaged under the name of "opportunity," "basic," or "enrichment," all holding low expectations for students.

- Students in tracked classrooms rarely catch up to their higher-achieving peers and are rarely provided opportunities for advanced classes (Barr and Parrett 2001).

- Students who do graduate following "slow-track" experiences demonstrate substantially less achievement and school success, often emerging from high school functionally illiterate.

Figure 2.2

Assignment to Special Education

With few other successful interventions or alternatives available, too often public schools evaluate and subsequently assign poor and culturally diverse students to special education based on learning disabilities, hyperactivity, or attention deficit disorders. These diagnoses unfortunately may relate primarily to the learning environment. For at-risk students, this assignment further separates them from the opportunities and high expectations held for regular education students (see Figure 2.3).

Results of Inappropriate Assignments to Special Education

- Special education placements have doubled during the last fifteen years in the United States. The majority of these placements are for learning disabilities.
- Pressure on schools and districts to finance increased special education services diverts needed resources away from other interventions.
- Students assigned to special education almost never get out.
- Students who do graduate following placement in a special education track demonstrate substantially lower achievement than other graduates.

Figure 2.3

Prescription Drugs

During the last two decades, as students have been intensely encouraged to "Just Say No to Drugs" through a number of national campaigns, millions of children have been prescribed and placed on medication intended to assist in improving their school behavior and achievement. Today, as many as one in ten students in the United States is medicated. Boys are medicated five times more often than girls. While such medication does indeed render many students more passive, less active, and more obedient, questions abound regarding the scope of the effectiveness and long-term effects of medication being overprescribed.

Pullout Programs

Many enrichment programs, like the federal government's Title I Reading Program, have historically removed students from their regular classrooms to provide instruction in reading. Unfortunately, while students are engaged in these pullout programs, they miss regular classroom instruction and the many benefits of working with their teachers and peers. Years of study have documented how little success these programs have had on at-risk students.

Large Schools

The United States is a nation of large schools. Yet for at-risk learners, a small school with a personalized environment is essential for their educational needs. In large schools, these students often feel isolated, anonymous, and alienated, and they sometimes become disruptive, bullies, or victims of bullies. Others simply underachieve or drop out. The larger the school, the more student disruptions can be expected. For every additional 600 students, there exists a corresponding increase in negative student behavior. Conversely, studies demonstrate an almost total lack of violence and considerably higher student academic success in small schools (Howley and Bickel 2002).

Expulsion

Most public school districts have established zero-tolerance policies. Unfortunately, for at-risk youth, many of whom have been retained, tracked, humiliated, and sometimes medicated, expulsion is used to counter student anger and disobedience. Expulsion serves a simple, single purpose: to get the student away from the school. Yet studies have shown that as an intervention, expulsion rarely, if ever, serves to reconnect a student with the goals of public education. Many expelled students progress from being in trouble at school to being in trouble with the police, which often ends with the expelled student being incarcerated (Colorado Foundation for Families and Children 1995).

Unsupportive Teachers

At-risk students report that too many teachers do not call on them in class, do not answer their questions, and are not supportive. These students are often written off as uncooperative and descend into further alienation from their teachers and schools. Research has clearly documented that students reciprocate the negative attitudes of teachers (Sanders and Rivers 1996).

So many of these destructive policies, programs, and practices are used despite decades of research that has documented their ineffectiveness. One explanation of their continued use is that the activities are so ingrained into the culture of schools that they are justified, not by thoughtful research but through unfortunate and widely believed mythologies about teaching and learning.

THE MYTHS THAT PERPETUATE INEFFECTIVE PRACTICES

Far too many educators employ instructional approaches based on a number of faulty assumptions. Unfortunately, these practices have a negative effect on many children and youth. To effectively teach all students, educators and schools need to examine their programs and rid them of practices that perpetuate myths and undermine student success (see Figure 2.4).

Confronting Mythology: Exorcising the Evils of Failed Education

Myth	Reality	Strategies* to Use
At-risk youth need slow learning.	At-risk students need intensive remediation and accelerated learning. At-risk students need personalized education. At-risk students need mastery learning. At-risk students must access their multiple intelligences.	3, 4, 5, 8, 26, 31, 37, 39, 41, 42
At-risk youth should be retained.	At-risk students should be offered before- and afterschool and summer programs to remediate, catch up, and accelerate. At-risk students should receive intensive focus on skills. At-risk students should be tutored.	6, 8, 14, 24, 28, 33, 50
At-risk youth can be educated with the same expenditures as other students.	All students can learn effectively and achieve high academic standards, but: It is not easy. It is not inexpensive. At-risk students need educational "intensive care." Districts and schools must provide targeted intervention.	7, 8, 13, 27, 31, 35, 47, 50
Classroom teachers alone can adequately address the needs of at-risk youth.	The complex needs of low-performing and other at-risk students demand schoolwide and community interventions. While one teacher can make an enormous difference, teams of teachers with shared visions can have a transforming effect on at-risk students. Communities of support multiply and enrich the impact of individual teachers.	14–17, 21, 28, 44, 45, 50

Figure 2.4 *(Continued)*

(Continued)

Myth	Reality	Strategies* to Use
Some students can't learn.	Schools must "leave no child behind."	5–8, 14, 21, 25, 33, 34, 37
	Schools must ensure that each student is learning, whatever it takes.	
	A good school can overcome the debilitating effects of poverty and a dysfunctional family.	
The most effective way to improve instruction for at-risk youth is to reduce classroom size.	While low student-teacher ratios are important and desirable, they are very costly and alone do not guarantee student success.	17, 19, 20, 21, 31, 44, 45
	Creating small schools and small learning communities does guarantee success.	
	Alternative schools are the single most effective approach for keeping students in school and learning effectively.	
	The most effective programs for eliminating school dropouts are alternative schools and service learning and mentoring programs.	
At-risk students need special education.	For many students, a smaller, more personalized learning environment is more effective than special education.	4, 8,19–21, 17, 25, 30, 47
	Schools need a range of options beyond special education.	
	Effective alternative schools create a community of support that may be more effective than special education for many students.	

Figure 2.4

NOTE: These strategies will be discussed in Part II of this book.

At-Risk Youth Need Slow Learning

The idea that at-risk children and youth need slow learning cannot be further from the truth. Over the past twenty-five years, research has clearly documented the damaging effects of slow-learning tracks and classes for low-performing and other youth at risk.

At-Risk Youth Should Be Retained

While retention seems so logical and is usually employed out of concern for the needs of at-risk youth, research has clearly documented the disastrous effects of this practice.

At-Risk Youth Can Be Educated With the Same Expenditures as Other Students

While many effective interventions may, indeed, be initiated with existing resources, programs for at-risk students usually require additional funds. A large number of public school students with severe problems need immediate, long-term, intensive educational care. And while this care is often expensive, it is critical to the students' improved achievement and school success.

Classroom Teachers Alone Can Adequately Address the Needs of At-Risk Youth

The challenges confronting at-risk youth are often so complicated; so pervasive and long-term; and so rooted in the home, community, culture, and socioeconomic conditions that it is all but impossible for a classroom teacher alone to significantly address the needs of these students. The most effective approaches are targeted schoolwide interventions and programs with strong community support.

Some Students Can't Learn

Almost every school in America has signs and slogans hanging in its halls, classrooms, and offices lauding the fact that "All students can learn," yet considerable evidence continues to suggest that many teachers and administrators not only doubt that fact but also seem motivated to ensure that these "dumb kids" don't interrupt or interfere with students they feel can indeed learn.

The Most Effective Way to Improve Instruction for At-Risk Youth Is to Reduce Class Size

One of the most widely held beliefs regarding teaching effectiveness centers on classroom size. Following teachers' salaries, it has often been the second issue to be considered in teacher contract negotiations. Given the growing diversity of the nation's classrooms, it is logical that reduced student-teacher ratio is an essential goal. A number of studies have questioned the cost of lowering class size because of the minimal gains in student achievement that tend to follow. Yet politically, smaller class size continues to be an attractive educational reform. Reducing the size of a class is an important step toward personalizing education, yet evidence shows that it is clearly not enough to counter the complex needs of at-risk students.

At-Risk Students Need Special Education

With few other options available, teachers tend to seek to identify students having difficulty learning as qualifying for special education. The most frequent special education designation is learning disabled (LD), which includes attention deficit disorder (ADD) and attention deficit with hyperactivity disorder (ADHD). If a student is not learning or is misbehaving, there is a strong tendency to refer the child for evaluation. Unfortunately, special education is not the answer for the majority of at-risk students. There are less expensive and far more effective approaches to educating these learners.

Considerable evidence exists to support changes in intervention practices currently being employed in public schools to "help" youth at risk. Despite decades of comfort with practices such as retention, tracking, expulsion, and inequitable funding, public education today must confront the proven reality of these failed practices and implement far more effective approaches to educate at-risk students.

Establish the Commitment to Educate Children and Youth At Risk

The risk for our children in school is not a risk associated with their intelligence. Our failures have nothing to do with IQ, nothing to do with poverty, nothing to do with race, nothing to do with language, nothing to do with style, nothing to do with the need to discover new pedagogy, nothing to do with the children's families. . . . We have only one problem: do we truly will to see each and every child in this nation develop to the peak of his or her capacities?

—Asa G. Hilliard III

The common school emerged in America more than 150 years ago as our democratic society's chosen process to provide the opportunity of basic literacy and education to the growing populace of our emerging nation. Compulsory education and child labor laws followed as state after

---

Note: The authors are particularly grateful to Kati Haycock and her colleagues (Barth et al. 1999) and Craig Jerald (2001), of the Education Trust (<www.edtrust.org>), for their landmark works, which have contributed to the development of this chapter.

state assembled legal support and policies to ensure educational opportunity for children. By the middle of the twentieth century, the vast majority of America's youth were completing elementary school, and more than 50 percent were earning high school degrees. By the year 2000, more than 70 percent of the students in the United States were completing twelve years of schooling. America's public schools were driven by the concept of equal opportunity—a concept that worked for many but, unfortunately, failed many others. For almost two centuries, our nation's policymakers and citizenry accepted this success rate as reality. At the dawn of 2002, equal opportunity to learn was being replaced in a most dramatic manner. Academic standards and rigid assessments in almost every state now demanded a new reality, one in which every student would learn at least to acceptable levels of achievement. Policymakers have replaced expectations of equal opportunity with statutes requiring equal acceptable performance.

It is no longer tolerable in the United States for significant numbers of students to underachieve, fail, and drop out of public education. No longer will public schools be allowed to ignore underachieving, at-risk students. High expectations will no longer apply only to "good" students. This sea change of policy requiring acceptable performance of all students either has affected or soon will affect every public school in America, with the promise of finally delivering basic literacy and education for all of our youth. As a society, we will move from "opportunities for all" to the new reality of acceptable performance for every student.

TAKE A STAND

As public school districts and their schools wrestle with the new reality of high-stakes tests, performance rubrics, tiered diploma structures, and other measures to establish acceptable performance, our nation's educators are confronted with a singular basic challenge. Will we seek to significantly improve our efforts to teach all students, or not? For those committed to teaching all students, please read on.

LESSONS LEARNED

Hundreds of school districts (see some examples in sidebar), found in all states, have redirected their efforts to significantly improving the achievement of their low-performing students. Select cases may be found where entire districts are elevating student performance.

Thousands of individual schools have significantly transformed their learning environments to reach their desired goals of increased achievement for all students. The landmark work of the Education Trust (2002), *Dispelling the Myth Over Time*, identified and followed many of the more than 4,500 high-poverty schools and/or high-minority schools in which children score in the upper 75 percent of their respective states in reading, math, or both. Their research along with our analysis of eighteen other studies, evaluations, and data analyses provide compelling evidence that poor and/or minority students in distressed communities can and indeed will achieve high levels of academic performance. The Education Trust's work identifies seven characteristics that drive the successes (see Figure 3.1).

RAISING STUDENT PERFORMANCE DISTRICTWIDE

Visit or contact school districts in

- Brazosport, Texas, (979) 265-6181, <www.brazosport.isd.net>
- Union City, New Jersey, (201) 348-5851, <www.union-city-nj.org>
- Chugach School District in Anchorage, Alaska, (907) 522-7400, <www.chugachschools.com>
- Johnson City School District in New York, (607) 763-1230, <www.jcschools.com>

Seven Characteristics That Drive Success

- Extensive use of state and local standards to design curriculum and instruction, assess student work, and evaluate teachers
- Increased instructional time for reading and math
- Substantial investment in professional development for teachers focused on instructional practices to help students meet academic standards
- Comprehensive systems to monitor individual student performance and to provide help to struggling students before they fall behind
- Parental involvement in efforts to get students to meet standards
- State or district accountability systems with real consequences for adults in the school
- Use of assessments to help guide instruction and resources, and as a healthy part of everyday teaching and learning

Figure 3.1

SOURCE: From *Dispelling the Myth Revisited: Preliminary Findings From a Nationwide Analysis of "High-Flying Schools,"* by C. D. Jerald. © 2001 Education Trust. Used with permission.

HIGH-PERFORMING SCHOOLS

- Central Park East Secondary School in East Harlem, New York, (212) 427-6230, <www.ashinstitute.harvard.edu/ash/central park.htm>
- Lapwai Elementary School, Lapwai, Idaho, (208) 843-2960,
- Norview High School, Norfolk, Virginia, (757) 852-4500, http://ww2.nps.k12.va.us/education/school/school.php?sectiondetailid=368

Every educational leader in the United States should visit the Education Trust Web site (<www2.edtrust.org>) and review *Dispelling the Myth* as well as visit or contact high-performing schools (see sidebar) or any of the schools identified by the Education Trust to observe firsthand how these schools have accomplished their goals.

Be advised that comparing data from these districts and schools will produce no "yellow brick road." Yet, in every case, specific components of process and action are clearly evident (see Figure 3.2). These components intertwine to create a critical web of commitment to the success and achievement of all students. No two schools or districts employ exactly the same "recipe" to achieve their goals; yet all subscribe to critical aspects of each component.

LOW-PERFORMING SCHOOLS CAN IMPROVE

Improving the nation's schools to ensure an equal minimal performance of all students presents a daunting challenge. Yet there is abundant evidence that educators, schools, and school districts are succeeding in their efforts to accomplish this goal. Saving at-risk students is the cornerstone

---

Formula for Success: Commitment + Process + Action

- A critical mass of educators committed to act
- District and/or school leadership (teachers and administrators)
- A school/districtwide commitment to using data
- Clearly established goals
- The selection and deployment of research-based practices and interventions
- Clear measures of progress
- Improved communication and engagement with community stakeholders
- A commitment to continuous school improvement

Figure 3.2

of success in each of these examples. A comprehensive knowledge base of research and practice now exists to guide the efforts of public education to successfully educate these students. *The Kids Left Behind* (Barr and Parrett 2007), a recent review of eighteen major studies, reports, and data analyses that sought to explain how high-poverty schools reverse age-old trends of underachievement, further supports this database. The fifty essential strategies explained in the remainder of this book encapsulate the successes of thousands of efforts by educators, schools, and communities that have proven successful in the pursuit of our most critical goal: ensuring the success of every student.

Districts and schools that are serious about improving practices to ensure success for every student must plan accordingly. These districts and schools expect immediate results and celebrate progress. They also begin their efforts with the knowledge that this work will never be complete, that the challenge of educating all students, especially those who are at risk, will never be finished, and that the need for targeted professional development toward the continuous improvement of classroom instruction and service will never end.

PART II

50 Proven Strategies for Schools and Classrooms

Fifty strategies have been identified that have a remarkably positive effect on student learning, school achievement, and the educational success of at-risk children and youth. The more the strategies are used together, the greater the predictability in influencing both student behavior and academic growth. Many of these strategies are directly focused on classroom teaching practice; others address school, district, and/or community policy and practices.

These strategies are based on reliable, valid educational research. Yet it is commonly recognized that the craft of teaching is unquestionably influenced by the "art" of effective classroom instruction. To portray this realm, examples of the "unconventional wisdom" of experienced classroom teachers and school leaders are provided. These strategies and lessons are offered as recognition of the wealth of reflective insight available from experienced practitioners. The implementation of these practices and examples of unconventional wisdom in the classroom, school, and community provides a springboard to successful learning for all students, even in the most challenging circumstances.

This book offers a blend of research and practice reflecting both the science and art of teaching. The strategies will prove essential to any school or teacher committed to "leaving no child behind."

4

Understand the At-Risk Student

I used to think at-risk students were poor, often minority, or living in some type of difficult family situation. Well, have I changed my mind. It is blatantly obvious to me now that any student can in fact become at risk. Teachers and parents must be ever alert to changes in student behavior and dispositions and care enough to find out what's going on.

—Teacher, Georgia

Research over the past fifteen years has provided a highly accurate and growing body of knowledge about students at risk of failing in school, dropping out, and then entering society with few of the skills necessary for economic success. Part of this research has provided a striking profile of students from families living in poverty. Other equally compelling research has identified students who have unusual resilience in overcoming the challenges of poverty. Years of study on these topics has yielded important findings regarding both the identification of and intervention for these students. The Search Institute, a nonprofit research and development institute, has identified a set of *developmental assets* in the home, school, and community that contribute to establishing important predictions concerning youth behavior, values, attitudes, and school success. The Search Institute has also developed an inventory process and actually assists schools and communities with both the study of these assets in its student population and the design of appropriate interventions.

Another notable effort is a biennial survey conducted by the National Centers for Disease Control (CDC). Beginning in 1984, the CDC has coordinated the efforts of nineteen other federal agencies to administer, analyze, and report the findings of the Risk Behavior Youth Surveillance survey. This study provides invaluable feedback to schools and communities that assists in local efforts to track trends in the risky behavior of teens.

Taken together, these research efforts provide a wealth of insight into students at risk and the types and degrees of teenage behavior that can place any student at risk. This information is not only valuable for educators but also essential for families, community members, law enforcement, the faith community, youth service agencies, hospitals, and a host of other agencies. Data from these efforts help educators and communities better understand the nature of contemporary American youth and provide excellent tools for monitoring and evaluating the effect that a variety of service providers (such as churches, community agencies, and the family) have on the behavior and success of teenagers in their communities. For teachers, these data provide helpful information that can lead to more careful and effective classroom instruction and intervention. Information gleaned from these efforts often paints in stark contrast the challenges that schools and communities face in ensuring that each and every student learns effectively and succeeds in school.

The strategies described in this chapter grew from a rich body of research efforts conducted by the CDC, Phi Delta Kappa, the Search Institute, and the Northwest Regional Educational Laboratory, as well as a number of recognized independent scholars.

Unconventional Wisdom

What Works for Experienced Teachers

Personalize your classroom.

It's such a little thing, but I greet my high school students at the door, welcome them by name, and I tell each one how glad I am that they are in attendance. I have found that for so many students, my greeting and support may be the only positive comments that they hear all day.

—Teacher, Idaho

Become a student advocate.

So many of my students work really hard in my class but struggle with other teachers. I try to get to know my students, and once I find out about their lives, the remarkable thing is that they come to school at all. Some of my high school students are homeless, and others have "divorced" their worthless parents and have become legally emancipated. Here they are on their own, working, paying rent . . . and still trying to go to school. I began making a point of sharing the students' situations and problems with other teachers. I really go to bat for my kids. I do everything possible to advocate for them and try to negotiate problems with some of the more difficult teachers and occasionally even the principal. When a particular student is having significant problems, I get as many teachers as possible to be especially supportive, and together give the student praise and support. When we all work together, great things can happen for these kids.

—Teacher, Washington

STRATEGY #1

Recognize That Any Student May Become At Risk

I had always heard that any kid could become at risk. I guess on some intellectual level I understood that. I just never considered that it could be that kid sprawled on the couch in my family room watching TV. I never believed it could be my kid. Was I ever naive.

—Parent, Nebraska

A traditional profile of at-risk students has evolved over the years, which enables critical predictions to be made regarding a student's self-concept, behavior, and educational needs. This profile often describes the low-socioeconomic students living in homes of poverty, often with only a single parent, grandparent, or foster parent. These students, often identified prior to arriving at school through interaction with social agencies or identified through free and reduced lunch program applications, often constitute a significant percentage of the school's enrollment. Educators need to learn more about these students and the culture of poverty in which they live and strive to better anticipate their needs. These students can be taught effectively and can achieve high levels of academic success.

Another challenging reality is the fact that any student may become at risk of failing in school, dropping out, or even turning violent. Some recent tragic acts of school violence have been committed, not by the children of poverty, but by students living in affluent, two-parent, middle- or upper-middle-class homes. Educators have always recognized that emotional events in students' lives, such as the death of a parent, divorce of parents, the breakup of a teen romance, taunting, bullying, and so on, can suddenly place even the most successful student at risk. Even more distressing is recent research that tracks the risky behaviors of all teenagers (see Figure 4.1).

This effort to identify and monitor the risky behaviors of teenagers in the United States is the previously mentioned study of the Risk Behavior Youth Surveillance survey coordinated by the CDC. The goal of the CDC's work is to focus the attention of the nation on behaviors among the young that cause the most significant health risks. The survey monitors the use of alcohol, tobacco, drugs, sexual activity, safety, and nutrition. Results of the 2003 and 2005 surveys not only dramatize the many risky behaviors of teenagers today but also report an alarming percentage of youth involved in these behaviors (see Figure 4.1). The biennial data have

Risky Student (Grades 9–12) Behavior: 2003–2005

2003	2005	Alcohol and Drugs
44.9%	43.3%	drank alcohol on one or more days during the preceding month
12.1%	9.9%	drove a vehicle after drinking alcohol
30.2%	28.5%	rode with a driver who had been drinking in the preceding month
28.3%	25.5%	drank five or more alcoholic drinks on at least one occasion in the preceding month
12.1%	12.4%	have sniffed or inhaled intoxicating substances (glue, contents of aerosol cans, or spray paint)
22.4%	20.2%	used marijuana in the preceding month
5.8%	4.5%	used marijuana on school property in the preceding month
3.2%	2.1%	have injected an illegal drug

2003	2005	Sex
37%	37.2%	of sexually active students used a condom during most recent intercourse
46.7%	46.8%	of the students have had sexual intercourse
34.3%	33.9%	were sexually active within the preceding three months
14.4%	14.3%	have had four or more sex partners
17%	17.6%	were on birth control during their most recent sexual intercourse
4.2%	4.7%	had been pregnant or had caused a pregnancy
87.9%	87.9%	learned about HIV in school

2003	2005	Suicide
16.9%	16.9%	thought about committing suicide in the preceding year
8.5%	8.4%	attempted suicide in the preceding year

2003	2005	Safety
33%	35.9%	were in a physical fight in the preceding year
12.8%	13.6%	were in a physical fight on school property in the preceding year
17.1%	18.5%	carried a weapon (gun or knife) at least once in the preceding month
6.1%	6.5%	carried a weapon on school property in the preceding month
5.4%	6%	missed more than one day of school in the preceding month because they felt unsafe at school or when traveling to and from school
18.2%	10.2%	had rarely or never worn a seatbelt when riding in a car driven by someone else

2003	2005	Tobacco
21.9%	23%	smoked cigarettes in the preceding month
6.7%	8%	chewed tobacco in the preceding month

2003	2005	Nutrition
78%	80%	ate fewer than five servings of fruits and vegetables during the seven days preceding the survey
55.7%	54.2%	were enrolled in a physical education class (mostly ninth and tenth graders)
43.8%	45.6%	were attempting to lose weight
29.6%	31.5%	thought they were overweight

Figure 4.1

SOURCE: Eaton et al. 2006. Use "Eaton et al. (2006) and Grumbaum et al. (2004). Available from National Centers for Disease Control (n.d.) at <www.cdc.gov/mmwr/preview/mmwrhtml/ss5302a1.htm> and <www.cdc.gov/mmwr/preview/mmwrhtml/ss5505a1.htm>

demonstrated the existence of a continuing crisis in adolescent health caused by risky behaviors and provides schools and communities with the ability to monitor behavior trends over time.

Trend data from the last two surveys illustrate the changes in rates of incidence of multiple-risk behaviors that place many youth at risk. Coupled with recent profiles of violent youth, these data make it clear that many of our nation's youth encounter multiple situations that at some time during their adolescent years may place them at risk (see Figure 4.2 on page 36).

RESEARCH

- At-risk youth are present in all socioeconomic groupings of United States adolescents.
- Any child may become at risk during the years of formal schooling.
- Significant populations of high school students regularly participate in a variety of risky behaviors that involve alcohol, tobacco, illicit substances, sex, safety, and nutrition.
- Violent youth often do not fit the traditional definition of students at risk.

TAKE ACTION

- ☑ **Know your students.** Establish expectations that all students will become connected with a caring adult at school. When schools place a priority on educators and staff developing positive relationships with all students, negative behavior and dropout rates can rapidly diminish.
- ☑ **Stay informed.** Monitor the Youth Risk Behavior Surveillance survey in reference to all standards and pay special attention to recent research on the complex nature of school violence and perpetrator profiles.
- ☑ **Schedule community meetings. Disseminate information and initiate community meetings.** Discuss the biennial report from the CDC at these meetings. Because of the large size of the study and the random selection of participants, these data can be used to make predictions about youth behavior in your area. Community meetings might include law enforcement, the faith community, and youth service clubs, as well as parents and school staff. Discussion of the youth surveillance data by a cross-section of the school and community can lead to consistent, comprehensive efforts to address youth problems and behavior.

Factors That Place Students at Risk

(Ranked from most serious to least serious)

- Attempted suicide during the past year.
- Used drugs or engaged in substance abuse.
- Has been a drug "pusher" during the past year.
- Sense of self-esteem is negative.
- Was involved in a pregnancy during the past year.
- Was expelled from school during the past year.
- Consumes alcohol regularly.
- Was arrested for illegal activity.
- Parents have negative attitudes toward education.
- Has several brothers or sisters who dropped out.
- Was sexually or physically abused last year.
- Failed two courses last school year.
- Was suspended from school twice last year.
- Was absent more than twenty days last year.
- Parent drinks excessively and is an alcoholic.
- Was retained in grade (i.e., "held back").
- One parent attempted suicide last year.
- Scored below twentieth percentile on standardized test.
- Other family members used drugs during past year.
- Attended three or more schools during past five years.
- Average grades were below C last school year.
- Was arrested for driving while intoxicated.
- Has an IQ score below ninety.
- Parents divorced or separated last year.
- Father is unskilled laborer who is unemployed.
- Father or mother died during the past year.
- Diagnosed as being in special education.
- English is not student's primary language.
- Lives in an inner-city area.
- The mother is only parent living in the home.
- Is a year older than other students in same grade.
- Mother did not graduate from high school.
- Father lost his job during the past year.
- Was dropped from athletic team during past year.
- Experienced a serious illness or accident.

Figure 4.2

SOURCE: Adapted from "Growing Up Is Risky Business and Schools Are Not to Blame" by Frymier et al. *Final Report, Phi Delta Kappa Study of Students At Risk*, v. 1. © 1992, Phi Delta Kappa. Used with permission.

See the "50 Strategies Suggested Reading" section for a list of resources selected to complement the fifty strategies as you put them to use in your classroom.

SAVING MY STUDENTS, SAVING MY SCHOOL

How can **Strategy #1: Recognize That Any Student May Become At Risk** be put to use in your classroom? What can you do to increase awareness and education among your group of colleagues?

_____

_____

_____

_____

_____

_____

_____

_____

_____

_____

Share your thoughts with a colleague or group of colleagues.

STRATEGY #2

Predict Youth Behavior Based on Developmental Assets

I had little idea what was going on with kids in our schools, and I was on the school board! After seeing a report of our Community Asset Survey, I was suddenly struck with how much work we really have to do.

—School Board Member, Oregon

Beginning in 1989, the Search Institute has conducted research that has identified a framework of forty factors that have a direct effect on the behavior of adolescents. These factors, referred to as *developmental assets,* have been found to have highly predictable implications of the positive and negative behavior of students. Scholars have studied these assets and concluded that the more developmental assets of support that teens or preteens experience in their homes, communities, and schools, the less likely they are to engage in negative behaviors. Examples of these positive assets include

- commitment to learning,
- positive values,
- social competence, and
- positive identity.

Beginning in 1989 and continuing through the 1990 school year, the Search Institute surveyed more than 250,000 students from 600 communities in thirty-three states. The goal was to identify the essential developmental assets that youth need to live healthy lifestyles. In 1996, the survey was revised and administered to 1 million students (Grades 6–12) from 213 communities in twenty-five states. Results of the two studies confirmed a direct relationship between the developmental assets students experience and their behavior.

Communities throughout the United States have begun to use the Developmental Assets Survey to determine the degree of support that is occurring with students in their communities and to mobilize the community to increase and enrich the developmental assets available to students. The Search Institute has also identified more than 500 strategies for building community and developmental assets.

The number of assets a teenager perceives in his or her home, community, and school has a direct relationship to his or her behavior. The greater the number of assets, the more positive the behavior a student will exhibit. If students have more than thirty of the assets, they are less likely to engage in risky behaviors that involve the use of alcohol, drugs, sexual activity, and violence. Fifty-three percent of students who report having more than thirty assets are also successful in school. With more than thirty assets, 87 percent of the teenagers report they value diversity, 88 percent report they maintain good health, and 72 percent report they practice delayed gratification (Search Institute 1997).

The developmental assets can also be used to predict negative attributes, values, and behaviors. Of teenagers who perceive fewer than ten assets, more than 50 percent report problem alcohol use, 42 percent report illicit drug use, 33 percent report sexual activity, and 61 percent report some form of violent activity. Only 7 percent report succeeding in school (Search Institute 1997).

RESEARCH

- Cumulative positive assets in the home and community significantly contribute to student success in school.
- Negative assets contribute to risky behavior and signal a need for intervention.
- Communities that actively engage in the study of developmental assets are more likely to create needed systems of youth support.

TAKE ACTION

- ☑ **Foster school and community collaboration and advocacy.** Take the lead in developing collaborative relationships within your community. Bring various agencies and municipal services together to address the needs of youth at risk. Neither schools nor communities can successfully meet these challenges alone.
- ☑ **Conduct a Developmental Assets Survey**. Consider conducting the Developmental Assets Survey with the teenagers in your community. Conducting the survey provides an engaging opportunity for the entire community to support the survey and gain insights into the youth in your area. The mayor's office or a consortium of schools, law enforcement, and religious groups, as well as social agencies, may often sponsor the Developmental Assets Survey. Communities have found it very beneficial to

repeat the survey every two to three years to identify trends both positive and negative in youth behavior in their area.

☑ **Conduct community forums to review survey results.** Organize a number of parent and community forums to review results of the Developmental Assets Survey. The results are usually published in the local newspaper and presented at chamber of commerce meetings, service clubs, and scheduled sessions with law enforcement and religious groups.

See the "50 Strategies Suggested Reading" section for a list of resources selected to complement the fifty strategies as you put them to use in your classroom.

SAVING MY STUDENTS, SAVING MY SCHOOL

How can **Strategy #2: Predict Youth Behavior Based on Developmental Assets** be put to use in your classroom? What can you do to increase awareness and education among your group of colleagues?

_____

_____

_____

_____

_____

_____

_____

_____

_____

Share your thoughts with a colleague or group of colleagues.

STRATEGY #3

Appreciate the Resilient Student

This student is just incredible. It's like I sometimes wonder whether or not he understands how bad his life really is. His parents are alcoholics. They are abusive. He lives in such a sad state of poverty . . . but somehow he makes it to school every day, and his smile just lights up my classroom.

—Teacher, Nevada

Despite a substantial and ever-growing body of knowledge that defines the characteristics, causes, and consequences of low-performing and other at-risk youth, it is crucial that educators not use this information to make quick, stereotypical judgments about their students. Adults must remember that there is an exception to virtually every rule or research conclusion. Scholars have not only identified the characteristics of at-risk youth but have also identified students who have many of these characteristics and yet somehow are successful in their academic achievement. These resilient students often defy all conventional logic, to the surprise and pleasure of their teachers and families.

Research conducted at the Johns Hopkins University Center for the Study of Disadvantaged Youth and elsewhere has focused on identifying the characteristics of children and youth who seem to succeed in school and life despite possessing significant characteristics of an at-risk youth. Resilience appears to enable many young people to succeed despite severe living situations in their homes and communities. The Northwest Regional Educational Lab has also synthesized research on factors of resiliency and has urged schools to attempt to reinforce and cultivate the personal attributes that strengthen the protective factors in individuals, families, schools, and communities. The attributes of a resilient child are listed in Figure 4.3 on page 44.

These attributes combine to provide a powerful force that effectively mitigates what in other students are debilitating factors and impediments to success in school.

RESEARCH

- The characteristics common to resilient children can be developed and cultivated in an educational setting. These students and their resilient behaviors may benefit many others through modeling appropriate behaviors; peer mediation and tutoring; and academic, social, and civic leadership.

Attributes of the Resilient Child

- **Social Competency.** Resilient children tend to have qualities of "responsive-ness, flexibility, empathy and caring, communication skills, a sense of humor, and other pro-social behavior." Resilient children tend to be more responsive, more active, and more flexible. Because of their flexibility and interpersonal skills, especially a sense of humor, the resilient child seems to develop more positive relationships and stronger friendships.

- **Problem-Solving Skills.** Resilient children tend to have skills that include the ability to think abstractly, reflectively, and flexibly and to look for and attempt creative, alternate solutions to both cognitive and life problems. Such characteristics have been identified in street children who are able to survive in the midst of extremely difficult life situations.

- **Autonomy.** Resilient children tend to be far more independent, have a greater sense of personal power, and have a stronger self-esteem than their other at-risk peers.

- **Sense of Purpose and Future.** Resilient children tend to have realistic, healthy, goal-directed, and optimistic expectations regarding their future lives.

Figure 4.3

- Research data, profiles, and characteristics regarding violent and at-risk students must be used only as a warning to teachers, counselors, and school administrators. Careful evaluation, investigation, and observations of student behavior and academic work over a period of time must be used to determine the degree of problems or lack of problems that an individual student may have in school.
- Resilient youth can rise to the occasion when challenged. Educators must maintain the highest expectations for these youth.

TAKE ACTION

☑ **Treat each student as an individual.** Never quickly conclude that a particular student is at risk. Just because a student qualifies for the free or reduced lunch program, has worn or dirty clothes, or comes from a single-parent home does not mean that the student is at risk.

☑ **Expect all students to learn.** Recognize that all students can and will learn and, thus, organize your classroom in a way that both expects and facilitates the satisfactory achievement and learning of every child.

☑ **Know your students.** Actively seek to become as well acquainted as possible with each student. This effort will result in developing a better understanding of all students, particularly those at risk and those who are resilient.

☑ **Collaborate with others.** Actively collaborate with other adults, both in and out of school, to best address the needs of students. In addition, resilient students themselves can be great resources for developing the attributes of resiliency in students.

See the "50 Strategies Suggested Reading" section for a list of resources selected to complement the fifty strategies as you put them to use in your classroom.

SAVING MY STUDENTS, SAVING MY SCHOOL

How can **Strategy #3: Appreciate the Resilient Student** be put to use in your classroom? What can you do to increase awareness and education among your group of colleagues?

_____

_____

_____

_____

_____

_____

_____

_____

_____

_____

Share your thoughts with a colleague or group of colleagues.

STRATEGY #4

Address the Differences Between Boys and Girls

These little boys are just ruining my classroom. They won't sit still, they won't stop talking, and they want to argue about everything. I have recommended six of them to be tested for special education. They must be ADD or ADHD.

—Teacher, Oklahoma

What has happened to our girls? Through Grade 5 they have all been so wonderful—great students and never any trouble. But this year, they are dressing like Britney Spears, showing their tummies and unbuttoning their blouses, and academics is only a fading memory. Now these girls have only one focus . . . boys.

—Teacher, Illinois

To observe that boys and girls are different should not be considered any great intellectual brainstorm. Yet research has begun to systematically define a number of male/female differences that have great importance to public education in general and to classroom teachers in particular. In fact, researchers have identified a number of key gender differences that affect teaching and learning. They have also documented how these differences evolve as boys and girls grow and develop. Boys tend to score poorly on language arts sections of standardized tests and are five to ten times more likely to be disciplined during the elementary and middle school years. The majority of students (two-thirds) identified as qualifying for special education are boys. Most of the students who are identified and medicated are boys (Gurian 2001).

Experts are increasingly helping teachers and schools understand the differences between boys and girls. They have helped to show that the structures of schools and the types of instruction that are used can lead to great problems for one gender or the other. Many researchers have concluded that schools in general are not user-friendly to boys (Gurian 2001). Boys perform best academically when they can move around the classroom, and they need frequent recess breaks. Young boys love to talk and love classroom arguments or discussions. Unfortunately, these traits are often discouraged in classrooms.

For girls, there is a significant research base supporting the difficulties that young girls have in mathematics. Yet by focusing on this problem, public education has achieved rather dramatic improvements, such as an increased number of girls who are taking advanced mathematics and science courses and achieving higher levels of success. A number of authorities now agree that the gender gap in math is on the decline (Gurian 2001). Figure 4.4 lists and describes additional areas of gender difference.

There is also a growing body of neurological research that has identified significant differences in the physiology of boys and girls. Because of chemical, hormonal, and functional differences, girls mature earlier than boys. There are significant structural differences between the brains of boys and girls. The brains of boys and girls process emotion in dramatically different ways.

Different Learning Styles

The end result of the physiological differences in boys and girls is the development of significantly different learning styles (see Figure 4.5 on page 50). Current research on gender differences, while constantly evolving, can prove most helpful for teachers in analyzing and evaluating the effectiveness of learning activities for boys and girls (Gurian 2001). Girls and boys do indeed learn differently and will react to and perform uniquely when charged with similar tasks. An effective classroom teacher both acknowledges and responds to these differences in the planning and delivery of instruction.

RESEARCH

- Research has documented distinct differences in the chemical/ structural aspects and functioning of the brains of boys and girls.
- These physiological differences are revealed in rather distinct social, intellectual, and emotional behaviors of boys and girls.
- The physiological differences of boys and girls contribute to the presence of distinctly different learning styles.
- The culture of schools, instructional approaches, and how classroom learning is structured will directly influence the academic success for boys and girls.
- Boys and girls differ significantly, and these differences continue to evolve as children grow and develop.

TAKE ACTION

- ☑ **Seek professional development.** Research on boys and girls is such a new area of study that most teachers have little or no

The Differences Between Boys and Girls

- When they enter kindergarten, girls are more able to stay on task, better able to pay attention, and are more eager to learn than boys.

- More boys experience developmental delays during the primary years. Girls are more pro-social and less prone to behavioral problems.

- During the late elementary years, boys enter a time of macho pretense that makes learning difficult.

- Boys are much more likely to be referred to special education because of behavioral problems.

- Early adolescence is a time of emotional turmoil for girls; boys experience a similar turmoil, but it occurs during early childhood.

- During early adolescence, girls' math and science scores drop significantly.

- In early adolescence, girls become increasingly unhappy with their bodies, self-critical, deferential, and depressed.

- As boys grow older, they lose the social skills of attentiveness, articulation, and responsiveness. Much of this seems to be the result of enculturation of the concept of "Boys don't cry."

- In early adolescence, girls lose resiliency, optimism, assertiveness, risk-taking, and energetic behavior.

- During preschool, boys are able to form more meaningful relationships than in later life and are able to talk about those relationships.

- Research on single-sex classrooms indicates the effectiveness for both boys and girls of these programs.

- Girls significantly outachieve boys in language usage and reading.

- Boys and girls have a number of distinctly different learning styles.

Figure 4.4

Learning Styles of Boys and Girls

Deductive/Inductive Reasoning

Boys tend to be more deductive, working from the general to the specific; girls are just the opposite. Girls are more inductive, moving from isolated examples to generalizations.

Abstract/Concrete

Boys tend to be more abstract and like philosophical and moral debates. Girls tend to be more concrete.

Use of Language

Girls tend to use more words than boys and are better readers.

Logic and Evidence

Girls are generally better listeners; boys tend not to listen well and demand clear evidence from the teacher to support the teacher's conclusions.

Boredom

Boys tend to become bored more easily than girls. As a result, boys are more prone to act out and disrupt classrooms.

Space/Movement

Boys demand more space when learning, especially at a younger age. Girls need less space and do not need to move around as much as boys.

Sensitivity and Group Dynamics

Cooperative learning tends to be easier for girls rather than boys. Social hierarchies are extremely important to boys. In school classrooms, girls are not recognized and called on as often as the more demanding boys.

Symbolism

Especially in the upper grades, boys tend to become more adept at using symbolism, diagrams, and graphs.

Learning Teams

Because of the differences between boys and girls, learning teams can be unusually effective, especially if the teacher recognizes the distinct differences between boys and girls and plans learning experiences appropriately.

Figure 4.5

SOURCE: From Gurian (2001, pp. 44, 49).

professional understanding regarding the physiological differences and the associated learning styles. Familiarize yourself with the emerging research on this intriguing topic.

☑ **Understand gender differences.** Gain a better understanding of how gender differences are played out in classrooms and be careful not to perceive natural gender behavior as simple acts of disobedience or disruption.

☑ **Relate classroom structures to gender differences.** Recognize the intellectual, social, and academic differences between boys and girls and how they relate to effective classroom structures and schedules to ensure learning for all students. Classrooms need to be both "girl-friendly" and "boy-friendly."

☑ **Plan differentiated learning experiences.** Acknowledge gender differences and plan lessons that relate to the strengths of both girls and boys at their specific age levels. Explore the use of cooperative learning as an effective approach to gender differences.

See the "50 Strategies Suggested Reading" section for a list of resources selected to complement the fifty strategies as you put them to use in your classroom.

SAVING MY STUDENTS, SAVING MY SCHOOL

How can **Strategy #4: Address the Differences Between Boys and Girls** be put to use in your classroom? What can you do to increase awareness and education among your group of colleagues?

_____

_____

_____

_____

_____

_____

_____

_____

_____

Share your thoughts with a colleague or group of colleagues.

Educate Poor and Culturally Diverse Students

Strategy #5
Connect Culturally for Effective Teaching and Learning

Strategy #6
Work With the Externally Centered Student

Strategy #7
Understand the Problems of Low-Income Students

Strategy #8
Eliminate Ineffective and Destructive Interventions

Strategy #9
Use Effective Programs for Teaching Low-Income Students

We have almost 50 percent of our students on the free lunch and breakfast program, but by the time the kids get to the junior and senior high, many of them are too embarrassed or too proud to take advantage of the program.

—Principal, Texas

I couldn't believe how many "emancipated" students were attending our high school. These are kids who just gave up on their parents and moved out. We have three guys who share a heated ministorage shed to sleep in and take their showers each day at school.

—Teacher, Alaska

These families may be poor and living in desperate conditions, but they love their kids and want them to learn. The more we partner with families, the more we understand our students' needs. When we work together, the payoff is that our kids learn better.

—Principal, Minnesota

The greatest challenge facing public education in the United States today is the goal of teaching all students effectively, especially children and youth living in poverty. These students live in homes and communities that surround them with an overwhelming set of complex problems, which often makes teaching and learning extremely difficult. These are the "invisible" children, the "forgotten" children, the children of the "other America." These are the children who are lost in the "digital divide." Dale Parnell, former president of the American Community College Association, has referred to these students as the "neglected minority." Too often, these students are described as being "disengaged" or "disconnected" from the basic functions of our society; others label these students with more dramatic and simplistic terms: *deprived, disadvantaged,* or *dumb.* In Tucson, they are referred to as "gutter punks." In New York, where homeless families live underground in abandoned rooms in the Manhattan subway system, they are the "cave children," in Texas, the "grits." Regardless of how or what these students are labeled, they represent the greatest challenge to schools and teachers who are attempting to teach all students effectively.

These students grow up in a "third-world" environment while looking out at the richest nation that has ever existed on the face of the earth. These are the children who grow up eating clay out of the dirt floors of their homes in the Mississippi Delta or the lead paint peelings from the walls in their apartments in Chicago or Los Angeles. These are the children who suffer rat bites in Detroit and live in abandoned automobiles in Boise. These are the Native American children living in double-wide trailers on reservations across the nation. These are the children who fill the homeless shelters throughout the United States. At least 20 percent of America's children line up each day for the free and reduced breakfast and lunch programs of public education; and, too often, this is the only nutritional food they receive each day (U.S. Bureau of the Census. 2004). These are the children of abusive and abused parents, of disrupted and dysfunctional families. These are the nation's newest mobile migrants, moving again and again and again when the monthly bills come due. These students represent all ethnic groups, and in 2004, the U.S. Census Bureau reported that there were nearly 13 million children in America living in families with incomes below the poverty line.

The public schools of America are populated with African American, Hispanic, Asian American, Native American, Eastern European, and other groups who bring both cultural richness as well as significant challenges to the traditional institution of American schools. When these students live in poverty, the challenges are compounded. Today, with the continued and sometimes dramatic growth of many cultural groups, the use of the term *minority* is or will soon be inaccurate and inappropriate. In a growing number of states and in thousands of communities, the minority population has already emerged as the majority population. For public education, the demographics of these student groups demand understanding, recognition, and dramatic changes in the curriculum, instruction, and management of the school.

In 1990, it was estimated that at least 40 percent of the children in the United States were at risk of school failure and these numbers would continue to increase well into the 2000s. Since that time, there have been significant enrollment increases of African American, Hispanic, and Asian children. By the late 1990s, more than 45 percent were characterized by one or more of the following factors, which researchers have identified as placing students at risk (Land and Legters 2002: 11–12):

- Culturally diverse students living in poverty
- Limited English proficiency
- Poorly educated mother and/or living with a single parent

Researchers have concluded, "Approximately 33.1 percent of black and 30.3 percent Hispanic students lived below the poverty line in 1999, compared to 9.4 percent of white children" (Land and Legters 2002: 6). Over the past twenty years, the enrollment of Hispanic students in public education has increased more than 150 percent and currently is similar in number to African American enrollment in the United States. Most states are projecting 20 to 40 percent increases in Hispanic student enrollment in public schools during the next twenty years (Land and Legters 2002).

Rather than using terms like *majority* or *minority* to describe groups of students in public education, it is more accurate today to describe our student body as a *cultural mosaic*. Even in the large ethnic groups, there are wide variations of student backgrounds and cultures. Hispanics are composed of Mexicans, Central and South Americans, Cubans, Puerto Ricans, plus a variety of other backgrounds. African Americans are composed of Jamaicans, Haitians, Africans, Middle Easterners, and many others. The same is true of the Native Americans living in many tribes throughout the United States, as well as increasing numbers of Asian and Eastern European immigrants.

The vast majority of teachers enter their profession with backgrounds in content knowledge, effective instructional approaches, and educational philosophy and theory. Unfortunately, many teachers, even graduates of the nation's most prestigious universities, enter their classrooms with little or no understanding of the historical backgrounds, languages, religions, cultures, social structures, social classes, community norms, and other characteristics of the students they find there (Epstein 2001). As a result, too many teachers are unable to communicate effectively with parents and students and are unable to teach effectively in the cultural mosaic of the nation's schools.

Because of the large and growing number of culturally diverse students, educators must work diligently to connect culturally with these students. It is critical that all educators identify and combat racial stereotyping and other racist practices still present in many of America's institutions, especially public education. Schools need to recognize the value of parental partnerships and customize their instructional strategies to capitalize on the strengths and learning styles of their culturally rich student populations. The challenge of providing effective education for these students is compounded by the fact that so many come from families living below the poverty level.

The problems associated with poverty are so pervasive, so complex, and so debilitating that an earlier generation of educators concluded that schools could have little positive effect on poor students. In the 1966 Equality of Educational Opportunity report, eminent sociologist James Coleman concluded that the quality of a poor student's schooling accounted for only 10 percent of the variation in student achievement. This meant that the impact of attendance in a good school rather than a poor school was almost negligible. The other 90 percent of the factors that affected teaching/learning were found outside of the influence of the school: in the home environment, socioeconomic status, and the natural abilities of the students. The vast majority of the factors that influence learning, Coleman concluded, were beyond the control of the school.

For children of poverty, it is fortunate that James Coleman was wrong. Yet it is most unfortunate that it has taken educators so long to acknowledge his incorrect conclusions. As of 2008, we know conclusively that poor and culturally diverse children can learn and achieve acceptable academic standards and, with appropriate help, that these students can and will succeed on high-stakes tests. None of this, of course, is easy or inexpensive. In this section, five essential strategies are presented that provide a blueprint for action designed to transform the educational success of poor and culturally diverse students.

Unconventional Wisdom

What Works for Experienced Teachers

Drive a wooden stake into the normal curve.

This just makes me crazy! Every teacher comes out of college with a big dose of educational psychology, where they still emphasize the "normal curve." That is so sad, because teachers use the normal curve concept to justify failing students in their classes. If we are serious about teaching all students successfully, we need to drag the normal curve out to some highway cloverleaf and drive a wooden stake through its heart, burn it up, and then scatter the ashes over a landfill. The normal curve is an evil thing. In this day and age, where every student needs to learn effectively, we have got to replace the normal-curve mentality with mastery learning.

—Teacher, Oklahoma

Offer multiple graduation options.

At our school in Rochester City, New York, we have reorganized our high school and permit students to complete graduation requirements in three years. We also provide students who are really struggling with the opportunity to choose a five-year schedule for graduation. Each of these high school options serves a large group of students. For at-risk students who previously failed or dropped out of high school because they couldn't keep up with the pace of the regular high school schedule, the five-year schedule offered a reasonable approach to graduation. Now these at-risk students and their parents can agree to a more reasonable pace, and in many instances, students are provided with the opportunity to find a part-time job. College students have always had these kinds of options for graduating from college. It makes sense to us to provide such an opportunity at the high school level.

—Teacher, New York

STRATEGY #5

Connect Culturally for Effective Teaching and Learning

The thematic, interdisciplinary focus nights have really worked for us. Once a month, we invite all families to the school for our evening event that features one of our themes for the year. Our parent advisory board joins us in planning for each of these schoolwide events as we use these evenings to celebrate our cultural diversity. We mix academics with food, dancing, and issues of cross-cultural understanding and appreciation around a theme. Almost every parent comes with his or her kids. These events have really built our home/school community.

—Teacher, Michigan

Our entire high school faculty is just going crazy. How can the state expect us to get all of our students passing the new graduation test? It's just crazy. How can we be as effective as all of those suburban schools in rich communities? There is just no way. Doesn't anyone understand the kind of families that make up the majority of our school district? We are not failing; it's the kids' families that are failing.

—High School Teacher, Washington

One of the greatest challenges facing public schools in the United States is the successful education of all students. In a growing number of schools and school districts throughout the United States, poor students from a range of backgrounds are achieving up to the academic standards of their more advantaged classmates. The Education Trust has identified more than 4,500 such schools. To be successful with all students, schools must focus on eliminating the factors that schools can control that place students at risk. In addition, schools must stop blaming students and their families for their economic circumstances and, instead, capitalize on the personal, social, and community assets that enrich the resiliency and learning styles of poor and culturally diverse students.

Unfortunately, the cultural strengths, values, and historical richness of many groups too often stand in stark contrast to those of the prevalent culture in public schools, which is usually dominated by a middle-class and Anglo-American ethos. For so many students, life at school and life at home (and in the community) require diametrically opposed survival skills. This cultural collision frequently creates personal and family conflict with schools and results in behaviors and actions that undermine student academic success.

To make matters even more challenging, educators often point to the cultural traits of different ethnic groups as the reason why some groups of students have difficulty adjusting to public education. "In the past, low academic achievement in the African American, Hispanic and American Indian population was interpreted as resulting from a 'deprived home environment'" (Padron, Waxman, and Rivera 2002: 67). Unfortunately, this negative attitude continues to persist.

A growing number of public school teachers are effectively teaching poor and culturally diverse students. Both practicing teachers and recent research have documented how important it is for schools to understand and capitalize on the cultural backgrounds of students, access the "funds of knowledge available within the community," and integrate these strengths into the educational program of local schools (Padron et al. 2002: 67). A growing number of studies have shown how to effectively engage parents in the instruction, curriculum, and school management of public education to create what former American Educational Research Association (AERA) president Gloria Ladson-Billings calls "cultural congruence." For classroom teachers, this means relating effective practices to the social, cultural, and historical characteristics and backgrounds of students and eliminating school and classroom practices that actually place the culturally diverse student at risk (Ladson-Billings 1994).

Schools Place Students At Risk

Too often, the negative stereotyping of students in public education has led to the assignment of these students to remedial and low-track classes and to their be retained in grade, placed in special education, and even suspended. African American, Hispanic, and Native American students are much less likely to be placed in gifted and talented classes, advanced placement, college preparatory, or other accelerated educational programs. Such stereotyping often places students into personal dilemmas of adapting either to "street culture" values that glamorize academic underachievement or feeling that they must "act white" to succeed (Kuykendall 1992). Senator Herb Kohl (D-Wisconsin) believes it often becomes a point of personal honor for students to simply respond with "I will not learn from you" (Kohl 1994). To successfully address the conflicts between family culture and values with those of public education, parents and families must have courage and be willing to work with the school bureaucracy.

Research on public education serving low-income and culturally diverse students has also identified other examples of institutional racism. Schools for poor and culturally diverse students are too often poorly maintained, often supported by significantly fewer financial resources, and staffed with less qualified and less experienced teachers. Too many public schools continue to use instructional practices that are not effective for culturally diverse students and constitute what some researchers have called the "pedagogy of poverty." These ineffective practices focus on the overuse of teacher-controlled discussion and decision making, emphasizing lecture, drill and practice, remediation, and worksheets (Padron et al. 2002: 70). Other researchers have identified school characteristics and practices that create an at-risk environment for the culturally diverse student. These characteristics include

- cultural alienation,
- low standards,
- low quality of education,
- low expectations, and
- classroom practices unresponsive to students (Jagers and Carroll 2002; Ladson-Billings 1994; Padron et al. 2002).

Such school conditions lead to discipline problems, low achievement, high truancy, suspension, and high dropout rates.

Mavis Sanders's (1996) work at Johns Hopkins University identifies five critical areas in need of attention by policymakers. These include

- school expenditures to address past and present inequities;
- focused educational policy on the most pressing needs;
- quality of teaching and the school experience;
- effective partnerships between the family, community, and school; and
- improved preservice teacher education and professional development.

Until the issues Sanders highlights are sincerely recognized and meaningfully addressed, it must be concluded that the poor and culturally diverse student is not innately at risk; the school practices place the student at risk.

Culturally Relevant Teaching

To be effective with culturally diverse students, teachers must ensure that their schools and classrooms are culturally relevant and responsive. This means emphasizing the everyday concerns of students, families, and communities; it means valuing cultural diversity and celebrating cultural differences and values. Culturally relevant teaching builds on student knowledge and skills and relates school lessons to real-life situations. For African American students, culturally responsive instruction means a "communal orientation" rather than a "competitive environment," high teacher expectations, a curriculum rich in the social ethos of the community, and a "caring community of learners" that includes teachers, students, and parents (Jagers and Carroll 2002: 51–57). For Hispanic students, using "learning activities based on foundational concepts" from the home and community helps facilitate literacy and content learning and helps Hispanic students feel more comfortable with and confident about their work (Padron et al. 2002; Peregoy and Boyle 2000). And while the bulk of research on culturally diverse students has focused on African American and Hispanic students, there is a growing research base regarding effective practices for Native American students.

Culturally relevant teaching also includes schoolwide and community celebrations, festivals, and holidays. It includes culturally diverse teachers in classrooms and principals in schools—not just teacher aids, cafeteria workers, janitors, and bus drivers. Research by Ladson-Billings (1994) has identified a number of principles that she believes guide the culturally relevant classroom. She has found that teacher-student relationships in the "culturally relevant" classroom are fluid and humanely equitable, involve cultivation of relationships beyond the boundaries of the classroom, involve practices that are careful to demonstrate correctness with each of their students, and are characterized by practices that encourage a community of learners. To address issues of stereotyping and censorship in school textbooks, narrowly focused history curriculum, and restricted use of approved texts and reading lists, Ladson-Billings further emphasizes that educators should view knowledge critically, be passionate about knowledge, help students develop necessary skills, and ensure that student diversity and individual differences are always taken into account.

Full-Service Schools

Because of the complex social and economic problems facing the children in poverty, schools must work with a wide variety of social service agencies to ensure that families receive the services that are so essential to the effective education of poor children. In addition to effective education, poor students and their families often need

- emergency aid,
- nutritional food,
- warm clothes,
- mental health services and health services,
- counseling,
- child care, and
- legal advice.

For better or worse, public schools tend to be the single institution in our society that can coordinate all of these needs. (See Strategy #50.)

Understand Community Norms

So many schools in poor and culturally diverse neighborhoods institute parent training programs, but, too often, these good intentions end in failure because they attempt to impose a set of middle-class values on parents. Too often, the failure of these efforts serves only to reinforce the stereotypical perceptions of middle-class teachers. To be effective with culturally diverse students, teachers and school administrators must work hard to overcome their cultural misperceptions and to learn about the attitudes, values, and customs in their students' families. So much conflict between schools and families can be avoided if educators expend the effort to understand values, not just impose them. Lisa Delpit (1995) tells the moving story of Hispanic mothers violating school rules by bringing their children into their classrooms prior to the school day rather than leaving them outside the school door as the school required. Only after prolonged conflict did the school come to understand that Hispanic mothers thought of their children as "babies" and were not willing to leave them unattended in the school yard.

Effective Practices for Culturally Diverse Students

In addition to culturally relevant or responsive teaching, research has identified a number of other instructional practices that are successful with culturally diverse students (see Figure 5.1).

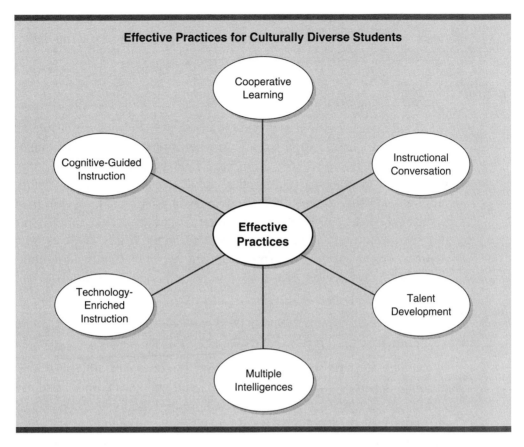

Effective Practices for Culturally Diverse Students

Figure 5.1

Cooperative Learning

Cooperative learning involving small teams of students working and sharing together has proven to be far more effective for culturally diverse students than the largely passive, teacher-directed instruction of an entire class. By directly assessing and defending their ideas, culturally diverse students are encouraged to develop higher-order thinking skills and come to complex understanding (McLaughlin and McLeod 1996).

Instructional Conversation

Instructional conversation is an extended discourse between teachers and students that combines relevance to students' personal lives with a focus on areas of educational value. At best, the dialogue grows out of student-initiated questions or comments that the teacher encourages and helps relate to important educational issues (August and Hakuta 1998; Padron et al. 2002).

Talent Development

A talent development approach is based on the philosophy that "all children can learn to high standards when there is a supportive environment, when high expectations are held by all stakeholders, and when there is clear accountability on the part of students, staff, families, and the community" (Boykin 2000: 7). Talent development involves the use of multiple activities, outcomes that relate to both formal education and the personal lives of students. It also involves high expectations coupled with a respect for the social and cultural dynamics of student, families, teachers, and other school personnel (Jagers and Carroll 2002: 49–51).

Multiple Intelligences

Schools and classrooms should employ the concept of multiple intelligences to ensure that the unique talents and abilities of each child are identified, strengthened, and celebrated. Some schools and classrooms choose to focus instruction around and celebrate a different intelligence each week or each month. Multiple-intelligences teaching acknowledges the whole learner and helps to ensure that the unique gifts of each child are recognized and developed (Gardner 1999).

Technology-Enriched Instruction

Some of the most powerful individualized teaching approaches are technology based. Appropriate technology-enriched instruction not only helps students "cross the digital divide" but also provides them a way to catch up and accelerate their learning (Thorsen 2003).

Cognitive-Guided Instruction

Sometimes referred to as *reciprocal teaching,* cognitive-guided instruction helps students process four specific comprehension monitoring strategies (Padron et al. 2002). These strategies include summarizing, self-questioning, clarifying, and predicting. To aid students in cognitive-guided learning, teachers must focus as much on students' psychological processing as on what is taught and how it is presented.

Partnerships and Collaboration
With Parents and Communities

In addition to using research-based instructional practices, teachers and administrators must work to establish collaborative community partnerships that extend beyond the classroom and the school. The partnerships of a school should empower students, parents, educators, and community leaders to work together as full partners in the instruction, curriculum, and management of the school. Such partnerships enrich teaching and learning and connect school goals to family and community goals. The fruits of these partnerships lead to higher academic achievement for all students. Some of the most effective approaches for working with culturally diverse families have been developed by Joyce Epstein (2001) and her colleagues at the School, Family, and Community Partnership Program at Johns Hopkins University. Very specific approaches have been developed, and a national network has been established to share information and support for schools and communities that are working with families of low-income and culturally diverse students.

Effective Schools: The Comer
School Development Program

Educators are fortunate to have a number of real-life successes in teaching poor and culturally diverse students. In addition to the 4,500 schools identified by the Education Trust, there are a number of highly successful program models with clear evidence of sustained effectiveness.

The Comer School Development Program, since the 1970s, has recognized "different and troubling student behavior as social underdevelopment or development appropriate for another setting, and recognizes low achievement as reflective of cognitive underdevelopment" (Comer, Haynes, Joyner, and Ben-Avie 1996: 8). With more than two decades of evaluation, research, and development, the Comer School Development Program has emerged as a powerful, effective approach for educating poor and culturally diverse students. The Comer program is neither a quick fix nor an add-on; rather, it is a long-range, comprehensive, schoolwide approach that examines and improves both the environment of the school and the behavior of students. This program is built and operates around three core teams:

- The Parent Team
- A School Planning and Magnet Team
- The Student and Staff Support Team (formerly the Mental Health Team)

These teams establish a school improvement plan and then regularly monitor the plan's implementation and effectiveness over time. The dynamics of this process hinge upon each team accepting equal responsibility for change, with "consensus, collaboration, and no-fault" as the watch words for constructively confronting challenges.

The Comer School Development Program, implemented in more than 541 elementary, 107 middle, and 73 high schools in twelve states, has impressive assessment data documenting the positive impact of this program on student achievement, behavior, and school adjustment, as well as the self-concept of students.

Other schoolwide improvement models with evidence of considerable success with culturally diverse students include Accelerated Schools PLUS, America's Choice, ATLAS Learning Communities, Coalition of Essential Schools, Core Knowledge, Direct Instruction, Expeditionary Learning/ Outward Bound, First Things First, High Schools That Work, High/Scope, KIPP, Making Middle Grades Work, Middle Start, Modern Red School-House, More Effective Schools, Onward to Excellence II, Project GRAD USA, School Development Program, Success for All—Middle Grades, Talent Development High School, Turning Points, and the wide and growing array of alternative, magnet, and charter schools (Comprehensive School Reform Quality Center [CSRQ] 2006a, 2006b).

RESEARCH

- Schools must understand and address the underlying problems of family stress and student underdevelopment in areas necessary for school success.
- Students from poor or culturally diverse families arrive at school with rich social and survival skills, resiliency, and an eager desire to learn, which schools must recognize and support.
- The more schools and classrooms become culturally relevant and responsive, the more effective they will become with poor and culturally diverse students.
- The more schools engage in partnering with families and the community to enrich instruction, curriculum, and school management, the more effective they will be in increasing student achievement, behavior, and positive self-concepts.

TAKE ACTION

☑ **Address funding inequity.** States, communities, districts, and schools need to focus attention and action on funding inequities that contribute to placing poor or culturally diverse students at risk.

☑ **Create partnerships.** Welcome parents and community leaders into comprehensive partnerships that engage the entire community in the instruction, curriculum, behavioral standards, and management of the program.

☑ **Learn from successful programs.** Don't reinvent the wheel. A growing number of approaches and model programs have substantial evidence documenting their effectiveness with poor or culturally diverse students. Teachers, parents, school administrators, and community leaders should learn about and visit successful school models and programs.

☑ **Assign the right teacher to the right classroom.** Work to ensure that the most qualified and effective teachers are assigned to (and want to teach in) classrooms populated by culturally diverse or poor students.

☑ **Seek professional development.** Join parents and community leaders in intensive, targeted professional development to gain enhanced understanding of and appreciation for the positive and negative effects of schools on poor or culturally diverse students, and to learn from the successes of others.

☑ **Develop plans and monitor progress.** Develop short- and long-term plans for improving student learning as well as plans to monitor the effectiveness of the efforts over time.

See the "50 Strategies Suggested Reading" section for a list of resources selected to complement the fifty strategies as you put them to use in your classroom.

SAVING MY STUDENTS, SAVING MY SCHOOL

How can **Strategy #5: Connect Culturally for Effective Teaching** be put to use in your classroom? What can you do to increase awareness and education among your group of colleagues?

_____

_____

_____

_____

_____

_____

_____

_____

_____

Share your thoughts with a colleague or group of colleagues.

STRATEGY #6

Work With the Externally Centered Student

This kid makes me crazy! If he fails a test, it is my fault. I made the test too hard. If he passes a test, he says that he just got lucky. . . . I can never get him to understand that what he does or does not do makes all of the difference.

—Teacher, Montana

The first and perhaps most important lesson for educators to learn about low-performing and other at-risk children is that educators and their students are often very different from one another. Teachers and school administrators have by and large experienced a successful K–12 education and graduated from college. Most educators have also completed graduate degrees, or at least some graduate work, and model the success of hard work, dedication, and delayed gratification. Teachers often exemplify self-determination and have an ingrained belief in cause and effect. They believe that hard work leads to success. When confronted with failure or lack of success, they have learned to take charge and try harder, invest more time, and increase their work and their output. All successful people have learned that what they themselves do can largely ensure their personal success. As a result, they can set long-term goals, identify what they need to do to accomplish their goals, and develop a personal plan to ensure success. Successful adults *internalize* an understanding of self-reliance and self-determination.

Far too many children and adults living in poverty have learned that regardless of how hard they work, there are often few rewards. Many have developed feelings of utter helplessness that, at best, lead them to passive acceptance of their plight or, at worst, to harmful addictions, substance abuse, or other debilitating behaviors. Rather than working harder to improve their condition, they tend to surrender to what they perceive as the inevitable. Too often, they simply give up.

The culture of poverty tends to make people externally centered. They come to learn that events and forces outside their own lives and control often overwhelm their best efforts and hard work. Jerry Conrath (2001) has attempted to explain the externally centered student. Conrath believes that far too many children of poverty see hardworking parents laboring in low-paying jobs that do not provide medical care or opportunities for advancement and they develop a sense that effort makes very little difference in their lives. Because children of poverty have often seen little possibility of hope for a better economic life, they frequently question the value of working hard in school. Many children of poverty live in homes where none of the adults have a job and perhaps have never had one. Others live in homes where adults work in the most low-paying, menial jobs, serving as field workers, house cleaners, fast-food employees, security guards, hourly workers in sweatshops, and on and on. Many adults with families living in homeless shelters today actually have jobs, often two or three part-time jobs. Unfortunately, even with minimum wage, far too many working parents do not earn enough to afford a place to live.

Children of poverty grow up being externally centered and believing that external events control their lives. They see no relationship between hard work, sacrifice, self-reliance, and success. These students often arrive at school with little or no concept of educational success and the reality that this success often depends on their efforts to conform to classroom procedures. As Conrath has reported, many at-risk students have an *external* explanation for everything, both the good and the bad that happens to them:

- If at-risk students pass a test, they often say, "the test was too easy" or the "The teacher didn't grade us very hard." These students do not see their success on the test as relating to anything that they did as an individual accomplishment.
- If at-risk students fail a test, it is usually because "It was too hard," "That teacher is a bitch," or "This course sucks." They rarely see their failures as relating to the fact that they did not do their homework, missed too many classes, or did not study for the exam.
- If externally centered students are asked why they are late for class, they often explain, "The bell already rang." When asked why they were absent, they say, "I was home."
- One teenage mother interviewed by the authors explained why she had become pregnant: "Well, this guy bought me a Coke and a Big Mac. . . ."

Externally centered students not only fail to understand the relationship between personal effort and success, they have also learned a variety of self-destructive behaviors:

- They are frequently absent.
- They do not do their schoolwork or their homework.
- They frequently complain to teachers or respond to questions during class with "This is boring" or "Why do we have to learn this?"

Challenging Students to Take Responsibility for Their Learning

The primary challenge for teachers of at-risk, externally centered students is to help them understand that they must take responsibility for what they learn. This is easier if it starts during the early elementary grades, but it must be attempted at any age. Teachers and schools must work to develop authentic responsibility in their students. This can be accomplished through a variety of effective school programs, such as service learning projects in the community, cross-age tutoring, and career internships in the adult workplace. But at the basic level, it means that teachers must do everything possible to ensure that students are welcome in their classrooms, punctual, engaged in learning, and successfully completing assigned work. Because at-risk students too often have home situations that make it difficult or impossible to do class assignments, schools must make time during the day to do classwork and assigned homework. If classwork and homework time are important to the successful education of students, that time must be allowed during the school day. Many schools extend class periods so that students can complete schoolwork while the teacher is present to assist them. Other schools encourage students to participate in before- and afterschool programs.

Teachers must never allow at-risk students to evade learning. Teachers must direct questions to all students and expect answers. They must always respond to all student questions and provide the necessary support to help at-risk students to complete their work. Teachers must effectively communicate to students that they care for them and hold high expectations for their performance and that students must be engaged in learning.

RESEARCH

- At-risk children and youth are often externally centered, especially those living in low-socioeconomic homes. These students believe external forces and events, not personal efforts, determine personal success or failure.
- Understanding poverty significantly enhances a teacher's ability to work effectively with poverty-level students and helps to culturally connect their teaching with the background of their students.
- Over time, educators can help low-performing and other at-risk students understand their potential for affecting their own lives. They can help students learn to take personal responsibility for their behavior and success in school.

- Service learning projects, cross-age tutoring, and practical internships in the workplace can help externally centered students acquire internally centered attitudes and behaviors.
- Schools are more effective with all students when they work closely with parents and attempt to understand and support the cultural backgrounds of their students' families.

TAKE ACTION

☑ **Learn about the culture of poverty.** This can be accomplished through readings, professional development activities, interactions with colleagues, visits to students' homes, and a variety of other activities.

☑ **Engage parents in the instruction, curriculum, and management of the school.** Build relationships with parents to help them become connected to all aspects of the school. This effort will both support and enrich school-based teaching and learning and will also ensure that the rules, regulations, curriculum, and behavioral expectations are not in conflict with those of the family.

☑ **Engage at-risk students in learning.** Be purposeful and creative in integrating at-risk students into classroom learning. Students should not be allowed to disengage through sleep or other inappropriate behavior. They must be required to complete classroom assignments, and they should be expected to contribute to classroom discussions.

☑ **Help poor students understand the hidden rules of the middle class.** Middle-class values should not be imposed on poor students. Students living below the poverty level should be taught about the hidden middle-class cultural rules that govern so much of public school—not to force students to accept them, but to help these students understand the complexity and choice of cultural values that are available to them.

☑ **Teach social responsibility.** Arm students with the social skills necessary to succeed in school. These skills range from appropriate communication to acceptable dress to a variety of behavioral expectations. All of these skills can and should be taught and reinforced. Without an understanding of appropriate social expectations, a student's academic progress will suffer or, in many cases, not be allowed to develop.

☑ **Create a structure for successful homework completion.** If homework is important, schedule time during, before, or after the school day for students to work on assignments and seek assistance if needed. Many students' homes simply do not provide an appropriate setting to complete out-of-school work.

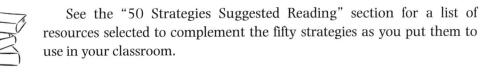 ☑ **Develop school responsibility.** Employ strategies that develop authentic, personal responsibility. School programs such as service learning, cross-age tutoring, and career internship have a powerful ability to enhance personal . . . responsibility in students who are low-performing and otherwise risk.

 See the "50 Strategies Suggested Reading" section for a list of resources selected to complement the fifty strategies as you put them to use in your classroom.

SAVING MY STUDENTS, SAVING MY SCHOOL

How can **Strategy #6: Work With the Externally Centered Student** be put to use in your classroom? What can you do to increase awareness and education among your group of colleagues?

_____

_____

_____

_____

_____

_____

_____

_____

_____

Share your thoughts with a colleague or group of colleagues.

STRATEGY #7

Understand the Problems of Low-Income Students

We try to schedule some type of event at the reservation school at least once a week. We have Family Computer Night, Traditional Arts and Crafts sponsored by the Cultural Center, and even a Jack-o'-Lantern Carving Night. For each event, we provide a nutritional meal and invite the entire family. Tonight, as families enter the cafeteria for dinner, we have nurses sitting at display tables distributing information about childhood diabetes—a particularly widespread disease among Native American children. We also have great basketball teams, and everyone turns out for the games. Our school is so important to this community. We try to educate both the children and their families, try to provide as many nutritional meals as possible, distribute health information, and offer blood tests. Our school is open about twelve hours each day, and it is the center of our entire community.

—Administrator, Reservation School, Wyoming

While it is difficult to effectively educate any unmotivated at-risk student, those from low-socioeconomic families represent a very special challenge. While poor students arrive at school with a rich variety of complex skills associated with personal and social resiliency and what researchers have defined as cultural strengths and supports, too often, these students come from homes where there are few conditions that stimulate, enrich, or support the kind of teaching and learning that typifies so much of public education in the United States.

For these students, the start of school often precipitates a collision of different values and cultures. Too often, these students and their families must make a great effort to maintain their personal and cultural integrity (and for some, their language) in the face of pressure to assimilate into the middle-class culture that pervades American public education. This effort often becomes a protracted power struggle between schools and families that makes teaching and learning all the more difficult. For many, this conflict manifests itself in students consciously choosing not to learn.

Poverty-level students may also come from homes in which the culture differs dramatically from the type of behavior and learning that characterizes much of public education. These homes have few books, magazines, and newspapers, and most have no reference materials or computers. Many children from these homes suffer from inadequate nutrition and the compromised mental and physical health related to the complex problems associated with poverty. In addition to health problems, poverty-level children often grow up with significant deficiencies in communication skills that impair their ability to read, write, and spell. Gerald Bracey (2002), a noted educational authority, reviewed a study of class differences in verbalization for children ages one to three. The study found that parents employed in professional occupations talked to their children using almost 2,200 words an hour, blue-collar parents spoke about 1,300 words per hour, and welfare parents spoke only 600 words per hour to their children. The impact of this lack of communication with adults severely affects children living in poverty. These children may arrive at school with significantly fewer communication skills than their more advantaged peers, and, too often, teachers fail to appreciate or capitalize on the rich, nonstandard forms of communication used by these students.

Children living in poverty may have cultural supports and experiences that enrich and strengthen their resiliency, but, too often, they have few of the opportunities that characterize middle-class culture. These kids usually have far fewer opportunities to travel, participate in organized sports activities, join clubs, participate in private lessons, and other types of social engagements. Many children of poverty live in disrupted and/or dysfunctional families where the stress level is unusually high on a day-to-day basis, making it a challenge even to find a quiet place to work or reflect. Unfortunately, families living in poverty may operate on a completely different set of attitudes, beliefs, and social rules that differ dramatically from the hidden middle-class rules and assumptions that govern both schools and workplaces. Often these differences lead to power struggles and clashes between families and schools. Families living in poverty tend to be externally centered, believing that their lives are swept along by external events. Few families living in poverty understand the causal relationship between personal hard work and sacrifice and success in school or the world of work.

"As a result of the enormous cultural differences between the world of poverty and the middle-class world of public education, poor children often arrive at school lacking the skills that schools tend to expect and emphasize. Public education emphasizes listening, following directions, pencil-and-paper exercises, reading, writing, tests, and obedience rather than the hands-on, problem-solving, and experiential skills that are often highly developed in poor children. As a result, schools frequently fail to effectively teach these children. The unfortunate consequence of this can be that students' self-concepts suffer. They are often unable or unwilling to do their schoolwork and their homework. They fall further behind educationally, are retained or placed in slow-learning tracks, and rarely catch up. These students are all too often destined for dropping out (see Figure 5.2).

To effectively educate poverty-level children, teachers must become more understanding of the speech patterns, communication styles, and participation structures of their students. The more teachers understand

---

**Important Insights Into the Lives and Learning Styles
of Children of Poverty**

- Poverty occurs across all ethnic groups and creates a special set of problems that complicate all other factors that influence teaching and learning.

- Children of poverty-level families can learn effectively and achieve high academic standards.

- The culture of poverty-level children often conflicts with the middle-class culture that pervades public education.

- Partnerships between schools and families of poverty-level students in the management of the school and in the education of poverty-level children can ameliorate or at least diminish the complex power struggles that can inhibit teaching and learning.

- A good school can overcome the debilitating effects of poverty and even those of a dysfunctional family.

- Good teachers, even in a failing school, can have a significant long-term positive effect on the students in their classrooms.

Figure 5.2

the culture of poverty and the ethnic cultures of their students, the more teachers can work together with parents and families as partners in education (Ladson-Billings 1994). We know this because a growing number of studies have documented that schools can, in fact, teach all children and youth effectively, even poor and/or culturally diverse students. As noted earlier, the Education Trust has identified more than 4,500 schools throughout the United States with more than 50 percent of students living at poverty level, being culturally diverse (African American or Hispanic), or both, in which students are achieving in the top one-third of academic performance measured by their respective states.

Research such as the Louisiana School Effectiveness Study, alternative and magnet school studies, and testing by the National Assessment of Educational Progress has documented the fact that poor children can learn effectively and achieve high academic standards. Perhaps most revealing is research on the importance of individual teachers. In one study, researchers analyzed the achievement scores of more than 100,000 students in hundreds of schools across the nation. They were able to refute the myth that teachers cannot make a difference with poor students. The study documented the following:

> The most important factor affecting students' learning is the teacher. In addition, the results show wide variation in effectiveness among teachers. The immediate and clear implication of this finding is that seemingly more can be done to improve education

by improving the effectiveness of teachers than by any other single factor. Effective teachers appear to be effective with students of all achievement levels, regardless of the level of heterogeneity in their classrooms. If the teacher is ineffective, students under the teacher's tutelage will show inadequate progress academically regardless of how similar or different they are in their academic achievement. (Wright, Horn, and Sanders 1997: 63)

Research continues to explore the positive and negative effects of teachers. Reflecting on a study of teachers in Tennessee in 1996, noted researcher William Sanders (Sanders and Rivers 1996) reported the following sobering conclusions:

- If a student has an ineffective teacher during the elementary years, it will take him or her up to two years to recover academically.
- If a student has two ineffective teachers during the elementary years, he or she may never catch up.

Sanders's conclusions are frightening because, sadly, children of impoverished families are often subjected to ineffective teachers.

While we know that children of poverty can learn effectively, there is also greater understanding today of the effects that an impoverished home life has on student learning (see Figure 5.3).

Effects of Economic Impoverishment on Student Learning

- Poor nutrition has a debilitating effect on children of poverty.
- Homes of poor children often lack the education enrichment supports to maintain and enrich what happens during the school day. As a result, poverty-level children have a poor record of completing homework assignments and arrive at school the next day less prepared than their more advantaged peers. Over time, if the school does not intervene and develop an effective partnership with parents, the gap between poor and advantaged children increases.
- Children of poverty suffer significantly during the summer months. A study analyzed by Bracey (2002) found that advantaged students spent their time during the summer going to city and state parks; taking swimming, music, and dance lessons; visiting parks, museums, science centers, and zoos; participating in organized sports programs; and going often to the public library. For poor children and youth, few of these activities were available. The summer months were too often spent without books, educational stimulation, or even nutritional meals. As a result, students from poor families suffered a significant drop in academic learning when compared with their more advantaged classmates, who not only maintained their level of achievement over the summer months, but actually increased their achievement through nonschool activities.

Figure 5.3

Understanding the culture and problems of poor children and their families is the first step in developing effective programs to address student needs. It is essential that educators equip themselves with reliable research-based information on the effects of poverty and the positive contributions of culture. They must join the effort to dispel the tragic myths perpetuated by an earlier generation of researchers regarding how little effect schools can have on the children of poverty. Without accurate information, too often,

- teachers and administrators do not expect poor children to learn, and they blame both the students and their parents for not learning;
- public school educators apply the concept of the bell curve to justify failing a percentage of their students, and these students tend to be children of poverty; and
- middle-class teachers often lack the cultural sensitivity to connect with the cultures of the students they are teaching.

As researchers have begun to understand that children and young people from poverty-level backgrounds can learn effectively, they have also begun to learn how schools can achieve such success with low-socioeconomic status students.

Before schools can undertake the actions listed in Figure 5.4 (page 80), many schools will have to make other significant changes. (See Figure 5.5 on page 80.)

Schools and teachers can make the difference for poverty-level children. Understanding these students and their lives must become a priority of every public school in America.

RESEARCH

- Poverty-level and culturally diverse students have rich social and cultural skills that often are not valued by or compatible with the prevailing middle-class culture in many public schools.
- Partnerships between schools and families are essential to ensure the effective teaching and learning for poverty-level students. When schools work with the families of these students, significant, measurable improvement in student skills, knowledge, and attitude can occur (Comer, Ben-Avie, Haynes, and Joyner 1999; Epstein 2001).
- An effective school can overcome the debilitating effects on children of poverty and dysfunctional families.
- Positive teacher attitudes informed by culturally congruent instructional strategies have a powerful effect on the achievement of poor children.

School Imperatives for Achieving Student Success

- Develop effective partnerships with all parents, particularly poverty-level families, to overcome distrust and cultural misunderstandings and actively invite parents to participate in the instruction, curriculum development, and management of the school.

- Help parents understand how they can help their children learn by enriching and supporting school efforts.

- Focus on enriching and effectively using the time students are in school.

- Intensify the teaching of basic skills. To achieve high academic standards, students must first obtain a strong foundation in the basic skills.

- Work to individualize and accelerate learning so that poverty-level students catch up academically as quickly as possible.

- Surround students with caring and demanding teachers who are culturally sensitive and believe that all children can learn, work to support students in their educational endeavors, and hold high expectations for academic achievement.

Figure 5.4

Readying Schools for Change and Success

- Work closely with parents as partners in their children's education to ensure student achievement.

- Lengthen the school days by establishing before- and afterschool programs to provide as much educational enrichment as possible while the students are at school.

- Reorganize the school day and the school week to provide intensive instruction to poor students. (Many schools have reorganized the school day to provide as much as an hour every day for intensive instruction in basic skills, tutorials, remedials, and enrichment. Other schools have created four-day academic programs to provide time one day a week for enrichment and remediation.)

- Develop summer programs or year-round schools for poor students to enrich social and academic learning during the summer months.

- Provide nutritional meals, books, and other educational stimuli on a year-round basis.

- Identify poor children and enroll them in high-quality preschool programs and full-day kindergarten.

Figure 5.5

TAKE ACTION

☑ **Review research on the nature of poverty.** Carefully review research regarding the characteristics of poverty, the culture of poverty, and the effects on teaching and learning.

☑ **Seek professional development.** Participate in professional development programs to learn more about the culture of poverty and effective approaches for working with poor children and their families. Keep abreast of the new and growing number of programs that have positive effects on poor children.

☑ **Conduct home visits and form partnerships with parents.** Conduct home visits to the families of poverty-level students and seek to develop a constructive partnership based on the mutual desire for all students to learn, which can be invaluable to the students' success.

☑ **Implement early and continuous assessment.** Identify and diagnose the problems and needs of at-risk children. Assess the achievement of poverty-level children prior to first entering school and frequently throughout the school year to determine the effectiveness of school programs.

 See the "50 Strategies Suggested Reading" section for a list of resources selected to complement the fifty strategies as you put them to use in your classroom.

SAVING MY STUDENTS, SAVING MY SCHOOL

How can **Strategy #7: Understand the Problems of Low-Income Students** be put to use in your classroom? What can you do to increase awareness and education among your group of colleagues?

_____

_____

_____

_____

_____

_____

_____

_____

_____

Share your thoughts with a colleague or group of colleagues.

STRATEGY #8

Eliminate Ineffective and Destructive Interventions

My parents didn't have much schooling. There were no books in our house. My vocabulary was limited to what I learned on the streets. When I started school I was already behind. After being retained in the third grade, I was placed in special education. Looking back, I wonder if the teachers really thought that they were helping me.

—Student, New Mexico

The culture of poverty combined with the family conditions associated with poverty create a complex set of debilitating problems that make effective teaching and learning an enormous challenge for at-risk students. Unfortunately, in addition to the cultural conflicts that exist between families of poverty and schools, a number of school policies, practices, and programs that compound the problems of poor children and youth have long-term, negative effects. Rather than assisting low-socioeconomic students to remediate, catch up, and accelerate, schools too often use failed and failing approaches that tend to brutalize, stigmatize, isolate, and abandon the very students they purport to help. Taken as a group, these school traditions in effect "wage war" on poor children and youth. Unfortunately, while educators have long understood that there is little they can do to improve the home and community environmental factors that negatively affect the ability of students to learn, teachers and administrators have been slow to identify ineffectual and destructive school philosophies, policies, programs, and practices that confound and exacerbate the problems of poor children and youth. After decades of research documenting the tragic effects of particular practices in public education, the only logical conclusion that can be reached is, "We have met the enemy . . . and the enemy is us."

The challenge of eliminating failed, destructive philosophies, policies, programs, and practices has become a sobering, ethical call to action. It is hard enough to help poverty-level children to learn effectively without assaulting them with public school traditions that all but doom these students to frustration and failure. Parents, teachers, administrators, school boards, and state and federal legislators should confront the destructive aspects, as shown in Figure 5.6 (page 84), inherent in public education and ban them from use.

Schools Must Vanquish the Enemy Within

Schools must banish the following practices:

- Embracing the outmoded philosophy of equal educational opportunity
- Blaming poverty-level families and their children
- Continuing unsound testing practices
- Using the normal curve
- Perpetuating flawed school practices and policies

Figure 5.6

Embracing the Philosophy of Equal Educational Opportunity

During the past fifty years, the legal operating philosophy of public education has changed from the "separate but equal" policy of racial and socioeconomic segregation to "equal educational opportunity for all." Unfortunately, the philosophy of equal educational opportunity has proven almost as destructive as the earlier "separate but equal" concept. First, for poor families and their children, there has rarely been equal educational opportunity. Using geographic boundaries to assign families to public schools has led to the continuing challenges posed by segregating schools based on socioeconomic status. In most communities, poor families and their children suffer great inequality by being assigned to inferior schools with other poor children. Research continues to document that the schools serving poor children and youth have fewer resources than schools in advantaged neighborhoods, as well as more inexperienced teachers, fewer teachers teaching in the areas of their credentials, inferior instructional materials, and, too often, failing levels of achievement (Haycock 2006). Few issues in public education have proven as tragic and destructive as the philosophy held by so many educators who continue to espouse this faulty assumption: "We give these kids every opportunity to learn. If they don't take advantage of our educational programs, it's their fault, not ours." Finally, today, this flawed philosophy is being legislatively replaced at the state and national level with the mandated philosophy of "Leave no child behind."

Blaming Poor Families and Their Children

Too often, teachers, administrators, and school boards explain the failures of public education by blaming the students. Schools and school districts all over the country serving poor neighborhoods have argued and often pleaded with educational policymakers to exempt them from newly legislated academic expectations because their schools serve large percentages of poor and minority students. Schools and school districts across the nation with low achievement scores explain their failing by blaming the families and students they serve: "Well, if you knew our students or visited their homes, you would understand why our achievement test scores are so low" is all too frequently an explanation. To blame poor children for their deficits is no more productive than blaming underdeveloped children for lack of proper nutrition. Today, we have a better understanding of the problems associated with poverty, and we have nearly three decades of research documenting that schools can effectively overcome these challenges.

Continuing Unsound Testing Practices

In addition to the problems posed by the environment and poor families, schools often contribute to the difficulties of poor children. Too often, public schools camouflage the challenges faced by poverty-level children with two unfortunate practices.

Hiding the Trees With a Forest

First, many schools report school and district achievement test scores with aggregate averages. As a result, the test scores of underachieving poor children are rendered invisible and compensated by the high performance of other, more advantaged children. Many school districts that report their students' scores as higher than state and national averages distort the reality of poor children and generate an unfortunate misunderstanding about the effectiveness of schools' and districts' performance. School districts must begin to disaggregate the scores of students so that comparisons can be made between those living in poverty and the more advantaged students in the school or district.

Reporting Achievement Annually

Too many schools fail to assess student progress and report frequently enough; instead, such schools comply only with annual state reporting requirements. Because poverty-level children often suffer a significant loss of academic achievement during the summer months, annual reporting of scores tends to support a conclusion that schools are failing these children, when, in fact, the gap between poor students and other students may be narrowed during the school year, only to fall farther apart during the summer months. Schools and school districts need to assess students during the early fall, midyear, and again at the end of the school year to evaluate student progress and the effectiveness of the instructional program. This practice will also help identify students for summer remediation and acceleration programs.

Misusing the Normal Curve

One of the unfortunate realities of public education is the continued misuse and misunderstanding of the concept of the "normal curve." Far too many educators still maintain that there will always be a percentage of students who will fail, and they dignify their conclusion by referring to the normal curve of probabilities. Far too many teachers, especially at the middle and high school level, believe that it is their responsibility to fail a percentage of students. Until rather recently, this concept has been used as a school or departmental philosophy. While there will, in fact, always be a range of achievement levels, the goal must be to raise the minimum level of expectations to significantly high levels and ensure that all students achieve this level of excellence. The expectation of mastery learning must replace the "normal-curve mentality."

Perpetuating Flawed School Practices and Policies

While poverty-level students suffer significantly from differences between the home and the community, too often schools employ practices and policies that tend to complicate the problems of these students. These include the following:

- Failing to identify poor children prior to kindergarten or the first grade and failing to provide early childhood enrichment programs.
- Failing to teach poor children to read at grade level during the early years.
- Continuing the use of the ineffective practices of tracking, retention, and pullout remedial, which isolate and stigmatize students. The evidence of the destructive effects of these practices on low-performing and other at-risk students is overwhelming.
- Incorrectly diagnosing large numbers of students as attention deficit disorder (ADD), attention-deficit/hyperactivity disorder (ADHD), or both, and assigning them to special education. Also, large numbers of these students are medicated. Many students simply need smaller, more personalized learning environments with caring teachers who hold high expectations for all students.

RESEARCH

- Research on effective schools has documented that all children, regardless of socioeconomic levels, can learn effectively.
- Research on effective schools has documented the flaw in the concept of equal opportunity and confronted the tragic practice of blaming poor families and their children for their educational deficits.
- Research has documented the brutal effects of tracking and retention on student self-esteem and academic performance.
- Research on Title I and special education has documented the lack of academic gain that occurs when students are pulled out of their classes for remediation programs.

TAKE ACTION

☑ **Consider recent research on failing programs.** Review research reports that summarize the destructive effects of many traditional programs and practices used in public education.

☑ **Improve assessment and testing practices.** Develop new policies regarding student assessment and testing that tend to camouflage the performances of poor children and youth.

☑ **Monitor and compare achievement of poverty-level students.** Disaggregate school and district data according to students' socioeconomic levels to carefully document and frequently monitor student achievement, attendance, failing grades, discipline referrals, and so on

☑ **Work to change school policies.** Help school boards and legislators to better understand the destructive impact of failed educational philosophies and work to change the operational philosophies and policies that negatively effect poverty-level children.

 See the "50 Strategies Suggested Reading" section for a list of resources selected to complement the fifty strategies as you put them to use in your classroom.

SAVING MY STUDENTS, SAVING MY SCHOOL

How can **Strategy #8: Eliminate Ineffective and Destructive Interventions** be put to use in your classroom? What can you do to increase awareness and education among your group of colleagues?

_____

_____

_____

_____

_____

_____

_____

_____

_____

_____

_____

Share your thoughts with a colleague or group of colleagues.

STRATEGY #9

Use Effective Programs for Teaching Low-Income Students

It will break your heart. We have a dropout rate of 50 percent in Tucson and literally hundreds of homeless teenagers living on the streets in the downtown area.

—Teacher, Arizona

Hey, it's not my fault these kids don't learn. I give them every opportunity to learn. . . . You don't know our kids. . . . They just do not take advantage of what we offer them.

—High School Administrator, Georgia

Research has not only documented that low-socioeconomic students learn effectively and can achieve established academic standards; it has also identified a number of school programs that have proven to be highly effective in addressing the challenging needs of these students. For poverty-level children to learn effectively and achieve high standards of academic performance, a number of conditions must occur:

- **Partnerships** with families must be developed for the management of the school.
- **Parents** of poor students must become partners in the instructional delivery and be enlisted to assist with their children's education when the children are at home.
- **Teachers** must be sensitive to their students' cultural backgrounds and take care to see that their instruction is culturally congruent with their students (Ladson-Billings 1994).
- **Schools** must likewise recognize and support their students' cultures and work with parents to make certain that the school's rules, regulations, and behavioral expectations are not in conflict with those of the family.

The school day and school year need to be extended to include opportunities for remediation, acceleration, and enrichment. Poor students need additional support as early as possible during the preschool years and once in school require extended-day and summer programs. To be effective with poor students, schools must implement programs with solid evidence of positive results and success (see Figure 5.7 and the discussion that follows.)

Programs That Yield Positive and Demonstrated Results

- Parental Partnerships (Strategy #15)*
- Child Care, Preschool, and All-Day Kindergarten (Strategy #34)
- Effective Basic Reading Skills Instruction (Strategy #32)
- Personalized and Computer-Assisted Instruction (Strategy #37)
- Extended-Day Programs (Strategy #50)
- Summer Programs and Year-Round Schools (Strategy #50)
- Service Learning and Career Practica (Strategy #45)
- Cross-Age Tutoring (Strategy #44)
- Mentoring (Strategy #44)
- Alternative Schools (Strategy #19)
- Full-Service Schools (Strategy #50)

Figure 5.7

NOTE: Each of these programs is discussed further in later strategies. See the strategy listed in parentheses.

Parental Partnerships

To be effective, schools must develop strong, trusting partnerships with all parents, especially those of poor students. Schools with proven track records of successfully teaching all students effectively create partnerships with parents to help manage the school, support teaching and learning, enrich the curriculum, and help to bring about a positive, cultural consistency between families and schools.

Child Care, Preschool, and All-Day Kindergarten

It is essential to help children of poverty enroll in educational programs as early as possible. This includes high-quality child care and preschool programs, such as Even Start, Head Start, and all-day kindergarten. These early childhood programs have proven to be the most cost-effective, successful approaches to influencing long-term positive student achievement.

Effective Basic Reading Skills Instruction

A critically important goal in ensuring student success in school is effective basic reading skills instruction—regardless of the student's age or grade level. Since poor students often arrive at school with communication needs and are often not prepared for reading success, schools must focus increased energy and attention on reading instruction. Basic reading skills are the foundation for all of later academic learning, and, as a result, they must become the focus goal during the early childhood and early elementary years.

Personalized and Computer-Assisted Instruction

At all school levels, every effort must be utilized to address the particular deficiencies of poor students. This means that schools and classroom teachers must personalize and individualize instruction. A growing number of effective and interactive computer-assisted instructional programs have proven to be unusually effective in this effort.

Extended-Day Programs

To maximize the educational impact of any instructional program, the school day must be extended. Before- and afterschool programs should include breakfast and snacks, as well as intensive one-on-one tutorials to help poor students catch up and accelerate their learning.

Summer Programs and Year-Round Schools

Because of the unfortunate drop off in student performance during the summer months, schools must provide ongoing remediation, enrichment, and nutrition programs throughout the summer. Summer programs and year-round schools may be the most important approach to ensure that poor students catch up and accelerate their learning.

Service Learning and Career Practica

For older low-socioeconomic students, getting out of the school and into the real world of the community is a necessity. Research has documented significant, positive effects of service learning and career exploration and practica.

Cross-Age Tutoring

For older students with basic skill deficiencies, cross-age tutoring has proven to be particularly effective. The practice of older students tutoring younger students both enhances the self-esteem and strengthens the basic skills of the older students and is also very effective with the younger students.

Mentoring

A highly effective approach to positively influencing the development of poor students is an adult-student mentoring program. A positive relationship with one adult can represent the most powerful, positive influence in the life of a poor child.

Alternative Schools

Alternative education is often the most effective approach to keeping poor students in school and helping them catch up academically and achieve high standards. Effective alternative schools surround students with teachers who care for, support, and challenge the students to achieve high expectations.

Full-Service Schools

Effective public schools often coordinate a wide variety of services from state and local social service agencies. Many schools have established health centers to help teenagers living in poverty without health care. Others actively engage the social service and juvenile justice systems with their schools.

RESEARCH

- Head Start has been proven to be one of the most successful federal programs ever developed. Yet gains from the Head Start Program can decline during the early elementary grades unless students continue to receive enrichment and support.
- All-day kindergarten is one of the most effective interventions to prepare poor children for school.
- The National Dropout Center has identified alternative schools, mentor programs, and service learning as the three most effective ways to keep at-risk students in school, improve their self-esteem, and keep them learning effectively.

- Successfully mastering the basic skills in the early elementary grades has long-term benefits both in school and in later life, and it is highly cost-effective.
- Poverty-level children and youth respond positively to personalized learning in a curriculum that has been customized to meet their needs.

TAKE ACTION

☑ **Enrich students during early childhood.** Educate families living in poverty about the early learning needs of their children. Teach parents about high-quality child care, Head Start programs, and other preschool programs that have a positive impact on self-esteem and student achievement.

☑ **Conduct early assessment and diagnosis to identify poor children as early as possible.** Conduct student assessment and diagnosis during the preschool years so that problems can be identified and addressed as early as possible.

☑ **Expand breakfast and lunch programs, provide free health programs, and offer all-day kindergarten programs.** Coordinate resources and services from the district and state and local health and welfare agencies to ensure that children have access to services and programs that have a positive impact on self-esteem and achievement.

See the "50 Strategies Suggested Reading" section for a list of resources selected to complement the fifty strategies as you put them to use in your classroom.

SAVING MY STUDENTS, SAVING MY SCHOOL

How can **Strategy #9: Use Effective Programs for Teaching Low-Income Students** be put to use in your classroom? What can you do to increase awareness and education among your group of colleagues?

_____

_____

_____

_____

_____

_____

_____

_____

_____

_____

Share your thoughts with a colleague or group of colleagues.

Establish Priorities That Focus on Student Learning

Strategy #10
Develop a Comprehensive Plan

Strategy #11
Build a Profile by Collecting and Using Data

Strategy #12
Set Goals, Targets, and Timelines

Strategy #13
Create Time for Collaboration, Planning, and Development

Strategy #14
Facilitate Continuous Improvement: The Critical Importance of Results-Driven Leadership

Once we agreed that increasing student learning and achievement was what we were about, our planning and delivery became focused. That's why we're here. It's the core purpose of our work . . . and we're talking about all kids.

—Superintendent, Idaho

As long as public schools have existed, educators and parents have worried about students who, for whatever reason, struggle to achieve. For many years, once a child completed compulsory education, low performance or other indicators of at-risk behaviors were often greeted with a recommendation that the student seek other opportunities—work, the military, or simply something else, as long as it was outside of school. Those days are now gone forever, for a student without an adequate education faces a bleak future of economic and social challenge and hardship.

State legislatures across the nation have confronted this reality by enacting educational standards and assessments. From state capitols to district boardrooms to classrooms, the concept of equal educational opportunity is being replaced by state and federal assessments that demand acceptable performance. What differs today from accountability efforts of the past are the state and federal consequences applied to educators, schools, and districts for repeated failure to reach stated expectations for student achievement. While these consequences vary, from punitive to incentive based, they all share a common purpose: all students must reach acceptable stated levels of achievement.

Educators rarely welcome legislated and often unfunded mandates. Yet few school board members, superintendents, principals, or teachers would disagree with the moral intent of the expectation that all children can and will achieve and reach acceptable levels of performance. The "how" of accomplishing this endeavor represents the challenge facing public education today.

Improving the achievement of low-performing students begins and ends with the system. Most districts and schools in the United States could share historic examples of the remarkable successes of individual students, often taught by a nurturing teacher with high expectations. Yet on the other side of the tracks or even the hallways of the school, the dismal failure of other students is perpetuated. Those districts, schools, and classrooms that demonstrate that all students will achieve to acceptable performance standards possess a simple yet forceful commonality: they establish priorities and focus on the goal of educating all students, including low performers and others at risk.

The five strategies presented in this chapter provide a framework for creating or improving student and educator performance in classrooms, schools, and districts. This improvement begins with one student, teacher, leader, school, and district at a time. Improvement becomes embedded as a way of life only when the individual parts work as a system. Throughout our nation, thousands of successful schools have begun and are continuing this journey by systematically establishing priorities and relentlessly focusing on the goal and work of "leaving no child behind."

Unconventional Wisdom

What Works for Experienced Teachers

Guarantee your graduates.

At our high school, we decided to impose the ultimate accountability. With the support of the school board, we established a program for our high school graduates that guarantees that they will satisfactorily pass college freshman English and college algebra. Should any of our former students fail either of these college courses, we pay for tutorial remediation and cover the cost of tuition to retake the courses. I can't tell you what a change this idea has caused. Our teachers are working harder than ever before to teach all of our high school students, and it's working!

—Principal, Wyoming

Have students plot their progress.

After attending workshops on total quality management and data-driven decision making and monitoring progress toward established goals, I got this idea of trying out several of these concepts with my students. I teach an adult learning evening class made up primarily of school dropouts. The first night of class, I explained my goals for the class and how I planned to monitor the performance of the class to assess my effectiveness. I also invited the students to discuss their goals and to try to think of ways to measure their performance and progress over time. By the end of the first week, we had all sorts of graphs and charts hung up around the room, and every week we reviewed our work, adding new data and discussing our progress. I couldn't believe it. These often sullen, unmotivated students just came alive. They had their goals, and they could see that they were making progress toward attaining them. How great to find something that works!

—Teacher, Indiana

STRATEGY #10

Develop a Comprehensive Plan

We had to make our at-risk kids a priority; they never had that status before . . . but why shouldn't they be? They're our kids . . . just like the kids with so many advantages.

—Superintendent of Schools, Wyoming

Throughout the country, districts like this one in Wyoming have concluded that without a focused plan, progress toward improving the performance of at-risk students is at best a gamble, and at worst a solemn, sad passing of yet another year of dropouts or underprepared students from our public schools. Districts, schools, and classroom educators who are both serious and committed to improving the performance of students at risk must first establish this mission as a top priority. This effort requires far more than compassion. It often means confronting the sensitive issues of socioeconomics, poverty, bigotry, prejudice, and their accompanying politics. To successfully undertake this endeavor, whether at the district, school, or classroom level, requires effective leadership and the commitment necessary to forge and implement a comprehensive plan of improvement. Most superintendents, principals, or teachers know this part: making it happen successfully is the challenge.

Most scholars of school improvement argue that sustained change must occur at the district level. Yet most examples of improved achievement of low-performing students reside at the school level, primarily due to district- and state-level accounting of quantifiable assessment data. Common sense dictates that the classroom teacher is the one who holds the key to unlock individual student achievement. School improvement scholars, while championing the necessity of systemic improvement at the district level, will acknowledge both the multiple challenges of this effort and the scarcity of models and examples that demonstrate the success of this approach. In practice, improvement efforts must occur in partnership between administrative leadership and classroom teachers.

A first, critical step in this process is the creation of a *districtwide design team,* composed of a small group of representatives from classrooms, schools, the district, and the community. The team should share a common vision: that at-risk, low-performing students can and will succeed.

Can low-performing students dramatically improve? *Dispelling the Myth Over Time* (Education Trust 2002), the study of schools and classrooms with high-poverty and/or minority enrollments, lists more than 4,500 examples in which these students outperform two-thirds of the students (reading and/or math achievements) in their respective states. Further study of these schools revealed the use of careful planning, which drives the characteristics listed as common to the schools (see Figure 6.1).

Characteristics of High-Flying Schools

- Extensive use of state and local standards to design curriculum and instruction, assess student work, and evaluate teachers

- Increased instruction time for reading and mathematics

- Substantial investment in teachers' professional development focusing on instructional practices to help students meet academic standards

- Comprehensive systems to monitor individual student performance and to provide help to struggling students before they fall behind

- Parental involvement in efforts to get students to meet standards

- State or district accountability systems with real consequences for adults in the school

- Use of assessments to help guide instruction and resources and as a healthy part of everyday teaching and learning

---

Figure 6.1

SOURCE: Adapted from Jerald (2001).

These characteristics form the basis of common practice that drives planning in these successful schools. Undoubtedly, educators in the identified schools and classrooms place ultimate credit for their impressive improvements on those who work with the students day in and day out—the classroom teachers and support staff.

Where to Start: The District, the School, or the Classroom?

Despite disagreement over point of departure, most would agree that the needs of low-performing and at-risk students require immediate intervention and support from the classroom, school, and district. Planning and delivering these intervention strategies becomes a shared responsibility, with the students and classrooms becoming the primary focus of the work. These efforts must also be supported by school leadership; clear, measurable goals; an accurate and honest data review to establish baselines; results-driven instruction practices and interventions; and necessary district support, resources, and policies. Frequent communication and review of progress across all levels of participants are essential to the success of this work.

Starting at multiple levels does, however, imply specific areas of responsibility and leadership for specific functions. Figure 6.2 suggests initial responsibility for specific activities.

Comprehensive Planning for Low-Performing Students			
Task/Activity	District	School	Classroom
Strategic planning	X		
Establish a design team	X	X	
Stakeholder communications	X	X	
Development of critical mass of support	X	X	
Educator collaboration and teamwork	X	X	X
Data baseline and monitoring	X	X	X
Goal setting	X	X	X
Selection of intervention(s)	X	X	
Creation of professional learning communities	X	X	

Figure 6.2

RESEARCH

- At-risk students need comprehensive intervention.
- Schools and classrooms that target intervention through comprehensive planning can and do raise achievement levels of low-performing students.
- Teachers who deploy supportive and collaborative efforts to meet the needs of at-risk students will succeed in raising the achievement of these students.
- Districts and schools must establish priorities and commit resources to improving the achievement of low-performing and other at-risk students.

TAKE ACTION

☑ **Collaborate and cooperate at the district, school, and classroom levels.** Form a design team composed of educators committed to helping youth at risk. Collect data, develop a baseline, and monitor the team's progress frequently.

☑ **Develop student-needs-driven measurable goals and monitor progress.** Focus on the learning needs of at-risk students. Draft needs-driven goals and seek approval from wider stakeholder groups.

☑ **Complete a comprehensive plan.** Consider the systemwide needs and issues related to comprehensive long-term improvement and frequently communicate with all stakeholders within the district, school, and community.

See the "50 Strategies Suggested Reading" section for a list of resources selected to complement the fifty strategies as you put them to use in your classroom.

SAVING MY STUDENTS, SAVING MY SCHOOL

How can **Strategy #10: Develop a Comprehensive Plan** be put to use in your classroom? What can you do to increase awareness and education among your group of colleagues?

_____

_____

_____

_____

_____

_____

_____

_____

_____

_____

Share your thoughts with a colleague or group of colleagues.

STRATEGY #11

Build a Profile by Collecting and Using Data

What gets measured gets done.

—Tom Peters (1987), p. 486

Districts and schools are overrun with data. We collect and store file cabinets and storerooms of the stuff. Federal programs (such as the No Child Left Behind Act and others) and external grants require volumes. State departments of education expect even more. We test students often, comply with frequent district requests for information, monitor attendance and behavior, and sometimes survey our stakeholders. We collect and archive far more data than are ever used or understood. Yet the mention of a need to collect and use data rarely elicits cheers of support from educators.

Some blame this reluctance to use data on years of collected and unused data, misinterpreted analysis, ignored recommendations, or fear of actions based on interpretations. At-risk students often suffer further indignation due to the typically poor state of maintenance of their own personal records. Their files are frequently incomplete, lacking in substance, poorly maintained, or missing. The mobile nature of many of these students further complicates the ability of schools to present clear, data-driven portraits of their most needy students.

Fortunately, a careful approach to collecting, monitoring, analyzing, and prescribing interventions from well-kept and well-maintained data on a low-performing child may provide the approach needed to unlock the student's potential to succeed. When actions based on accurate data are carefully collected, monitored, and analyzed, the intended results, successes, and shortcomings of an intervention may be far better understood, disseminated, and continuously improved.

Build a Profile

Who are your low-performing students? Who are your youth at risk? How does your district or school compare with others? Do the community and school board recognize the complexity of student needs in the district or school? Do teachers and staff know the extent to which at-risk students are impacting classrooms other than their own? The answers to these and other questions can be addressed through the development of district, school, and classroom profiles. Profiles can be developed from the data at hand or from data that are usually easily accessible.

A district- or school-based design team starts by looking at available data on the needs of a specific grouping or cohort of students. While a systemic approach is advisable from the beginning, many educators have found the need to present a "snapshot" of needs before a school or district will commit the time and resources to mount a systemic effort. Figure 6.3 provides a simple format to target sources of data on any given group of students, staff, costs, or activities. The data necessary to address these areas and issues are surprisingly available, although some data are confidential, requiring approval and anonymity in analysis and reporting.

Information, trends, and findings from an initial look at available data will often be quite revealing. For example, teachers and principals have

---

Take a Look: Sources of Data

- Achievement data

- Retentions

- Suspensions/detentions

- Number of F's or D's

- Behavior reports/problems

- Low-level classes
  - How many?
  - Who's teaching them?

- Special education enrollment

- Student mobility

- Dropouts or teen pregnancy numbers

- Ritalin or prescribed medications

- Free and reduced lunch numbers

- Student absences and tardies

- Teacher sick days

- Student pullouts or interruptions

- Nominal costs of school participation
  - Sports
  - Activities
  - Yearbooks, and so on.

Figure 6.3

SOURCE: Adapted from Barr and Parrett (2001).

reported that merely tallying and reporting grades of D and F for eighth-grade students has a major impact when brought to the attention of the school faculty and district administrators. In cases like these, the information is not new; it has simply never been reviewed in any form of systemic, careful analysis.

Other sources of pertinent information regarding the performance and needs of low-performing students may be found through reviewing data on the following:

- Staff instructional assignments
- Counseling and advising groups and issues
- Course schedules and offerings
- Instructor experience compared with assigned classes and activities
- Professional development topics, issues, and participation
- Kindergarten screening
- School communications to parents
- State-reported/required data on special education, gifted and talented education, at-risk students and dropouts, and per-pupil expenditures
- Ethnic composition of staff and students
- Limited English proficiency (LEP), English language learners (ELL), and second-language learners (ESL)
- Student participation in extracurricular activities
- Teacher turnover
- Family engagement in school events and activities
- Family and student interviews

Another highly revealing data source is the assessment of education beliefs, perceptions, and perspectives regarding the demographics, needed services, and present program effectiveness of a district's effort to serve at-risk youth. Educator and student checklists and school profile tools can yield invaluable data needed for the effective development of immediate and long-term plans to improve services to these students.

Share Your Work

The initial goal of a design team's work should be to develop or build a preliminary profile or baseline portrait of the targeted student group. As one might imagine, the product of this effort could well range from simple to complex. School improvement specialist Dr. Edie Holcomb advises the "KISS" approach: keep it simple and succinct. Time constraints for the work and analysis may force the early effort to be focused on a few key issues. Clarity and accuracy of the initial profile are critical, as the results often open eyes and minds to current needs and foster further study. Thus the visual depiction through charts and graphs must be carefully constructed, easy to read, and free from clutter. The presentation of a few carefully prepared visuals should clearly display the findings and prompt discussion, recommendations, goal setting, and action.

RESEARCH

- The analysis of available data is critical to goal setting and identification of actions needed to help at-risk students achieve success in school.
- The requirement of state and federal assessments mandate districts, schools, and classrooms to become more data driven.
- Low-performing students will achieve and succeed in school if they are given appropriate interventions, opportunities to catch up and accelerate their learning, and ongoing attention to their immediate needs.

TAKE ACTION

- ☑ **Take an initial look.** Examine sources of data readily available regarding the school performance of students at risk.
- ☑ **Carefully select the categories of highest concern.** Listen to and assess the beliefs and perspectives of students, teachers, and administrators; review pertinent data; and develop categories for action.
- ☑ **Review and assemble the data.** Organize data into understandable visuals that clearly depict the needs of students.
- ☑ **Present the data to peers and school/district leaders.** Focus on preliminary recommendations for goals and actions, suggest a timeline for approval, and formally present the results to peers and school and district leaders.

See the "50 Strategies Suggested Reading" section for a list of resources selected to complement the fifty strategies as you put them to use in your classroom.

SAVING MY STUDENTS SAVING MY SCHOOL

How can **Strategy #11: Build a Profile by Collecting and Using Data** be put to use in your classroom? What can you do to increase awareness and education among your group of colleagues?

_____

_____

_____

_____

_____

_____

_____

_____

_____

Share your thoughts with a colleague or group of colleagues.

STRATEGY #12

Set Goals, Targets, and Timelines

Our school had no focus; the classrooms and students followed suit. Somehow, a few of our kids made it through, but so many disappeared. Once we got on the same sheet and began directing our efforts at our most pressing needs—attendance and student engagement— we experienced remarkable success in keeping and graduating many of our most at-risk kids.

—Principal, Alternative School, Florida

For decades, educational research has acknowledged the critical importance of goal setting, carefully monitoring progress, and frequent attention to needed midcourse adjustments in the process of guiding school improvement. A simple formula has emerged in which participants establish consensus around a few highly specific and measurable goals and then periodically assess the school's effectiveness in achieving these goals. When the formula is used, it does not take one to three years to see success; schools can expect immediate and dramatic increases in student performance.

Too often, over the years, school reform has focused on a variety of unrelated activities that have tended to become ends unto themselves: a daylong teacher inservice at the start of the school year, an adoption of a new textbook series, requiring teachers to complete a three credit hour graduate course on a new topic, sending teachers off to attend a conference, or even the creation of a site-based team to manage a local school. School reforms have attempted to improve schools through additional funding, smaller class size, infusion of technology, and a bewildering array of new approaches: everything including multiple intelligences, social and emotional learning, teaching styles, cooperative learning, and new forms of classroom management. While each of these ideas might, in fact, improve schools and classroom learning, if they are implemented without regard to long-term goals and improved student performance, they too often become little more than ends unto themselves. Improved student performance often begins with consensus building around a few carefully selected, measurable goals that is then followed by a systemic monitoring of the school and classroom progress toward achieving the goals.

Politicians have long recognized the power of well-stated goals to mobilize the citizenry around goal fulfillment. During his short tenure, President John F. Kennedy gave a ringing call for support when he stated,

"In this decade, we will place a man on the moon." The goal was achieved. Franklin Roosevelt challenged the country to the unlikely task of building more than 50,000 military aircraft during the early days of World War II. The country responded by manufacturing more than 100,000 aircraft. Perhaps the United States would have never stretched "from sea to shining sea" had it not been for Thomas Jefferson's challenge to send a team of explorers to find a Northwest Passage.

Goal setting drives successful business and industry in the United States. W. Edwards Deming (1986) championed the concept that any type of business improvement cannot be achieved until specific, widely shared goals are developed. Deming's first principle of business improvement is "Create a constancy of purpose."

Finally, the concept of setting goals, targets, and timelines is being employed in schools and classrooms across the nation. This essential component to school improvement can be approached in a number of very specific steps. (See Figure 6.4 and the following discussion.)

Use Data to Identify Problems and Establish Goals

Schools should develop goals that relate directly to identified, measurable challenges by reviewing data and building student and school baseline profiles.

Steps to Improving a School

- Use data to identify problems and establish goals.
- Target students who are not achieving.
- Develop shared goals.
- Carefully select two to four goals.
- Select measurable goals.
- Develop a plan to achieve the goals.
- Develop and agree to target short-term progress indicators and assessments.
- Establish a timeline and review progress monthly.
- Expect immediate, dramatic results.

Figure 6.4

SOURCE: From Schmoker (1999).

Target Students Who Are Not Achieving

Rather than waiting until the end of the school year, the semester, or the end of a grading period, teachers should use monthly data on student performance to identify students who are not achieving, and develop and implement strategies toward gaining more positive results.

Develop Shared Goals

The first and most important step is to gain schoolwide support for a set of specific goals. The greater the agreement in pursuing the goals, the greater the chance of success.

Carefully Select Two to Four Goals

Recognizing that a school cannot attempt everything at one time, it is essential that the school agree to pursue only a few very specific goals at one time. Usually, the consequence of addressing too many goals at once is minimal progress and loss of consensus.

Select Measurable Goals

Too often, district strategic plans, mission and vision statements, and school improvement plans are built around such large, general, and ambiguous goals that it is virtually impossible to determine whether the school is making progress toward achieving a particular goal. "Increase the number of students reading at grade level by 8 percentage points on the standardized measure by the end of the third grade" is a much more measurable goal than "All students learning . . . whatever it takes." One way to narrow the possible goals a school might pursue is to identify those that teachers, parents, and administrators believe will have the greatest, most immediate impact on the most pressing area of need.

Develop a Plan to Achieve Goals

Teachers, parents, administrators, and stakeholders can brainstorm a wide variety of activities that are believed to be important in achieving their goals. Small groups should then investigate the research and practice base for interventions using documented improvement and achievement results.

Establish a Timeline and Review Progress Monthly

Rather than waiting until the end of the year to evaluate progress toward a goal, it is essential that teachers recognize their accountability in achieving established goals and establish a timeline of expectations. For example, groups of first-grade, middle school science, high school algebra, or biology teachers could meet monthly to discuss and critique progress and student performance. Teachers who are experiencing success as well as those struggling with an agreed-upon intervention or approach should share strategies and plan adjustments.

Expect Immediate, Dramatic Results

Schools that follow this simple formula can not only expect school performance to improve but will also frequently experience immediate, dramatic results in student performance, particularly from low-performing students.

RESEARCH

- Low-performing students, classrooms, and schools often are characterized by an absence of clear, measurable goals. Failure to establish clear, measurable goals is a significant factor in the inability of a school to improve student performance.
- The most effective intervention programs for low-performing students employ a systematic, ongoing process of goal setting and performance evaluation.
- Frequent and regular assessment of student performance helps to document the success and failure of efforts to address school and student needs and provides a framework for continual school improvement.

TAKE ACTION

- ☑ **Review school data.** Review available data regarding school performance (e.g., attendance, failing grades, dropout rates, mobility rates, discipline or disruption referrals, standardized test scores, etc.) and use these data to develop a baseline profile that focuses on the most pressing needs.
- ☑ **Set goals.** Arrange a time for parents, teachers, administrators, and students to review problems and discuss goals for school improvement. Focus on the selection of a few (three or four) measurable goals that address the most serious challenges and hold promise for maximizing school learning.
- ☑ **Monitor progress.** Once shared goals have been identified, plan to monitor progress on an ongoing basis and meet monthly to evaluate progress and critique approaches to gain better student performance.

☑ **Celebrate success**. As soon as a goal is met or significant progress toward a goal is achieved, take time to appropriately recognize and celebrate the work and progress.

☑ **Seek continuous improvement**. The process of setting measurable goals, based on frequent progress checks of data, never ends. New goals must be set as efforts to improve student learning and school success continually cycle.

 See the "50 Strategies Suggested Reading" section for a list of resources selected to complement the fifty strategies as you put them to use in your classroom.

SAVING MY STUDENTS, SAVING MY SCHOOL

How can **Strategy #12: Set Goals, Targets, and Timelines** be put to use in your classroom? What can you do to increase awareness and education among your group of colleagues?

_____

_____

_____

_____

_____

_____

_____

_____

_____

_____

Share your thoughts with a colleague or group of colleagues.

STRATEGY #13

Create Time for Collaboration, Planning, and Development

I have always heard that trying to improve public education is like trying to change a flat tire while the car is moving. Well, it is no joke. That is exactly what it's like to be involved in a major school improvement project. I feel like we are all running along the side of the car and nothing very productive is getting done.

—Teacher, Missouri

One of the essential elements in data-driven school improvement is for teachers to learn how to collect, manipulate, and utilize data and then find time for ongoing collaboration, planning, and development. All schools contain a rich collection of all sorts of data. Unfortunately, this mother lode of information, including data about student performance, attendance, special education, discipline referrals, and so on, too often lies untouched on the shelves of various offices in schools and school districts. The reason for this is that most teachers lack the skills to analyze the data and have little or no time for collaborative work. Schools must work to move beyond what some educators call the "first order" of data-driven decision making (i.e., isolated and unrelated use of data by individual teachers or administrators) to the use of data as part of a schoolwide comprehensive effort that represents a more significant and productive "second order." To do this, a school needs to arrange time for training and the guided analysis of data.

Allison Cromey (2001), of the North Central Regional Educational Laboratory, proposes a data retreat to get the entire school community working together to learn how to use data, develop consensus around data-driven school improvement plans, "scour data sources," and search for patterns and interrelationships among data sources (see Figure 6.5).

While data retreats represent an effective means to initiate successful, data-driven school improvement plans, the most essential element of success is to ensure that teachers have time on a weekly basis to continue to meet together and continue their collaboration, planning, and development.

To improve a school, dedicated planning time is essential. Unlike business and industry, which are able to close down to retool, schools usually attempt to retrofit themselves while continuing the day-to-day,

Organizing Data Retreats

Before the Retreat:

- Develop a school improvement team.
- Collect and organize data.

During the Retreat:

- Analyze data and define needs.
- Pose hypotheses.
- Set improvement goals.
- Identify specific strategies.
- Define evaluation criteria.
- Make the commitment to implement specific strategies, apply criteria to evaluate attainment of goals, and adjust strategies as necessary.

Figure 6.5

SOURCE: From Cromey (2001).

stress-filled demands of educating students. Teachers contend with a daily schedule that typically provides only one preparation period; a required supervision assignment on the playground, hallway, or bus stop; and the remaining 80 to 90 percent of the day leading classroom instruction. There is simply little or no time for schoolwide or even department-wide collaboration in the typical school.

Successful schools work hard to provide teachers with time to discuss students, compare instructional approaches, design materials, conduct team planning, and critique one another. Inevitably, creating time is one of the most challenging aspects of school improvement. There are, however, a number of innovative and relatively inexpensive approaches that schools can employ to create the critical time necessary for collaboration (see Figure 6.6 on page 116).

One of the most useful ways for school boards or state legislators to help encourage school reform is by providing funding for additional substitute teachers and extended contracts to free up teachers for planning and collaboration.

A growing number of schools are using a four-day academic program (often in the form of a 2 × 2 block schedule) to free up one day each week for student makeup work, service learning, career internships, online research, and, of course, teacher collaboration.

Creative Approaches to Scheduling Collaboration Time

- Develop partnerships with colleges or universities so that professors may serve as teachers for a day.

- Have student volunteer service programs where students provide volunteer work in their community for one afternoon each week, proving a rich learning experience for the students while simultaneously providing time for teacher collaboration.

- Negotiate teacher contracts that increase class size by one or two students. This can yield funds for additional substitute teachers to free up faculty for collaboration.

- Provide groups of teachers with the same lunch period, followed by a planning period, so that they can work together.

- Permit schools to use professional leave in one- and two-hour blocks rather than using them as entire days. Three to five professional leave days can be scheduled over many weeks in short, one- to two-hour blocks of time.

- Lengthen the school day by twenty minutes four days a week and dismiss students at noon on Friday, allowing teachers to work together for a half day each week.

- Schedule hobby days or activity days one day or one-half day per week or on alternate weeks, and use community volunteers to work with students in their interest areas.

Figure 6.6

SOURCE: Adapted from Raywid (1993), Williams and Dunn (1999).

RESEARCH

- Data retreats can significantly alter the way teachers and administrators think, perceive, behave, collaborate, and even relate to the use of information and to one another.

- Conducted carefully, data retreats lead to profound, "second-order" changes in school that lead to comprehensive, schoolwide improvements.

- Systematic, long-term school improvement is impossible without regularly designated time for teacher collaboration, planning, and development.

- Research has documented a number of inexpensive and effective approaches for creating the critical time necessary for teacher collaboration.

TAKE ACTION

☑ **Collect data.** Identify, collect, display, disaggregate, interpret, question, and organize available data.

☑ **Plan and conduct data retreats.** A data retreat should be planned and conducted with the goal of using available data to identify problems; establish agreed-upon, schoolwide goals; identify patterns and relationships in data; and help local educators learn how to collect and use data in school and classroom decision making and planning.

☑ **Explore ways to create time for collaboration and meet regularly**. Many resources document practical, down-to-earth, and inexpensive ways to create collaborative time in a school day. Use these efforts to stimulate and create collaboration time.

 See the "50 Strategies Suggested Reading" section for a list of resources selected to complement the fifty strategies as you put them to use in your classroom.

SAVING MY STUDENTS, SAVING MY SCHOOL

How can **Strategy #13: Create Time for Collaboration, Planning, and Development** be put to use in your classroom? What can you do to increase awareness and education among your group of colleagues?

_____

_____

_____

_____

_____

_____

_____

_____

_____

_____

Share your thoughts with a colleague or group of colleagues.

STRATEGY #14

Facilitate Continuous Improvement: The Critical Importance of Results-Driven Leadership

We were thrilled! Our kids had outperformed our neighboring, more advantaged district for the first time ever in K–2 grade reading scores. We're now proof that a school filled with Native American students from mostly low-income families can improve. But this is one test, one semester, one group of kids. . . . It's scary how much work lies ahead.

—Teacher Leader, Idaho

Successful organizations continuously change and improve. Schools are no different. The record of improving public schools in the United States has all too often reflected a promising gain accompanied by stakeholder enthusiasm, only to be followed by a drop or flattening of the progress. Changes in funding, labor policy, school board composition, demographics, leadership, and/or a host of other factors might precipitate such an unwelcome change. Yet more than 100 years of experience with such a challenge teaches us that the issues confronting the success of our schools are and will remain fluid—requiring the effort of continuous improvement to be a constant force in education policy making, planning, and leadership.

Educational consultant Mike Schmoker (1999), in the bestseller *Results: The Key to Continuous School Improvement,* makes a cogent case for the obvious. Results must drive school improvement: results that satisfy all stakeholders' expectations, mandates, and policies represent the minimum for which educators should strive.

Schmoker's work provides a critical framework (see Figure 6.7 on page 120) and protocol for educators to follow to achieve the results they want and need to attain. Schmoker's approach provides structure and process to the difficult work of continuously improving schools. However, to continuously improve requires a school district or classroom to be in a position to accomplish such work. To be in a position to improve requires capacity. The Consortium for Policy Research in Education (CPRE) analyzed twenty-two districts in the historically reform-active states of California, Colorado, Florida, Kentucky, Maryland, Michigan, Minnesota, and Texas to determine the key stratagems used to help improve teaching and consequently learning (Massell 2000). The results of this study provide focus and direction for a district's efforts to build capacity to continuously improve.

The Schmoker Model

- Implement effective teamwork.
- Develop measurable goals.
- Focus on performance data.
- Seek rapid results and breakthroughs.
- Access and use best-practice research.
- Integrate classroom, school, and district leadership.

Figure 6.7

SOURCE: From Schmoker (1999).

The four approaches listed in Figure 6.8 represent those that occurred most frequently in the study's twenty-two districts. Clearly, school board, superintendent, and central office leadership play a critical role in a district's efforts to continuously improve results targeted by these four strategies. In fact, it might be suggested that absent district leadership, these four strategies might never be systematically implemented. Leadership is vital to the development of a district's capacity to continuously improve, but history has also taught us that district leadership alone is simply not enough. Being in a position to continuously improve requires leadership capacity at the district level as well as in schools and classrooms.

Continuous improvement at the school level demands principal leadership. Principal leadership requires a concerted effort to lead and support the challenging work of classroom teachers. In Carl Glickman's (2002) *Leadership for Learning: How to Help Teachers Succeed,* he suggests five structures administrators can use to best support teaching and learning in the classroom (see Figure 6.9). Any individuals or teams charged

Approaches for Building Capacity for Improvement

- Interpret and use data.
- Build teacher knowledge and skills.
- Align curriculum and instruction.
- Target interventions for low-performing students and/or schools.

Figure 6.8

SOURCE: From Massell (2000).

Structures for Classroom Assistance

- Clinical supervision

- Peer coaching

- Critical friends

- Classroom action research

- Study teams

Figure 6.9

SOURCE: From Glickman (2002).

with supervisory responsibility for supporting teaching and learning are encouraged to use Glickman's model.

Finally, the proverbial buck stops with the classroom teacher. Schmoker suggests the most interesting lesson of the past several years is that teacher leadership is indispensable to school improvement. Glickman's suggestions for teacher leadership are summarized in Figure 6.10.

Teacher leaders represent the linchpin for improving a school's service to low-performing students at the classroom level. They are a key support to a classroom teacher's endeavor to comprehensively address the needs of at-risk students. The work of teacher leaders, their contributions, and "frontline" efforts will enable districts to build the capacity critical to continuous improvement.

Formalizing Teacher Leadership

- Designate—and cultivate—talented teachers at every school.

- Pay teacher leaders a reasonable stipend. Leadership is not free.

- Provide teacher leaders with additional release time.

- Include teacher leaders in leadership training.

- Involve school faculty in the selection of teacher leaders.

Figure 6.10

SOURCE: From Glickman (2002).

Together, districts, schools, and classrooms must share the functions of leadership necessary to gain targeted results. To accomplish this requires what many refer to as "re-culturing" the educational community. Rick DuFour, educational consultant and former school superintendent from Illinois, recommends the creation and support of professional learning communities to meet this challenge of "re-culturing" and to address the critical needs of low-performing and other at-risk students (DuFour and Eaker 1998).

A simple yet powerful tool for any level of leadership to employ in the work of improving schools is the Shewhart Cycle (Shewhart 1939; see Figure 6.11). This cycle—plan, do, study, act, repeat—establishes the most important principle of continuous improvement: it never ends. You are never finished.

Research

- To build capacity for continuous improvement, schools and districts must focus on four key strategies: interpreting and using data,

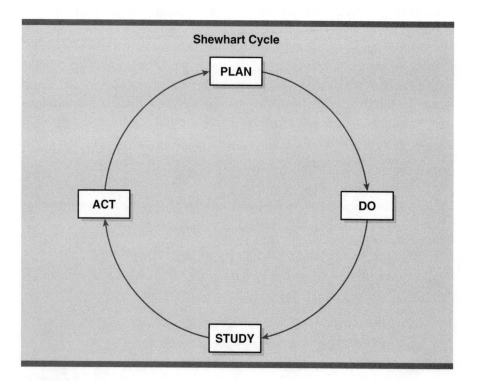

Figure 6.11

SOURCE: From Shewhart (1939).

building teachers' knowledge and skills, aligning curriculum and instruction, and targeting interventions for low-performing students or schools.

- District, school, and classroom leaders must work together to create a culture of continuous improvement for low-performing students.
- The creation of professional learning communities will improve district, school, and classroom capacity to continuously improve the performance of all students, especially those at risk.

TAKE ACTION

☑ **Focus stakeholder support and work.** Focus on the needs of low-performing students.

☑ **Establish proven models of improvement.** Actively engage in continuous improvement in the stages of implementation and review.

☑ **Engage district, school, and classroom leaders.** Key leadership must be active and connected to the design, implementation, and frequent progress monitoring of targeted efforts and interventions.

☑ **Develop professional learning communities.** Communities of support and assistance will dramatically enhance the achievement and school success of low-performing students.

See the "50 Strategies Suggested Reading" section for a list of resources selected to complement the fifty strategies as you put them to use in your classroom.

SAVING MY STUDENTS, SAVING MY SCHOOL

How can **Strategy #14: Facilitate Continuous Improvement: The Critical Importance of Results-Driven Leadership** be put to use in your classroom? What can you do to increase awareness and education among your group of colleagues?

_____

_____

_____

_____

_____

_____

_____

_____

_____

_____

_____

Share your thoughts with a colleague or group of colleagues.

Collaborate With Parents and Families

7

Strategy #15
Encourage Parent and Family Engagement

Strategy #16
Build Effective Partnerships Among Families, Schools, and the Community

Those teachers only call me when my son is in trouble.

—Parent, Kentucky

I really mean it when I say, "This is my school." I am not only welcome at the school, but my kids' teachers do all sorts of things to encourage my involvement. I have participated for over a year in the development of a shared long-range vision for the school. I have helped to identify the three goals that the entire school and community will be working on for the next three years. I am also in constant, continuing communication with the teachers regarding my kids' learning. I feel that I am truly a part of my children's education.

—Parent, Oregon

Everyone keeps talking about how schools are failing and must be reformed. Well, let me tell you, the schools are all right. The problem is the families—too many dysfunctional families, too many parents who just don't care. Schools aren't the problem. . . . It's families that need to be reformed.

—Teacher, South Carolina

Parents and families play a critical role in the education of children and youth. Unfortunately, family stability and the support of children have experienced a steady decline during recent decades. Today, almost 30 percent of the students in public schools live in single-parent homes. There are increasing numbers of families living in poverty and a growing population of households in which English is not the primary language. Even in families with two biological parents, the adults are often working in demanding jobs that decrease the opportunity for family activities and quality time with kids. The traditional family dinner has increasingly become a historical relic of a more casual way of life that is long gone. Complicating all of this is the dramatic mobility of more and more families today. This mobility has all too often created dysfunction between generations and eliminated traditional, extended-family support. So much of the child-rearing traditions practiced by earlier generations have been lost to contemporary parents. Collectively, these forces pose great new challenges for our public schools. Today, schools must

- help educate parents, who are their children's first teachers, and
- communicate with and engage families as partners in the education of their children.

The stakes are unusually high. Positive parent and family participation in education leads to overall academic achievement and improved cultural relationships between parents, teachers, and students. Without it, the outcomes have become all too often painfully clear.

Unconventional Wisdom

What Works for Experienced Teachers

Sandwich criticism between praise.

When working with students or talking to their parents, always start and end every conversation with legitimate praise. In between the praise, you can focus on areas of needed improvement. But it is important to blend criticism with praise. This approach works especially well when talking to parents.

—Teacher, Georgia

Hold student-led conferences and create videos.

Last year, I started having my students plan individual presentations for their parents during the conference evening. They select samples of their schoolwork and prepare portfolios to display their work. They include our classroom instructional goals and objectives so that parents can evaluate the degree to which their children have achieved the goals. This year, since some parents cannot or will not attend conference night, I have helped students prepare videotapes of their presentations. They use the videos to introduce their teachers and their friends, display their classroom work, and help their parents learn about their school setting as well as review their schoolwork. My students have told me that they often show them more than once to family and friends. Some kids have mailed them to their grandparents. I believe these videos will become historical documents in so many of the homes. These student-led conferences have been so successful. I now have most of my parents participating, some that never came before. I see so much care and pride in the students' work that I know that this has become very important in their lives.

—Teacher, Alaska

STRATEGY #15

Encourage Parent and Family Engagement

The greatest impact on student achievement comes from the family in well-designed, at-home activities—and this is true regardless of family, racial, or cultural background or the parents' formal education.

—Joyce Epstein

Successful teachers recognize the importance of actively engaging parents and families in the education of their children. Research is unequivocal regarding the importance of this connection, particularly with youth at risk. Yet the task of educating, communicating, and engaging parents and families in the education of their children places demanding new responsibilities on teachers that were far less emphasized and prevalent in earlier generations. Teachers of only a decade or so ago were required to do little more than provide family members with the opportunity to attend a yearly parent/teacher conference. Today, effective teachers actively engage families in their children's schooling, make family members aware of their important contributions, and encourage them to feel comfortable in working closely with schools. In engaging the parents of at-risk students, who themselves may have experienced long-term negative relationships with public education and are very uneasy about working with or even visiting schools, the challenge for educators is great.

Joyce Epstein, noted scholar and director of the Center on School, Family, and Community Partnerships and the National Network of Partnership Schools at Johns Hopkins University, puts it simply: "The way schools care about children is reflected in the way schools care about student families" (Epstein 1995: 701). Epstein further notes that to see children one-dimensionally, exclusively in their role as students, is to see the family as separate rather than an essential part of a child's academic success. Recognizing that families and schools have a shared interest to together create improved opportunities for student achievement is key to overall academic improvement. Epstein makes it clear that for at-risk children, creating effective family/school/student partnerships may well be the single most important factor contributing to student success.

When a student is without a parent or family with whom the school can connect, educators must attempt to connect with whatever external support system plays a role in the student's life outside of school, whether that is an extended family member, friend, or agency. In these cases, educators and schools must also assume a more prominent role themselves in the support of the child.

Effectively engaging families may require home visits or neutral location meetings, regular calls or contacts with parents that focus on positive reports about their children's work or that at least sandwich negative reports between elements of praise, and daily or weekly communication of detailed information regarding how parents can assist their children in achieving learning objectives. The growing number of home computers, even in poverty-level schools and homes, has led to an expectation for the use of e-mail and Web-based communications that include daily homework assignments, schedules of upcoming tests, field trips, parent opportunities to volunteer in the school or classroom, and other educational activities. The payoff for these new responsibilities for teachers is a stronger relationship with the home that leads to enhanced achievement for the student. (See Figures 7.1, 7.2, and 7.3 on pages 130–131.)

RESEARCH

- Parent and family engagement has a strong, positive relationship to student learning. It leads to increased student achievement, improved parent-child communication, improved student attitudes and behavior, and increased community support of the local school.
- Schools and educators play a critical role in initiating, maintaining, and improving family/school/student partnerships.
- Many schools actively seek and have successfully developed family partnerships with all types of families, not just those with the relative advantage of being composed of two parents.
- When parents/families/teachers agree on instructional goals, have a shared vision regarding the mission of the school, and work together to support classroom learning, academic achievement improves.
- Parent and family engagement leads to increased cultural understanding, provides essential insights into special problems and needs of students, and reinforces the behavioral norms of the home and school.
- When parents are engaged, students achieve more, earn higher grades and test scores, have better attendance, and complete homework more consistently, regardless of socioeconomic status, ethnic or racial background, or the parents' educational level.
- When programs are designed to engage parents in partnerships, student achievement for at-risk children not only improves, it can reach levels that surpass their more advantaged peers. In addition, the children who are farthest behind often make the greatest gains.

MEMO TO: Justin's parents

FROM: Mrs. Eldridge, Our School

I think that our concerted efforts are finally paying off! I can see so much improvement in Justin's homework now that you are providing direct attention and help each evening. Moving him closer to my desk and surrounding him with more engaged students also seems to have helped.

As we discussed earlier, I met with the music and P.E. teachers, and they have worked to break up the clique of students who seemed to have had such a negative impact on Justin's behavior. I think that praising his academic success both at school and at home has also had a positive payoff.

I will call you in a week or so. Perhaps we could meet for coffee one morning before the workday begins to compare notes.

   Thanks for all of your support and help.

Figure 7.1

Sample Fourth-Grade Teacher's Telephone Log

Date	Notes
9/14	Call from Stephanie's mother concerning classmates' teasing.
9/16	Called Roger's dad to see why his son has been absent.
9/21	Called Jacqueline's mother to see if our discussed actions are paying off.
9/23	Called Tiffany's mother; arranged for meeting to discuss gifted-talented program placement.
10/2	Talked to school counselor to request that she find out more about Roger's excessive absences.
10/5	Called Seth's parents to "brag" about his wonderful project.
10/12	Stephanie's mother called again—seems the girls are still teasing and taunting. . . . What to do?
10/15	Talked to 5 parents to express praise for their children's outstanding classwork.

Figure 7.2

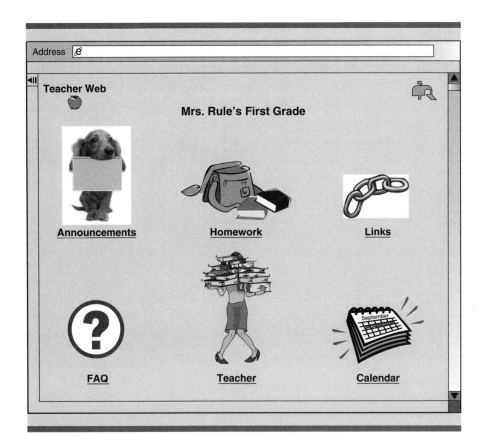

Figure 7.3

TAKE ACTION

☑ **Reach out.** Visit homes and expend extra effort to connect with poverty-level and culturally diverse families who may be less comfortable with the traditional avenues of family involvement at school.

☑ **Gather data.** Regularly communicate with parents and families to obtain additional information and insight into the unique needs, interests, and situations of children.

☑ **Create partnerships and facilitate collaboration**. Parents and families should be welcomed as partners in the curriculum, instruction, assessment, and management of the school. Create parent support groups, advisory councils, and visioning groups to help share information and advice and actively support the instructional program.

☑ **Use parents and families as resources.** Invite and engage parents and families to serve as tutors and classroom volunteers and to assist with out-of-school activities. Where appropriate, parents should assist with classroom instruction.

☑ **Seek professional development and create action plans.** Access the invaluable resources available today regarding the creation of effective family/school/student partnerships and create time to develop a school action plan.

☑ **Enhance assessment literacy.** Conduct regular parent/student conferences, frequently send home information and results regarding lessons and assignments, and actively include parents and students in the assessment of students and the instructional program.

See the "50 Strategies Suggested Reading" section for a list of resources selected to complement the fifty strategies as you put them to use in your classroom.

SAVING MY STUDENTS, SAVING MY SCHOOL

How can **Strategy #15: Encourage Parent and Family Engagement** be put to use in your classroom? What can you do to increase awareness and education among your group of colleagues?

_____

_____

_____

_____

_____

_____

_____

_____

_____

_____

_____

Share your thoughts with a colleague or group of colleagues.

STRATEGY #16

Build Effective Partnerships Among Families, Schools, and the Community

Our greatest allies are our parents. But they are often as at risk as their kids, and they need help. I have concluded that my job is to provide them with all of the help that I can, because in the end, it is the kids who benefit.

—Teacher, Maine

As a high school teacher, I never thought parents were interested in what happened in my class. I never really tried to communicate with them. Then I started a Web site for my history class, and all of this changed. I realized that these parents are interested in their kids and want to be involved in their school. Technology provided a way for it to happen.

—Teacher, Utah

Supporting parents in the education of their children and creating sustained effective communication are cornerstones of the home, school, and community partnership. For the families, and often for the communities in which at-risk children reside, the creation of effective partnerships with the school may well be the difference between success and failure. Joyce Epstein's work (Epstein et al. 2002) with the School, Family, and Community Partnership Program of the Center for Research on the Education of Students Placed At Risk has identified elements of successful partnerships and how those elements support Epstein's six types of involvement (see Figure 7.4).

Epstein's Six Types of Involvement

- Parenting
- Communicating
- Volunteering
- Learning at home
- Decision making
- Collaboration with the community

Figure 7.4

SOURCE: From Epstein et al. (2002).

One of the most important roles for educators is parent education. While this work has always been essential for elementary schools, it is now recognized as critically important at the secondary level as well. Elementary educators must not only work to educate the parents and families of their students but also strive to educate the parents of very young children. As children's first teachers, parents must understand how they can stimulate their children's neurological development and prepare them for school. Research has clearly identified a number of rather simple techniques that parents and families can employ to increase a child's intelligence; to help prepare children to read; to select effective child care; and to identify and address aberrant behavior, including bullying, in young children.

Research has also dramatized the importance of the education of parents of elementary-age students regarding human growth and development, behavior, discipline, and achievement. For parents of older students, educational issues often include information about drug and alcohol addiction, human development, media influences, gang activity, and the early warning signs of violence. It is equally important for teachers to learn from parents about a student's background, culture, and personal skills.

Figure 7.5 (page 136) and the discussion that follows identify key issues of which every parent should be aware.

Enhance Communication Between Families and Schools

Successful teachers acknowledge that communication between the school and the home is a prerequisite to successful parent and family education engagement in the classroom and the school. Especially for poor, culturally diverse students and those living in dysfunctional families, effective communication must be carefully and consistently employed to assist family members to develop trust and confidence in their children's teachers. For the parents and families of low-performing students, communication from teachers must often overcome the fact that these adults may have had negative experiences with their own schooling and are often initially suspicious of schools and educators. Compounding the problem is the reality that much of the communication with the parents and families of at-risk students may not have been pleasant, often coming in the form of reports of uncompleted schoolwork, failed tests and assignments, behavior problems, and school violence. The long-term goal is to develop effective, frequent, and positive two-way communication.

The initial objective of any two-way communication should be to establish trust between the teacher and the parent/family. Unfortunately, establishing trust may be a major challenge. To cultivate a trusting atmosphere with

What Parents of Young Children Need to Know

Pay attention to warning signs.

Parents need to identify warning signs in their children regarding violent, violence-prone, and bullying behaviors and know where they can find help in addressing problems. (See also Strategy #22.)

Interact with children.

Parents should interact and talk to their children, ask questions, and encourage children to make decisions. Talking with children about their experiences helps them to develop new words and to understand what they mean. Talking with children, asking them questions, and encouraging them to make decisions stimulates the young mind by encouraging the skills of expression, communication, and interpretation and helps students to become independent decision makers.

Stimulate children.

Parents should provide a stimulating environment with a rich variety of experiences to stimulate young children. Trips to shopping malls, grocery stores, parks, zoos, and museums all can provide stimulating learning opportunities for children. These excursions provide children with a forum for asking questions, talking, and experiencing real-life events that can be related to the stories that their parents read at home.

Monitor and control television viewing.

Parents should encourage responsible television viewing. There are many wonderful, enriching television programs that help children learn about reading and language. Parents should use these programs to intellectually stimulate young children and provide yet another experience about which to talk and ask questions. Careful selection of television viewing of up to ten hours per week can have a slightly positive effect on children's achievement later in school. As the number of hours increases beyond ten, television viewing becomes a negative influence. Children who watch more than twenty hours of television per week often do poorly in school.

Participate in school.

Parents should be interested and involved in their children's school. Research indicates that the more parents are interested and involved in children's schoolwork, the better children tend to do in school. Parents should regularly visit their child's school, become acquainted with the teacher, learn how they can help the child at home, and discuss how they can encourage their child to be more effective in school.

Provide love and security.

Parents must provide a safe, loving environment for young children. Overshadowing all other practices, parents must provide young children with love, care, and security in order for them to develop secure, positive self-concepts and self-esteem. In this age of rampant poverty, divorce, single and teenage parents, and latchkey children, the loving, secure environment that is so essential to a child's development is too often sadly lacking.

Figure 7.5

SOURCE: Adapted from *Hope fulfilled for at-risk and violent youth: K–12 programs that work,* 2nd Edition, by Barr, R. D. and W. H. Parrett, 2001. Used by permission of Allyn & Bacon, Needham Heights, MA.

students' families, it is essential that teachers, counselors, and parents pursue a positive approach to communication (see Figure 7.6).

As part of a school's overall improvement plan, educators should evaluate the effectiveness of their school/family communication approaches. Figure 7.7 (page 138) can be used for just such a purpose.

Figure 7.8 (page 139) lists a variety of successful communication tools, strategies, and approaches teachers and school leaders can use to improve communication with parents and families.

RESEARCH

- Attending to ways parents and families can support and promote their children's learning inside as well as outside of school will unquestionably help the achievement and school success of virtually any child. For at-risk students, this effort can mean the difference between graduating and dropping out.
- In recent years, research in the fields of developmental psychology, child care, and preschool education has made remarkable progress. Dramatic insights have been gained into the growth and development of infants and young children, providing the foundation for effective parent education.
- Child development studies provide parents with the critical knowledge of how to stimulate the brain of very young children and actually enhance their intelligence. These studies also give essential

---

Actions That Promote Positive School and Family Communication

- Be open, helpful, friendly, and respectful to student families.
- Communicate clearly and frequently about policies, programs, and student progress.
- Encourage family feedback.
- Foster an atmosphere of teamwork among the school, student, and family.
- Seek out and facilitate the involvement of all families in a two-way dialogue about student achievement and well-being.
- Engage parents and the larger community in volunteer activities and partnerships with the school.

Figure 7.6

SOURCE: From Decker et al. (1994).

Taking Stock: A Report Card

Directions: Grade each of the following on a scale of 1–4, with 4 being "excellent." Calculate the average for each category.

Reaching Out to Families	Grade	Final Grade
1. Communicating often and openly with families	____	
2. Reaching all cultural and language groups	____	
3. Reaching working and single parents	____	
4. Extra efforts to reach all families	____	
	____	

Welcoming Families to the School Building	____	
5. School's welcome to families	____	
6. Open and available school and staff	____	
7. Encouraging volunteers	____	
8. Active PTA/PTO activities	____	
9. Major PTA/PTO activities	____	
10. Reaching out to the community	____	
	____	

Developing Strong Relationships	____	
11. Teachers communicate with parents	____	
12 Parent-teacher partnership	____	
13 Parent-principal partnership	____	
14. Parents involved in decision making	____	
15. School-parent involvement policy exists	____	
	____	

Helping Parents Understand the Curriculum	____	
16. Information about the curriculum	____	
17. Goals for student achievement	____	
18. Information on student performance	____	
	____	

Helping Parents Be More Effective	____	
19. School supports parents	____	
20. School connects to community services	____	

Figure 7.7

SOURCE: Cooke, Gwendolyn (2007). *Keys to Success for Urban School Principals,* 2nd Edition. Thousand Oaks, CA: Corwin Press. Reprinted by permission.

**Characteristics of Successful Communication Programs
Between Parents and Educators**

1. Use a variety of communication tools on a regular basis, seeking to facilitate two-way interaction through each type of medium.

2. Establish opportunities for parents and educators to share partnering information such as student strengths and learning preferences.

3. Provide clear information regarding course expectations and offerings, student placement, school activities, student services, and optional programs.

4. Mail report cards and regular progress reports to parents. Provide support services and follow-up conferences as needed.

5. Disseminate information on school reforms, policies, discipline procedures, assessment tools, and school goals, and include parents in any related decision-making process.

6. Conduct conferences with parents at least twice a year, with follow-up as needed. These should accommodate the varied schedules of parents, language barriers, and the need for child care.

7. Encourage immediate contact between parents and teachers when concerns arise.

8. Distribute student work for parental comment and review on a regular basis.

9. Translate communications to assist non-English-speaking parents.

10. Communicate with parents regarding positive student behavior and achievement, not just regarding misbehavior or failure.

11. Provide opportunities for parents to communicate with principals and other administrative staff.

12. Promote informal activities at which parents, staff, and community members can interact.

13. Provide staff development regarding effective communication techniques and the importance of regular two-way communication between the school and the family.

Figure 7.8

SOURCE: From National PTA (1998: 10).

new understanding of the human bonding of infants with adults and the tragic effects of failing to bond.

- Research has clearly documented the power of high-quality child care as well as the essential components of effective programs for young children.
- Research has documented that parents can be taught to identify early warning signs and take preventative and corrective actions.
- Effective teacher communication with parents and families is the prerequisite to parent engagement and education.
- To be effective, communication among the classroom, school, and home needs to include open, candid discussion with all parties.
- Communicating regularly with parents and families can greatly enhance a child's academic performance, regardless of the parent's level of education or income.
- Communication among the classroom, school, and home is beneficial to students of all ages. When parents and educators communicate effectively, positive relationships develop, problems are more easily solved, and student academic performance improves.
- Education is critical in helping parents understand techniques that can significantly increase the intelligence of young children, mold the personality of children before the age of three, and lay a positive foundation for reading.

Take Action

☑ **Read to children.** Help parents understand how important it is for them to help their children learn to read. Inform parents about the importance of reading aloud to their children. Infants, even before they are able to comprehend the stories being read, greatly benefit from this practice. Many scholars contend that no other activity has a more positive, long-lasting influence as that of reading to young children.

☑ **Don't reinvent the wheel.** Access and implement instructional materials specifically designed for parent education. (See Chapter 7.)

☑ **Help parents learn.** Develop and frequently offer educational opportunities for parents with students of all ages. Learning packets should be sent home with clearly explained specific roles for parents to assist their children's learning.

☑ **Encourage parents to communicate.** Busy parents of today need as much assistance as possible to communicate with teachers. Use phone calls, voice mail, e-mail, classroom Web sites, and self-addressed postcards. Welcoming, friendly communications regarding the variety of classroom and school instructional activities, assessments, special events, and social gatherings will encourage parents and families to become regularly and actively engaged in the classroom and school.

☑ **Be creative; employ a variety of strategies.** Establish a variety of methods to maintain and enrich communication. Telephone calls, e-mail, Web-based communications, narrative written reports, parent/student conferences, and student-led conferences are all effective practices.

☑ **Arrange a comfortable meeting.** Welcoming parents and families to the school at times convenient for them is critical. Meeting parents in neutral sites may also be necessary to build effective relationships. Home visits, especially for young children, represent perhaps the best way to establish initial contact and open communication.

☑ **Facilitate two-way communication.** Effective communication includes an invitation for the adults in the home to respond and provide feedback through a variety of options. This kind of two-way communication is essential.

 See the "50 Strategies Suggested Reading" section for a list of resources selected to complement the fifty strategies as you put them to use in your classroom.

SAVING MY STUDENTS, SAVING MY SCHOOL

How can **Strategy #16: Build Effective Partnerships Among Families, Schools, and the Community** be put to use in your classroom? What can you do to increase awareness and education among your group of colleagues?

_____

_____

_____

_____

_____

_____

_____

_____

_____

_____

Share your thoughts with a colleague or group of colleagues.

Create Caring Classrooms, Schools, and Communities of Support

Strategy #17
Create a Community of Support

Strategy #18
Create a Common Vision

Strategy #19
Establish Alternative Schools

Strategy #20
Develop Small Schools and Schools-Within-Schools

Strategy #21
Provide Effective Transitions

I don't really know how to explain it, and when I try to, it sounds so corny. But this school is like my family. No, that's not right; this school is my family. It is the family I never had.

—Student, California

To ensure that all children and youth achieve, especially those whom teachers find particularly challenging, it is critical to provide an atmosphere of caring and support. It is not that these students cannot learn, but often that they choose not to learn. The reasons that these students are not learning effectively are complex. The magnitude of problems that surround them often overwhelm their academic interest, focus, and performance. Many of the challenges students at risk face are severe and have taken years to develop. Because of this, conventional academic instruction is all too often insufficient and ineffective.

Individual teachers are far more effective when caring classrooms are part of a schoolwide *community of support.* Such a community of support tends to take on the characteristics of a surrogate family, a place where students feel safe, cared for, and challenged. When this type of school atmosphere is established, at-risk students become actively engaged in learning. In fact, a community of support can do much, much more.

For at-risk children and youth, a supportive educational atmosphere has an overwhelmingly positive effect. It has the potential to improve their attitudes, help them learn effectively, and transform their lives. For at-risk children and youth who do not have a supportive, caring family or who may have had negative school experiences, the family atmosphere can have an immediate, positive impact. Effective schools and programs for at-risk youth often create an all-for-one, one-for-all camaraderie among teachers, parents, and students similar to that found in elite military organizations, superior athletic teams, cohesive private schools, and successful companies. Students in such programs become committed to their schools and peers, creating an environment of positive pressure to succeed. A positive, supportive atmosphere contributes directly to a student's improvement in school attendance, academic achievement, and attitude.

The school as a community of support is a broad concept that intertwines school membership and educational engagement. Productive school membership is the result of a sense of belonging and social bonding among the school and all members. Positive educational engagement focuses on school activities, but especially blends classroom academic work and extracurricular activities. For a school to develop a family atmosphere and serve as a community of support, teachers must possess a moral commitment to educating at-risk youth and sufficient autonomy and resources to develop the effective programs required to help these students.

Such a positive school climate fills a void in many students' lives and is critical to the mission and purpose of effective schools for at-risk youth. The goal of every school should be to create just such a caring community of respect, support, and challenge. With this community of support, all students will have the chance to succeed.

Unconventional Wisdom

What Works for Experienced Teachers

Talk to students.

We talk to and with our kids while they are studying, like you would have a dinner conversation at home. It isn't always about schoolwork. Sometimes a student's parents are getting a divorce, a student is having health problems, a student has broken up with a girlfriend or boyfriend, and so on. Everybody randomly joins in the conversation and discusses problems and issues while they still do their work. It's a very relaxed atmosphere, where students have an opportunity to talk about themselves and their lives. They help problem solve issues and give each other advice. We talk about world problems and current events. They have a voice, and we listen.

—Teacher, Indiana

Give students responsibility

All of our students are expected to help teach others. We have students do orientation for new students. They are expected to help kids in the class who need help. You frequently see kids get up and go to help others on the computers, with projects, or other coursework. When we are absent, we give our students our lesson plans. Our seniors are put in charge, and they run the class very smoothly. We have a legitimate substitute teacher in the class. They are usually astounded because they don't have much to do. We would prefer not to have substitutes, but the school system gets too nervous on this one. Our students actually do a much better job than the subs do. They like the responsibility, respect it, and take ownership. We have even had some students do work on an honor system. No, they do not have a valid teaching licenses or contract, but they have proven invaluable to our school.

—Teacher, Indiana

STRATEGY #17

Create a Community of Support

When I met with this really difficult student, I reminded him that he had earlier told me that there was "no way he could ever learn algebra." He hung his head and nodded. So then I asked him to explain to me how he had passed algebra with a grade of B. "Well," he said, with a huge shy grin, "that teacher just would not leave me alone. She wanted to help me before school, after school, and during lunch. She assigned another student to work with me. She even called me at home to see if I was having trouble with my homework." He looked up at me and shrugged, "I didn't have a choice. I had to learn the stuff to get that teacher off my back."

—High School Counselor, Arizona

I failed every class I took during the ninth grade except one in science, where I got an A. That one teacher really believed in me, and I would not let her down.

—Student, Ohio

So many of these kids come into our little alternative school as real thugs. They think of themselves as tough gangbangers. They wear leather jackets, sunshades, baggy pants, their caps are on backwards, and they always have all those chains around their necks. But when they get into our school and begin working with our teachers and the other students, an incredible change occurs. In only a few weeks, they begin to dress differently, act differently, and become engaged in learning. It's like magic. They become kids again.

—Teacher, Idaho

The challenging problems of the at-risk student are compounded by the negative attitudes held by far too many teachers. This is what President George W. Bush calls the "bigotry of low expectations." Herb Kohl (1994), in a short book titled *I Won't Learn From You and Other Thoughts on Creative Maladjustment,* explains that because many teachers often ignore the at-risk students, fail to call on them in class, or don't respond to their questions, many students simply respond in kind. They refuse to do schoolwork, homework, and participate in classroom activities. They also often become disruptive. Kohl maintains that all of this becomes a "point of honor" and a "matter of pride" to students. These students simply refuse to learn from noncaring teachers. For the at-risk student to learn, teachers must make sure that students feel cared for, supported, respected, and challenged. Only then will most at-risk students respond with positive effort. Unfortunately, even then, the most caring teachers and supportive classrooms cannot help every child.

It is critically important for teachers to care for at-risk youth, to believe that these students can achieve, to hold high expectations for them as learners, and to provide the essential support that these students must have to succeed. In each of these areas, teachers must be relentless. No matter how well an education program is planned, without such teachers, the program's effectiveness is jeopardized. Students live "up to" or "down to" the expectations of the significant adults in their lives. If teachers and parents expect great things of children and youth and provide essential support, students tend to excel. This may well be the most critical component in designing effective programs for these students. Programs that assemble a staff of caring teachers with high expectations and a shared philosophy and vision will greatly increase a school's potential for success. Teachers cherish the opportunity to teach with colleagues who share an educational philosophy and vision for their school. This combination of caring teachers who hold high expectations and a shared common philosophy and vision is the reason at-risk students in these schools and programs outperform their previous personal bests.

In a study of expelled students in Colorado, researchers asked the students if they could name one or more teachers during their elementary years who cared about them and worked hard to help them learn. Almost every student interviewed could recall teachers from their elementary school experiences. When asked the same question about teachers at the secondary levels, not a single expelled student could identify one teacher (Colorado Foundation for Families and Children 1995). This study offers a dramatic insight into the importance of caring adults in the lives of students. For students who are at risk of violent behavior, a positive connection with a caring adult may reduce harm, even save lives. Because many students do not have such a relationship at home, the school environment is even more important.

Treating students with respect is intimately related to a caring atmosphere. For high-risk students, there is little more antagonizing than being shown disrespect, especially by an adult. Disrespect often provokes anger and violence. (For more teacher behaviors that provoke student anger, see Figure 8.1 on page 148.) It is essential that teachers interact with students

Teacher Behaviors That Erode the Classroom Climate

1. Sarcasm — Students' feelings can be hurt by sarcastic put-downs thinly disguised as humor.

2. Negative tone of voice — Students can read between the lines and sense a sarcastic, negative, or condescending tone of voice.

3. Negative body language — A teacher's clenched fists, set jaw, quizzical look, or threatening stance can speak more loudly than any words.

4. Inconsistency — Nothing escapes the students' attention. They are the first to realize that the teacher is not enforcing the rules and consequences consistently.

5. Favoritism — "Brownnosing" is an art, and any student in any class can point out the teacher's pet who gets special treatment.

6. Put-downs — Sometimes teachers are not aware that they are embarrassing a student with subtle put-downs or insults.

7. Outbursts — Teachers are sometimes provoked by students, and they "lose it." These teacher outbursts set a bad example for the students and could escalate into more serious problems.

8. Public reprimands — No one wants to be corrected, humiliated, or lose face in front of his or her peers.

9. Unfairness — Taking away promised privileges, scheduling a surprise test, nit-picking while grading homework or tests, or assigning punitive homework could be construed as unfair.

10. Apathy — Students do not want to be ignored. Teachers who forget students' names or appear indifferent will lose students' respect.

11. Inflexibility — Teachers who never adjust homework assignments or test dates to meet the needs of their students appear rigid and uncaring.

12. Lack of humor — Teachers who cannot laugh at themselves usually don't encourage students to take risks and make mistakes. Humorless classes lack energy.

Figure 8.1

SOURCE: Burke, Kay (2000). *What to Do With the Kid Who . . . : Developing Cooperation, Self-Discipline, and Responsibility in the Classroom,* 2nd Edition. Thousand Oaks, CA: Corwin Press. Reprinted by permission.

in a respectful manner. If teachers are disrespectful of students, students are likely to reciprocate with disruptive, disrespectful behavior. Directly related is the need to develop a climate of respect in the classroom and the school, a climate that does not tolerate bullying, intimidating, and abusive behavior. Teachers must not only respect their students, they must also demand the students respect one another as well as teachers.

When such a classroom atmosphere of respect exists between teachers and their students as well as among students, it creates a community of caring and support that has a transforming effect on students. When such a condition occurs schoolwide, the positive effects are even more significant. The dynamics of interpersonal respect, caring, and support reflect the best of strong families. For at-risk students whose homes and families so often lack these qualities or, even worse, who have experienced abusive conditions, participating in a community of support in a school or classroom can have a dramatic effect. Communities of support seem to create a surrogate family atmosphere. Such an atmosphere surrounds students with positive interrelationships that impact everything from behavior to attitudes to improved academic achievement. For the schools' most needy youth, such an atmosphere appears to be an essential prerequisite for success in school. Communities of support can overcome the anger, distrust, and negative attitudes about schools and help students become more effective individuals in classrooms as well as in their personal lives.

RESEARCH

- It is difficult for at-risk students to invest real effort in academic learning unless they feel that their teachers are genuinely concerned about them, respect them, and are willing to provide the support that they need.
- Students live "up to" or "down to" the expectations of teachers. Teacher attitudes have an enormous influence on student academic performance and behavior. If teachers believe that students can learn, and hold high expectations for them, students will respond in a remarkably positive manner.
- Well-prepared teachers who keep current on the latest research and professional development on best practices in working with at-risk students have a significantly more positive impact on student learning than teachers with minimum preparation.
- Schools that create a climate of care, high expectations, and respect find unusual success in educating at-risk youth.

TAKE ACTION

☑ **Focus the school on success for all students.** Work with other teachers and administrators to ensure that all students have the opportunity to succeed. Schools must hire personnel and allocate resources to accomplish this vision.

☑ **Respect students.** Do everything possible to make each and every student feel welcome, accepted, encouraged, respected, and challenged. This begins by meeting the students at the classroom door and welcoming them by name, assuring them that you are glad they are there, and being supportive in the classroom and elsewhere.

☑ **Provide extra support.** Provide extra attention to students having difficulty learning. This may mean working with students outside of the classroom and providing additional supplementary materials. It means working closely with the home. It may also mean providing other students to tutor at-risk students.

☑ **Engage students.** Make every effort to engage at-risk students in their own learning. Take the time to answer their questions and provide extra individual support.

☑ **Seek professional development.** Keep abreast of new and ever-expanding research-based conclusions regarding the improvement of teaching and learning.

☑ **Be relentless.** Join other educators to form a common front of unwillingness to allow a child to not succeed. The staff must then be relentless in its work with every at-risk child.

 See the "50 Strategies Suggested Reading" section for a list of resources selected to complement the fifty strategies as you put them to use in your classroom.

SAVING MY STUDENTS, SAVING MY SCHOOL

How can **Strategy #17: Create a Community of Support** be put to use in your classroom? What can you do to increase awareness and education among your group of colleagues?

_____

_____

_____

_____

_____

_____

_____

_____

_____

_____

Share your thoughts with a colleague or group of colleagues.

STRATEGY #18

Create a Common Vision

We have been working for five years on a block schedule for the high school, and we still have about a dozen teachers who are adamantly against the idea. I have just about given up. We need to find some way to help those teachers who are against the idea to transfer out of our school. If we can help them find another school, we can reach a "common vision" for our school. I now understand why alternative and charter schools are so effective. Only those teachers who share a common vision work together.

—Teacher, Minnesota

In recent years, research on student performance has documented the importance of parents, teachers, and administrators developing a common vision for their schools. If all of the stakeholders in a school can agree on a common vision, develop a shared philosophy, establish short- and long-term goals, and together monitor the school's progress toward the goals, the goals are invariably met. It is almost like a self-fulfilling prophecy. If parents, teachers, and administrators can come to agreement regarding what they hope the school will achieve, that is the first step toward making their hope a reality.

Because most school districts continue to place students in schools based on their home address; assign teachers based on availability, resources, and seniority; and often employ policies that regularly reassign principals, teaching and learning tend to be inconsistent and based on each individual teacher's personal philosophy and teaching style. At best, such a variety of instructional approaches is awkward and inconsistent in quality; at worst, it is extremely detrimental to learning, particularly for at-risk students. Students often move through the first six years of school, each year having continually to adjust to a significantly different teaching philosophy and instructional approach and style. A student could have a teacher who

- emphasizes whole language one year and one who emphasizes phonics the next;
- offers a traditional, back-to-basics, teacher-centered approach one year and one who offers an cooperative learning approach the next; or
- welcomes parents into the classroom one year and one who doesn't the next.

If a school community can come to an overall vision and philosophy (e.g., a unified commitment that all students will learn and stay in school), parents, teachers, and administrators can mobilize around that vision. In addition, if a district can align its K–12 curriculum and a school can agree on a common instructional approach (e.g., core knowledge, multiple intelligences, expeditionary learning, etc.), the entire school can assume a consistent approach from grade to grade and from teacher to teacher. Such schoolwide consistency has great power to influence positive student achievement, especially for at-risk students.

In a conventional neighborhood school, it may take several years of hard work to develop a common vision with all stakeholders. Even then, some teachers and parents may need the opportunity to transfer to another school, where their beliefs are more widely held. Sometimes, irrevocable conflicts in educational philosophy can be accommodated by the development of schools-within-schools, where multiage grouping or a year-round calendar is practiced in one wing of the building and a more traditional approach to classroom teaching in another. The task of developing a common vision is far more attainable in an alternative, magnet, charter, or even a new neighborhood school, because parents, students, teachers, and administrators with similar goals and philosophies will choose to participate and work together in a school. New parents are carefully informed about the philosophy and instructional approach of the school and know what to expect. Seasoned parents demonstrate a willingness to collaborate and form a foundation of support for the school community as a whole. Yet regardless of the challenge or the time necessary to develop a shared vision, the value in terms of student achievement and positive attitudes is well worth the effort.

Shared vision provides focus. It allows goals to be established and potential to be realized. Shared vision has long been recognized as a critical factor in the success of any organization. It is no less important in a public school.

RESEARCH

- When teachers and parents work together to develop a shared vision—a long-range plan or short-term schoolwide objectives— everyone engaged develops a sense of ownership and participation that leads to increased student performance and improved behavior of all students, especially those who are low performing or are in other ways at risk.

- When teachers and parents develop a common vision, goals for their school, and regularly assess and evaluate the progress and success of the school in achieving the vision and goals, student learning will systematically move forward toward those established goals.

- Without consensus in direction, approach, and vision, a school program lacks guidance and goals and too often demonstrates inconsistent, ineffective, and even chaotic educational practices.
- A shared vision attracts a focused type of professional and thus contributes to successfully staffing the school with teachers and principals of common philosophies.

TAKE ACTION

☑ **Initiate a visioning process.** Each public school in the nation should initiate a process of reviewing and developing a consensus vision for their school.

☑ **Review successful visioning processes.** There are a number of carefully developed, successful models for creating a common vision. Two of the most widely used school-based approaches can be found in Accelerated Schools PLUS <www.accelerated schools.net> and the Comer School Development Program <www.info.med.yale.edu/comer>.

☑ **Use the school vision.** Once a school vision has been established, it must be used for recruiting and hiring new teachers, guiding professional development for all teachers, providing orientation to all new parents, and establishing stakeholder engagement.

☑ **Assess and evaluate progress.** Develop and initiate an assessment model designed to regularly monitor progress and to evaluate how successful the school is in achieving its vision and goals.

 See the "50 Strategies Suggested Reading" section for a list of resources selected to complement the fifty strategies as you put them to use in your classroom.

SAVING MY STUDENTS, SAVING MY SCHOOL

How can **Strategy #18: Create a Common Vision** be put to use in your classroom? What can you do to increase awareness and education among your group of colleagues?

_____

_____

_____

_____

_____

_____

_____

_____

_____

_____

_____

Share your thoughts with a colleague or group of colleagues.

STRATEGY #19

Establish Alternative Schools

What else can I say? This small alternative school just changed my life and rescued me from a free fall into self-destruction. This school saved my life . . . and I would give my life for this school.

—Student, Iowa

The kids in my school call themselves the ghetto kids, the rejects, and the throw-away babies. They feel they were not wanted, they say they couldn't get help, and they readily admit all their rebellious acts. They need a lot of care and lots of attention. They need time to heal. We laugh and tell them that they are high-maintenance kids who need intensive care. They're okay with this. Alternative school kids are not difficult kids; they are kids with difficult lives.

—Teacher, Indiana

Perhaps the most effective approach to addressing the needs of at-risk students is the establishment of *alternative schools*. Originally created to serve children who were not succeeding in public schools, an alternative school is a type of public school that has a small student enrollment and a unique curriculum tailored specifically to the needs of the students who choose to attend school there. In most districts, these schools are called *alternatives* or *magnets*, but they may also be called *academics, focus, career-themed*, or a host of other titles and names. A *charter school* is a special kind of alternative school, which, although a public school, operates outside the authority of a school district. These schools usually receive their mandate, or charter, from the state body that oversees that state's education system. Regardless of what they are called, all of these schools share a common set of components (see Figure 8.2 and the discussion that follows).

Choice

Each type of alternative school serves students and their parents through voluntary participation. Choosing to participate in an educational program has enormous importance in getting students and parents committed and students engaged in effective learning. It is equally important that teachers also choose to participate in educational alternatives. Only when teachers choose to be a part of a program that focuses its work

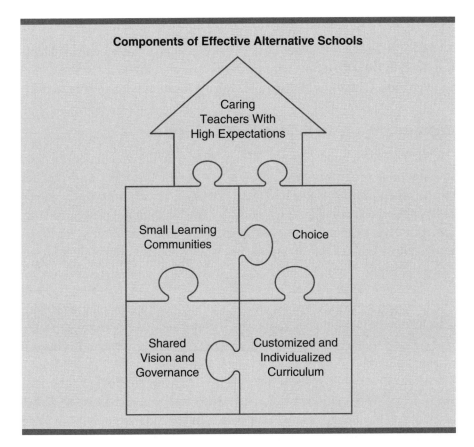

Figure 8.2

on at-risk students will there be a common philosophy and vision for the school and the appropriate care and respect for these challenging students that is a prerequisite to effective teaching and learning.

Small Learning Communities

The typical size of schools of choice in the United States is approximately 150 to 250 students. Most traditional high schools in the United States average more than 1,000 students. School enrollment has a greater effect on student performance and well-being than does class size.

Shared Vision and Governance

Because alternative schools involve students, parents, and teachers through voluntarily participation, a remarkable opportunity is gained to assemble students and adults who share a common philosophy and vision to cooperatively govern the school.

Caring Teachers With High Expectations

Because teachers choose to participate in alternative schools, students are surrounded with adults who want to work with them, assist them, and support them. These adults also hold high expectations for student learning.

Customized and Individualized Curriculum

Alternative schools provide an opportunity to design curriculum and instructional programs that address the needs, interests, and abilities of the students that the school attracts. As a result, schools of choice reflect the widest possible range of distinctive educational programs. This includes career-theme magnet schools, teen parent programs, multiple-intelligences schools, Montessori schools, last-chance alternatives for at-risk youth, and others.

The importance of each of the characteristics common to schools of choice is well supported by research. As a result, when the characteristics are clustered together, they represent a powerful force to improve academic performance and behavior and also to positively transform the lives of at-risk students.

Alternative public schools have been extensively studied over the past thirty years. At-risk students have been studied prior to arriving at and after attending alternative schools. Students in alternative schools have been compared with students in traditional neighborhood schools. Researchers have studied alternative-school students' performance with pre- and post-achievement performance measures. Follow-up studies have tracked students for years after they have graduated from alternative schools. Case studies have been conducted of individual alternative schools as have studies of large numbers of certain types of alternative schools, and a growing number of states (Oklahoma, North Carolina, Georgia, etc.) are conducting statewide, annual evaluations of the effectiveness of alternative schools.

Taken together, the body of research and evaluation data on alternative schools serving at-risk and a variety of other young people has been remarkably positive. It has helped to identify why these customized schools have continued to be so successful. This research has also helped to demonstrate that the success of alternative schools was not related solely to the specific components of the program, but rather a complex set of factors combined to create a surrogate family atmosphere. Researchers at the University of Wisconsin, Madison, concluded after in-depth case studies of alternative schools that "Effective schools provide at-risk students with a community of support" (Wehlage, Rutter, Smith, Lesko, and Fernandez 1989: 223). This atmosphere appears to be the single most important factor in ensuring an at-risk student's academic success.

RESEARCH

- Conventional, large, comprehensive schools cannot serve the complex needs of at-risk youth. Alternative schools have become recognized as an integral component of most public school districts in the nation.
- When students, even at-risk students, participate in public schools of choice (alternative schools, magnet schools, and charter schools) that demonstrate the previously identified characteristics, student attitudes and behavior improve, dropout rates are reduced, and academic achievement significantly increases.
- In a study of 24,000 students in Grades 8–12, researchers were surprised to discover that students in alternative career-theme magnet schools showed higher achievement scores than their counterparts in conventional high schools and in Catholic high schools (Gamoran 1996b). Even more impressive was the fact that these particular magnet schools enrolled a larger percentage of poor and minority students.
- When students choose to participate in magnet and focus schools and programs with a relevant, high-interest curriculum, they become highly motivated. Students appear to be unusually interested in learning when academic programs and real-life experiences outside of school are integrated into the curriculum.
- In a comparative study (Smith, Gregory, and Pugh 1981) of students attending alternative public schools and other more traditional public schools, students in the schools of choice felt that their needs, based on Maslow's hierarchy of needs (see Figure 8.3 on page 160), were addressed significantly better than did students in traditional education programs.

TAKE ACTION

- ☑ **Learn about schools of choice.** There is an impressive and growing body of research on all types of schools of choice. This research has not only identified and described a wide variety of established alternative models, with significant evaluation to document their effectiveness, but has also identified effective processes to start and improve schools of choice.

- ☑ **Participate in national and regional conferences.** A large number of state and national associations exist that provide periodic conferences, workshops, and technical assistance. There are national associations of alternative schools, magnet schools, charter schools, and teen parent schools. While the process of starting and improving alternative schools is a very personal,

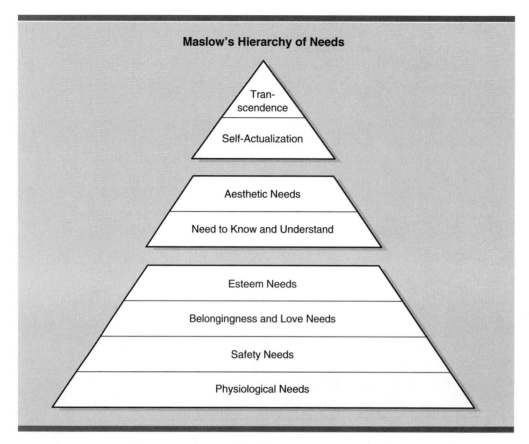

Figure 8.3

SOURCE: From Maslow (1962).

creative process, a review of the research will guide local work and help to avoid pitfalls and problems.

☑ **Network with schools of choice.** Visit established alternative, magnet, and charter schools in the region. Every successful program will testify to the importance of networking with effective models in the planning and improvement stages.

☑ **Involve the key players in planning.** Involve key stakeholders, including teachers, parents, administrators, school board members, and students in the planning, development, and approval of a new program.

See the "50 Strategies Suggested Reading" section for a list of resources selected to complement the fifty strategies as you put them to use in your classroom.

SAVING MY STUDENTS, SAVING MY SCHOOL

How can **Strategy #19: Establish Alternative Schools** be put to use in your classroom? What can you do to increase awareness and education among your group of colleagues?

_____

_____

_____

_____

_____

_____

_____

_____

_____

_____

_____

Share your thoughts with a colleague or group of colleagues.

STRATEGY #20

Develop Small Schools and Schools-Within-Schools

I was just lost in that big high school. There were thousands of students, but I didn't know anybody. Nobody knew me. None of my teachers would call on me in class. Even when I raised my hand to ask a question, they would look right through me. I was just another face in the crowd. Since no one seemed to notice me, I decided to disappear. One day about 10 o'clock I got up from my desk, walked out of that school, and I never went back.

—Student, California

Educators need to understand the powerful influence that a school's size exerts on student academic performance and behavior. Years of research offer compelling insights into how and why school size affects students, particularly at-risk students. Yet despite the fact that school size is a tremendously important factor in the education of K–12 students, it is one that is too often overlooked or ignored. Too many school districts throughout the United States choose to continue to maintain schools with huge enrollments. It is not unusual for urban and suburban elementary schools to enroll 600-plus students and for secondary schools to be as large as 2,000 to 4,000 students. A new high school that recently opened in Dade County, Florida, was designed to accommodate more than 6,000 students. These large schools, while efficient in operation, spell trouble and endless difficulty for many students, particularly those at risk.

Small schools or small schools-within-schools enable teachers and students to connect. They help students to feel accepted and develop a sense of belonging. Small schools foster personalized learning, individualized attention, and better academic performance. The inverse is also true, but in a negative sense. Any large gathering of people increases the sense of personal anonymity and the potential for disruptive behavior and even violence. In that sense, large schools are similar to other large gatherings of people—parades, football games, and concerts—all of which demand heightened security and similar crowd control techniques. The larger the school, the more likely the number of police assigned to the building; the more teachers and administrators assigned to observe hallways, restrooms, lunch rooms, and parking lots; and the more extensive the use of two-way communications, video cameras, and metal detectors. A primary reason that so many students drop out of school or fail academically is that they simply feel lost in big, intimidating, impersonal secondary schools. Certain isolating factors are always present in large schools:

- Students with few friends
- Students who have no special relationship to any teacher
- Students who feel that no one cares for or about them

Large schools are perhaps the least effective possible educational environment for these shy, isolated students. This is especially true when students make the transition from elementary schools to large junior high or middle schools. After attending school with a common group of peers and teachers for several years, students arrive at a junior high or middle school where they may be assigned as many as seven different teachers and grouped with different peers each hour of the day. But while it has long been recognized that large junior high, middle, and high schools contribute to the lonely isolation and alienation of so many teenagers, the impact may in fact be far more sinister.

Recent acts of teen violence have confronted society with a new concern: large schools may in fact generate violent acts. With media-immersed teenagers divided into athletes, preppies, punks, Goths, skaters, druggies, and so on, it takes only an added element of intolerance, racism, or social class antagonisms to lead to a wide variety of aggression and violence. The 1999 violence at Columbine High School in Littleton, Colorado, dramatized how student organizations, athletics, and social cliques of the student body engaged many of the 1,800 students but "locked out" others, causing them to feel isolated, victimized, and angry. Almost everyone—scholars, educators, parents, and students—agree: secondary schools, particularly high schools, are far too big, too impersonal, and, for too many of the nation's brightest students, boring.

Over a decade ago, the Carnegie Council on Adolescent Development (1989) recommended that large, impersonal junior high schools be divided into a number of small, interdisciplinary groups of teachers and students. In 2004, the National Association of Secondary School Principals National Report, *Breaking Ranks II: Strategies for Leading High School Reform*, recommended that each secondary school teacher be responsible for contact time with no more than ninety students in a given term so that the teacher can focus on the needs of every student. Schools with significantly smaller enrollments provide a dramatically different and more personalized educational environment. In a more intimate environment, everyone knows one another, and this familiarity tends to foster mutual respect and higher achievement, and it virtually eliminates violence. Small size alone often encourages a more personal, humanistic educational program that is virtually violence- and bully free.

The 2001 National Clearinghouse for Educational Facilities Center for School Change study, *Smaller, Safer, Saner Successful Schools,* identified six positive characteristics common to small schools (see Figure 8.4). Research clearly indicates the heightened success of small schools, particularly for students at risk.

Characteristics of Smaller Schools

- A safer place for students
- A more positive, challenging environment
- Higher achievement
- Higher graduation rates
- Fewer discipline problems
- Much greater satisfaction for families, students, and teachers

Figure 8.4

SOURCE: From National Clearinghouse for Educational Facilities Center for School Change (2001).

Many school districts in America have recognized the research implications of reducing school size and followed the advice and recommendations of scholars, research institutes, and professional organizations. New York, Chicago, and a growing number of other urban districts have launched a massive effort to transform large, inner-city schools into networks of small schools or schools-within-schools. Other schools across the nation are joining the Coalition of Essential Schools, which recommends significantly smaller schools-within-schools and encourages the personalization of learning. Many other districts and communities are creating new alternative, magnet, or charter schools specifically designed for enrollments of no more than 250 students. These schools complement small size with voluntary participation and an instructional program designed to address the needs and interests of certain students.

Recently, the William and Melinda Gates foundation has oriented significant funding toward its small high school initiative. This effort is designed to replicate existing highly successful small high schools throughout the nation.

RESEARCH

- National research studies over the past thirty years have established a direct relationship between small school size and increased student achievement, improved behavior and attendance, and reduced violence.

- Schools with more than 1,000 students tend to cause cliques, isolation, alienation, and anger. For every 600 additional students, disruptions increase significantly.
- The positive relationships between teenagers and teachers that tend to occur in small schools significantly increase academic performance and reduce risky behavior in students.
- The lack of violence in alternative schools has been attributed to school choice, customized curricula, personalized attention, caring and demanding teachers, and school size.

TAKE ACTION

☑ **Restructure large schools.** Restructure large existing schools into smaller educational environments of 400 students or fewer, where a group of teachers and students work exclusively together for much of the day. These smaller educational environments, sometimes called "houses," may be structured as teacher/student "teams," educational "families," schools-within-schools, or alternative programs. Such programs ensure that teachers and students know each other well and that no student feels isolated, overlooked, or alienated.

☑ **Create new small schools.** Create new, small schools as alternative public schools, magnet schools, or, where they are available, charter schools. These optional public schools should be available to students, parents, and teachers through voluntary choice, and the curriculum and instructional programs must be customized to meet the specialized needs of at-risk students.

☑ **Provide leadership for improvement.** Research clearly recognizes that district, school, and classroom leadership must converge to create smaller learning environments and schools. School boards and superintendents must actively support the creation of smaller schools. School principals must work collaboratively with classroom teachers, teacher leaders, and the school community to design and successfully implement smaller learning environments. These efforts take considerable time, reallocation of resources, and a firm commitment by all to the journey of improvement. Without substantial and sustained leadership, efforts to create smaller schools may achieve only piecemeal success.

☑ **Enhance collaboration through professional development.** Professional educators have rarely been prepared for the demanding work of restructuring schools or the complex challenge of creating smaller learning environments. Success in creating smaller schools rests to a large extent on the district's and the school's collective will and determination to support and enhance the professional development of educators. Professional development guided by a thoughtful, collaborative process is essential to accomplishing the work of creating smaller schools.

See the "50 Strategies Suggested Reading" section for a list of resources selected to complement the fifty strategies as you put them to use in your classroom.

SAVING MY STUDENTS, SAVING MY SCHOOL

How can **Strategy #20: Develop Small Schools and Schools-Within-Schools** be put to use in your classroom? What can you do to increase awareness and education among your group of colleagues?

\
\
\
\
\
\
\
\
\
\
\
\
\
\
\

Share your thoughts with a colleague or group of colleagues.

STRATEGY #21

Provide Effective Transitions

The scariest day in my life was the first day in middle school. After spending six years with my friends, I was suddenly lost in this huge, unfriendly school surrounded by strangers. I was afraid to get off the school bus; I was afraid to go to the restroom. I just hated the place.

—Student, Illinois

Family mobility and other types of school transitions have been identified as powerful forces in influencing students to drop out. Attending to the need for student support through educational transitions is very important (see Figure 8.5). For the at-risk student, these transitions are emotionally charged, stressful, and all too often unsuccessful.

In recent years, a new type of "migrant" student has emerged in public education. These new migrants are not the seasonal farm workers of an earlier generation; rather, they are poor families that tend to move and relocate when they are unable to pay their bills. In poor communities, the percentage of turnover is significant. It is no longer unusual for a school to experience a rate of mobility in excess of 30 percent per year. One of the great challenges of public education today is to assist these children during their lonely migrations through school after school.

Emotional and Stressful Transitions

- From home to kindergarten
- From elementary school to middle school
- From middle school to high school
- From postsecondary education to training or work
- From one school or school district to another
- From grade level to grade level

Figure 8.5

First Grade

While research has documented the significance of educational transitions and the negative impact of the transitions on at-risk youth, not enough is yet known about how to ease the impact of these transitions. The importance of the transition to the first grade is well documented. Some researchers have argued that the first few hours in the first grade can be compared to the imprinting process that occurs during the first twenty-four hours of a duckling's life. Yet one recent study found that few teachers do anything to help children and their families adjust to school before the critical first day (Pianta and Cox 1999). For too many at-risk children, the first days in the first grade mean a first encounter with failure. Recent studies report that more students are failing and being retained during the first grade than ever before.

Junior High/Middle School

The transition to a junior high or middle school is especially difficult, even more so for at-risk youth. Incoming students find themselves in large, complex schools, with as many as seven or more teachers each day, and around a different group of peers each period. In this situation, students tend to feel anonymous and unknown. It is easy for students to slack off in their academic work and make bad choices, because they feel no one will notice and no one will care.

High School

The transition from junior high or middle school to high school is also very difficult because high schools have traditionally been ineffective in remediating student deficiencies. Increasingly, schools and programs for at-risk students employ full-time transition counselors and specialists to coordinate efforts. Effective teachers of at-risk youth understand that the facilitation of successful transitions is extremely important work.

COMMON CREDIT-BASED
TRANSITION PROGRAMS

- Dual/Concurrent Enrollment
- Advanced Placement (AP)
- Tech Prep
- International Baccalaureate (IB)
- Middle College High Schools
- Early College High Schools

Learn more about these programs at <www.ed.gov/about/offices/list/ovae/pi/cclo/cbtrans/factsheets.html>. (For more on transition programs, see Strategy #21.)

Work or Postsecondary Education

The transition from high school to the world of work or postsecondary education is also challenging for many young people who do

---

LEARN MORE ABOUT EFFECTIVE
POSTSECONDARY TRANSITION PROGRAMS

- National Collaborative for Postsecondary Education Policy, <www.ecs.org/ecsmain .asp?page=/html/issuesPS.asp>
- GEAR-UP (Gaining Early Awareness and Readiness for Undergraduate Programs), <www.ed.gov/programs/gearup/ index.html>

---

graduate from high school. Recently, many high schools have begun to require students to develop carefully thought-out plans for both their high school years and their next stops after graduation. Often these postgraduation plans are incorporated into high school graduation requirements.

Assign Transition Responsibility

In this age of increased student mobility, schools at all levels should assign someone in the building the responsibility of assisting students to make the move from school to school. Often this responsibility is assigned to a counselor or to the building principal and includes required discussions with parents regarding the future plans for the student who is leaving, as well as the reasons for departure.

Experts agree that regardless of the grade level, successful transitions are critical for the at-risk student. Yet as more schools and districts have begun to develop transition or bridge programs designed to help students prepare and make these difficult transitions, studies report that most of these programs are established in middle-class and suburban schools, leaving America's inner-city and rural at-risk youth with little support at this critical time.

Because of the stress associated with school transitions, teachers at all levels should offer leadership in providing programs to help students and parents negotiate these transitions more effectively.

RESEARCH

- The long-term success of children and youth can be made more certain or placed in jeopardy by how well students negotiate school transitions.
- Student mobility is directly related to dropping out of school, especially when students move multiple times.
- The transitions from elementary to middle school and middle to high school are the most significant and difficult transitions in a student's educational life.
- Effective transition programs can alleviate much of the stress, anxiety, and failure associated with the challenge of moving through school.

TAKE ACTION

☑ **Plan a home visit.** Meet students and their parents in their homes prior to the start of school. The children and their parents need to meet their teachers, learn about what they will be doing in school, and gain information about their new classrooms. The home visit sets the foundation for a successful transition.

☑ **Arrange school visits and orientations.** Arrange for exploratory visits and orientations for students and parents prior to the transition to the next school level. Work to engage incoming students with expectations, opportunities, and the experiences of previously successful students.

☑ **Develop programs and interventions for students to assist in the transition to the next school level.** A growing number of schools have designed academies at the first year of middle or junior high school and high school to help students with transitions. The programs keep students together with a selected group of teachers for most of the school day. Some schools provide space for the academies' students in a particular wing of the building so that they spend much of their time with students of their own grade level. The academies focus on academic and social issues that contribute to successful passages.

☑ **Develop a senior plan.** A growing number of high schools have required a major senior project to culminate students' public education. Many schools also require students and their parents to develop a careful, detailed plan for what each senior student plans to do following graduation.

☑ **Prepare students for life beyond high school.** Prepare graduating seniors and potential dropouts for the array of possible educational opportunities that are available to them. This might include colleges and universities, GED programs, community college programs, on-the-job-training programs, the U.S. military, and others.

 See the "50 Strategies Suggested Reading" section for a list of resources selected to complement the fifty strategies as you put them to use in your classroom.

SAVING MY STUDENTS, SAVING MY SCHOOL

How can **Strategy #21: Provide Effective Transitions** be put to use in your classroom? What can you do to increase awareness and education among your group of colleagues?

_____

_____

_____

_____

_____

_____

_____

_____

_____

_____

Share your thoughts with a colleague or group of colleagues.

Create a Climate of Respect in Schools and Classrooms

9

I'm sick of the f-word. It's "Good f'n morning," "This f'n work sucks," or, "Get out of my f'n face." If it's not the f-word, it's the use of the word bitch. More than anything else, inappropriate, abusive language may drive me from teaching.

—Teacher, Florida

My son is afraid to go to school; he goes all day without using the restroom, because they are such isolated, frightening places. Why doesn't the school put an end to all of these cliques, bullying, intimidation, and violence?

—Parent, Oregon

I don't think schools should become like prisons, but maybe they should at least become more like airports. Why do we tolerate language and behavior in school that we would never tolerate in the

173

*home, the church, the shopping centers, and at public events. What's
wrong with this picture?*

—Parent, Iowa

*It's been a long, tough battle, but we have all worked together to
bully-proof our school and insist on a climate of trust and respect.
It's been worth all the hard work. Today our school is a totally different place.*

—Teacher, Arizona

The vicious teenage and child violence of the late 1990s stunned the
nation and moved the issue of school safety to the top of family and
educational priorities. The nation's schools had never experienced anything like it before: students killing students and sometimes teachers
and parents. At Columbine High School in Littleton, Colorado; Thurston
High School in Springfield, Oregon; and the public schools of El Cajon,
California; Jonesboro, Arkansas; Paducah, Kentucky; and Pearl, Mississippi,
we learned about sniper attacks, bombs and booby traps, assassinations,
and suicides. We learned about murder, mayhem, tragedy, and death.

Unfortunately, high-visibility school violence is only the tip of the ice-
berg. For each one of the dramatic school shootings, there are thousands
of other teenage murders or negligent homicides. Each year, between
2,500 and 3,000 teenagers are arrested and charged in the deaths of
other teenagers and adults. Between 1985 and 1994, the arrests of ten-
to seventeen-year-old children and youth for homicide, rape, robbery,
and assault increased by 70 percent. Based on surveys of students age
twelve to nineteen, violent crimes at school were reported by 42 percent
of the students in 1995, up 23.5 percent from six years earlier. In 1997,
one-half of all African American males eighteen to thirty-five years of
age in Washington, D.C., were either in prison, on probation, or under
the jurisdiction of the court. In a single month, one in nine of the
nation's high school students brought a weapon to school. By the year
2000, the number of teenagers in the United States was projected to
increase by more than 20 percent, the majority of them poor, minority,
and residing in inner-city impoverished neighborhoods (Burke 1998;
Walsh 1997).

Like a serial killer who leaves an accumulating amount of evidence,
each act of teenage violence has provided psychologists, criminologists,
sociologists, and educators with added data for a growing knowledge base

toward understanding the tragic phenomena of youth violence. This knowledge has articulated highly specific, predictive profiles and has led to higher confidence levels in the probability statistics used to forecast violence among youth. Research on troubled youth and adults has provided a growing understanding of the causes and ways to prevent youth violence. Unfortunately, it appears that the most recent acts of violence have mutated into new, more sophisticated, and even more sinister forms of teenage murder. As research efforts contribute increasing data on youth violence, a growing understanding of its causes, better insights into warning signs and the documented success of programs for addressing the needs of these violent young people have emerged.

Too often, at-risk young people feel like they are outsiders, that no one cares for them or about them. Too often, schools contribute to this feeling. These youth often experience an overwhelming loneliness and hopelessness. Media exposure tends to heighten their isolation and too often lures them into the virtual world. Today, many young people turn to school disruptions or violence. Many are reported to have

---

TWO MAJOR CAUSES OF YOUTH VIOLENCE

- Home life
- Peer harassment

---

had suicidal thoughts, and some have ended their violent episodes with suicide, or at least consideration of it. In survey after survey, many students, including honor students, say they feel increasingly alone and alienated, unable to connect with their parents, teachers, and sometimes even classmates. These teenagers seem desperate for guidance, and when they do not find it at home or at school, they cling to cliques of other isolated outsiders and, of course, immerse themselves in the brutal world of television, movies, computer games, and the Internet. Too often, the feelings of being slighted, ignored, bullied, and victimized lead to a growing internal rage. A national study of youth violence conducted in 2000 by the (then) Washington State Attorney General, Christine Gregoire, identified two major causes of youth violence: home life and peer harassment (National Association of Attorneys General 2000, citing Maine Department of the Attorney General's Civil Rights Team Project). The youth interviewed called for adults—both parents and teachers—to set boundaries and provide guidance and caring. Most violent youth, regardless of their family situations, tend to feel isolated, hopeless, and disengaged.

The problem, unfortunately, is larger than youth violence. Parents, neighbors, community members, students, and educators are equally concerned with a generation of "trash-talking" vulgar bullies who show little respect for teachers and fellow students. Surrounded by the ever-growing media impact of sex, violence, and in-your-face heroes and role models, the standard for acceptable language and behavior has significantly declined among our nation's youth. Today, children and youth see professional athletes choking coaches, pushing referees, and being charged with violent crimes, even murder. They watch prime-time television about schools and see senior boys demanding sex from fourteen-year-old girls, teachers having sexual affairs with students, and young bullies intimidating students and teachers alike. Our youth see movies where the f-word is used hundreds of times in a two-hour production, listen to obscene and violent rap music, and play violent video games.

The experts agree: today's media have led to an increased desensitization to violence and an increase in aggressive and antisocial behavior. By the time many children arrive at school, they have already seen 8,000 murders and 100,000 violent acts on television. They have spent more time watching television than they will spend in school for the next twelve years. Adding to the dilemma, with nearly all parents working and away from home until late in the day, many kids spend more than three-and-a-half hours alone each day. The traditional evening family dinner has become for many a memory of the past. With increased exposure to media and decreased involvement with family and adults, the media and peer pressure have become the most powerful forces in influencing youth attitudes and behavior. As a result of these changes in families and society, student behavior in school has declined markedly, perhaps even more so for at-risk youth.

Unconventional Wisdom

What Works for Experienced Teachers

Develop character.

One of the primary goals of our small charter school is to develop character. In the past, teasing, bullying, and taunting plagued our school. Rather than just disciplining offending students, we developed a kind of old-fashioned approach. First, we established a school goal of respect. Next, we made our hallways and restrooms quiet zones with no talking or touching. We also added playground and lunchroom supervision. Our school is not for everyone. But many parents see our children walking from class to class, to recess, or to the lunchroom in orderly, straight lines without talking, and the parents immediately try and get their children into our school. The interest has been so high that two other parent groups have started their own charters and have modeled their new school after our approach. It's really worked—we've helped the kids eliminate some behaviors that were really getting in the way of learning.

—Principal, Idaho

Declare a war on bullying.

So many parents work today and seem to have so little time to be with their kids. After school, our students are alone much of the time, and there seems to be little family time together when the adults finally get home from work. The teachers in our school believe that many parents simply do not know their children and are largely unaware of some very disturbing behaviors. This past fall, we began offering parents a short evening instructional program that focuses on early warning signs of violence and bullying in children. We provide each parent an information packet and have each adult complete a short questionnaire about his or her child's behavior. We share with each parent the same evaluation completed by their child's teacher, and then we talk about differences in the two surveys. I really believe that we are now working with parents to address troubling behavior as early as possible. This approach has led to wonderful discussions and some really positive follow-up. I am more convinced than ever that many parents need a lot of help in raising their children these days.

—Teacher, Wisconsin

STRATEGY #22

Recognize Early Warning Signs

Every time you have one of these horrible high school shootings, the news media interview the violent student's elementary teachers and they always say the same thing: "I knew he was going to do something like this some-day." What breaks my heart is that so many people are aware of the violent tendencies in a kid, but we rarely do anything about it.

—Teacher, Tennessee

In almost every incident of youth violence, parents, students, and teachers report that they knew the violent kid would someday get into real trouble. Research has clearly documented both violent profiles and early warning signs for teachers and parents. It is, however, essential that these profiles and warning signs not be used as absolute predictors of violence. These characteristics and behaviors can only alert parents and school officials to observe, conduct careful evaluation, and perhaps provide counseling. Research cautions that many resilient students may possess one or more of these profile characteristics and still be outstanding young people.

Recent study and analysis have provided educators, schools, and communities with an emerging profile of violent youth and a compilation of early warning behavioral indicators (see Figure 9.1). The emerging profile seems closer to that associated with teenage suicides than with the traditional characteristics of violent teenagers (see Figure 9.2). Violence all too often begets more violence. The circumstances that exist in the life of an abused child or young adult can be the catalysts for the abused to strike out as a violent abuser (see Figure 9.3 on page 180).

RESEARCH

- The traditional profile of abused youth has powerful predictability. While recent acts of school violence suggest a new and emerging type of violent youth, the traditional profile continues to serve to identify a subculture of violent youth.
- Educators and families can learn how to recognize aberrant or disruptive behavior that could be an indication of later violent acts.

Early Warning Behaviors

- Has a history of tantrums and uncontrollable angry outbursts.
- Characteristically resorts to name-calling, cursing, or abusive language.
- Habitually makes violent threats when angry.
- Has previously brought a weapon to school.
- Has a background of serious disciplinary problems at school and in the community.
- Has a background of drug, alcohol, or other substance abuse or dependency.
- Is on the fringe of his or her peer group, with few or no close friends.
- Is preoccupied with weapons, explosives, or other incendiary devices.
- Has previously been truant, suspended, or expelled from school.
- Displays cruelty to animals.
- Has little or no supervision and support from parents or a caring adult.
- Has witnessed or been a victim of abuse or neglect in the home.
- Has been bullied and/or bullies or intimidates peers or younger children.
- Tends to blame others for difficulties and problems caused by himself or herself.
- Consistently prefers television shows, movies, or music expressing violent themes and acts.
- Prefers reading materials dealing with violent themes, rituals, and abuse.
- Reflects anger, frustration, and the dark side of life in school essays or writing projects.
- Is involved with a gang or an antisocial group on the fringe.
- Is often depressed and/or has significant mood swings.
- Has threatened or attempted suicide.

Figure 9.1

SOURCE: From U.S. Department of Education (1998a).

Emerging Profile of Violent and/or Suicidal Youth

- Middle- or upper-middle-class family
- Intelligent
- Success in school
- Bored, isolated, angry, and disappointed
- Escalating history of violence and aggressive acts
- Access to guns and the Internet
- Fear of alienation and loneliness

Figure 9.2

SOURCE: From Barr and Parrett (2001).

The Powerful Predictability of Violence

Circumstances common to abused youth include the following:

- Poverty
- Dysfunctional families (youth often raised by grandparents or foster families)
- Childhood abuse
- Failure to bond with adults or to develop positive relationships with adults
- Exposure to media violence
- School failure and school problems

Add to this profile the following additional characteristics and the likelihood of violence is increased dramatically:

- Racial intolerance
- Access to guns
- A family with a history of criminal violence
- Abusing drugs and/or alcohol
- Belonging to a gang

The likelihood of violence is increased even further if the following characteristics are present:

- Has used a weapon in the past
- Has been arrested
- Has neurological problems

Figure 9.3

SOURCE: From Barr and Parrett (2001).

TAKE ACTION

- ☑ **Initiate professional development.** Make referrals. Refer students who exhibit early warning signs to school counselors and psychologists for careful evaluation and for discussions with parents.
- ☑ **Coordinate social services.** Often, youth with violent, violence-prone, bullying, or other disruptive behaviors require services far beyond the resources of local schools. Work closely with the associated agencies of the health and human services division and the juvenile justice system.

☑ **Work as a team.** The challenge of helping violent and violence-prone youth requires all available means of support coming to the aid of the student before the violence begins. No individual teacher, principal, counselor, or support staff should act alone. Get help—team up with colleagues to intervene with these students.

See the "50 Strategies Suggested Reading" section for a list of resources selected to complement the fifty strategies as you put them to use in your classroom.

SAVING MY STUDENTS, SAVING MY SCHOOL

How can **Strategy #22: Recognize Early Warning Signs** be put to use in your classroom? What can you do to increase awareness and education among your group of colleagues?

_____

_____

_____

_____

_____

_____

_____

_____

_____

_____

_____

Share your thoughts with a colleague or group of colleagues.

STRATEGY #23

Bully-Proof Classrooms and Schools

In the tentative handwriting of a child, she wrote: "Dear Mommy and Daddy, I know my death will shock you, but I had to do it. All my life I've been teased and harassed. I just couldn't stand it anymore."

—Jessica Portner

Recent research suggests that far more students than imagined are actively engaged in bullying. One study by Parents Resource Institute on Drug Education (PRIDE) (n.d.) reported that 40 percent of the students in Grades 6–12 threatened to hurt another student at school. Other researchers estimate that as many as 77 percent of adolescents have been bullied at some time in school and as many as 10 to 15 percent of students are bullied on a regular basis. A 2001 survey funded by the National Institute of Child Health and Human Development (NICHD) found that 16 percent of the 15,686 students in Grades 6–10 in public, parochial, and other private schools throughout the nation reported that they had been bullied during the current term. The study identified bullying as "physical, involving hitting or otherwise attacking the other person; verbal, involving name-calling or threats; or psychological, involving spreading rumors or excluding a person." The NICHD researchers also reported that while boys were both more likely to bully others and more likely to be victims of bullying than girls, bullying is not limited solely to boys. A Philadelphia study reported that 65 percent of the middle school girls engaged in some sort of bullying (NICHD 2001). Boys were more likely to say they had been bullied physically, while girls more frequently said they had been bullied verbally and psychologically.

Unlearning to Be a Bully

Violent and bullying behavior is learned, and, if identified sufficiently early and adequately addressed, it can be unlearned. There are excellent examples of schools that have been transformed from disruptive, intimidating environments to schools characterized by a climate of respect. Schools can develop bully-proof strategies that can transform students and create a positive learning environment.

Figures 9.4 and 9.5 on pages 184–185 suggest a number of strategies for educators and schools to employ related to the early detection of bullying behaviors and appropriate preventative measures for victims.

Bullying Behavior

- Pushes, shoves, hits, kicks, and/or makes fun of other kids, says mean things, or calls other students names.
- Manipulates relationships.
- Starts acting aggressively as early as preschool.
- Believes aggression is an acceptable way to solve conflicts.
- Is quick to react with hostility to neutral events.
- Gets into fights but blames others for starting them.
- Lacks empathy.
- Breaks rules aggressively.
- Needs to dominate others.
- Has two or three friends who are aggressive.
- Feels no anxiety.
- Generally feels well liked.
- Does not feel lonely.
- Hangs out with increasingly younger children.

Figure 9.4

SOURCE: Excerpted from *The Bully-Free Classroom: Over 100 Tips and Strategies for Teachers K–8* (Updated Edition) by Allan L. Beane, PhD, copyright © 2005. Used with permission of Free Spirit Publishing, Inc., Minneapolis, MN; 1-800-735-7323; www.freespirit.com. All rights reserved.

Dealing With Bullying: Actions for Parents

- If you think your child is being bullied, ask him or her. Kids are embarrassed. Parents need to take the initiative. Take notes.
- Believe your child if he says he is being bullied.
- Don't confront the bully or the bully's parents. This probably won't help and might make things worse.
- Don't tell your child to get in there and fight. Bullies are usually stronger and more powerful than their victims.
- Don't blame your child.
- Don't promise to keep it a secret. Explain to your child you will help and ask the teacher to help.

- Contact the teacher as soon as possible. Request a private meeting when other students won't see you.

- Seek the teacher's perspective. Stay patient. Ask what will be done and get specifics. Ask to be kept informed.

- Help your child develop bully-resistant skills. Enroll him or her in a class on assertiveness skills, friendship skills, or self-defense. Build his or her social skills by having him or her join clubs.

- Consider whether your child does something that encourages bullies to pick on him or her. Is there a behavior that needs to change? Ask the teacher for insights.

- Get involved with your child's school and volunteer in the classroom.

Figure 9.5

SOURCE: Excerpted from *The Bully-Free Classroom: Over 100 Tips and Strategies for Teachers K–8* (Updated Edition) by Allan L. Beane, PhD, copyright © 2005. Used with permission of Free Spirit Publishing, Inc., Minneapolis, MN; 1-800-735-7323; www.freespirit.com. All rights reserved.

RESEARCH

- If a child is a bully, there is a strong possibility that the child will grow up disruptive and violent and will end up serving time in jail or prison.
- By age thirty, 25 percent of the adults who had been bullies during childhood will have criminal records.
- Bullying behavior can be identified as early as age two.
- There is evidence that both the bully and the victim of the bully are vulnerable to long-term social and emotional problems.
- Bullying behavior can be unlearned and schools and classrooms can be bully-proofed with appropriate programs.

TAKE ACTION

- ☑ **Educate parents.** Help educate parents regarding bullying behaviors. Parents of all students need to be alert to situations where their children are being bullied as well as perpetuating the bullying and intimidating.
- ☑ **Make educators, parents, and community more aware.** A compendium of preventative measures for victims should be used in every school. These interventions should be acknowledged

and understood by all educators, parents, and community members.

☑ **Teachers and schools must take action.** Schools and educators possess vast resources with which to institute effective preventative and intervention programs to combat bullying. Successful models are readily available to be borrowed from other districts and schools.

☑ **Teachers and students must act decisively.** Engage in intervention practices. This begins by identifying the most critical issues and implementing a plan of intervention.

 See the "50 Strategies Suggested Reading" section for a list of resources selected to complement the fifty strategies as you put them to use in your classroom.

SAVING MY STUDENTS, SAVING MY SCHOOL

How can **Strategy #23: Bully-Proof Classrooms and Schools** be put to use in your classroom? What can you do to increase awareness and education among your group of colleagues?

_____

_____

_____

_____

_____

_____

_____

_____

_____

Share your thoughts with a colleague or group of colleagues.

STRATEGY #24

Create Reentry Opportunities for Expelled Students

Well, with zero tolerance, we expel the kids from school, but we cannot expel them from our community. They're still out there, but now they are no longer supervised. Should we be surprised that these kids get into trouble?

—Principal, Oregon

To ensure safety and a positive learning climate, disruptive, dangerous, intolerant, and bullying behaviors must not be tolerated in public schools. While schools must have zero-tolerance policies to suspend or expel these students from schools, expelled students should not be simply released to the community, where their learning is interrupted and they are not supervised. Communities must ensure that when students are forced from school through expulsion or incarceration in the juvenile justice system, every effort is made so that their education continues to be supervised and is not interrupted.

Unfortunately, in most communities, little collaboration or social structure exists between public schools and the juvenile justice system. As a result, when students are expelled, they step out into a vacuum. Expelled students tend to be no more successful outside of school than they were inside of school. In the 1995 study of 1,500 expelled students conducted by the Colorado Foundation for Families and Children, within the succeeding twelve months, almost 50 percent had been in trouble with the police and more than 33 percent were in jail. Once in jail or prison, these former students tended to continue their troubling behavior. As a result, the recidivism rate of juvenile offenders is high.

Youths incarcerated in the United States tend to be between fifteen and sixteen years old, out of school for more than a year, and lacking in basic skills. Once out of the supervised educational environment of public schools, the majority of these poorly educated youth are unable to find meaningful employment and many end up in trouble.

Attending to Suspended, Excluded, and Expelled Youth

There is an urgent need for schools and other social agencies to cooperate in the creation of highly structured, high-security educational programs for expelled students. It is essential that these students' education not be interrupted and that they be supervised in secure educational settings. Even if the human loss is minimized with programs like this, the financial cost of addressing the problem is significant. In most states, the cost of public education per student is between $6,000 and $9,000 per year. To incarcerate a youth in the juvenile justice system costs between $40,000 and $64,000 per year.

Several school districts have developed educational "boot camps," modeled after the military, to address the difficult needs of expelled students. The About Face Academy in Oklahoma City uses certified teachers who are retired military personnel to staff this school, which has gained impressive results through emphasizing structure, pride, and obedience.

FIND OKLAHOMA CITY'S "ABOUT FACE ACADEMY" ON THE WEB

- <www.okcps.k12.ok.us/eservices/aboutface.htm>

It is unfortunate, yet necessary, that today all schools must possess a range of intervention strategies for suspended, excluded, and expelled students. These services must focus on the needs of the student and incorporate positive approaches for extinguishing unacceptable behaviors and creating opportunities for reengagement in school. Many districts offer a menu of intervention programs for these students, depending on their offenses and their needs.

Figure 9.6 shows a variety of intervention services school districts can make available for suspended, excluded, and expelled youth.

A Range of Interventions for High-Risk Youth

- Alternative schools
- Transition programs
- Reentry programs
- Mentoring programs
- In-school suspensions
- Residential program services
- Counseling and support groups
- In-school tutoring
- Schools-within-schools
- Correspondence programs
- Web-based instruction

Figure 9.6

RESEARCH

- If expelled students are not supervised and if their education is interrupted, there is a high probability that they will quickly be in trouble and often find themselves in jail.
- Too many expelled students have never learned basic skills and, as a result, have often become disruptive and have failed in school.
- Expelled students with basic skill deficiencies have very limited employment opportunities.
- There is a high recidivism rate for expelled students who are arrested, convicted, and incarcerated in the juvenile justice system.
- Districts with reentry and other intervention programs for suspended, excluded, and expelled students experience dramatically higher success rates with these students.

TAKE ACTION

- ☑ **Develop a range of interventions.** Explore and implement a range of intervention programs to meet the needs of suspended, excluded, and expelled youth.
- ☑ **Create educational programs.** Provide high-security programs so that expelled students can continue their education. These educational programs should be modeled after effective alternative schools.
- ☑ **Explore cooperative programs.** Explore the possibility of cooperating with state departments of education, the criminal justice system, the juvenile justice system, and other agencies to fund and provide effective programs for expelled students.
- ☑ **Consider legislative action.** Several states have passed legislation that requires and funds multiple educational alternatives for expelled students. Often, because the legal issues involving expelled students are so complex, legislative action is necessary.

 See the "50 Strategies Suggested Reading" section for a list of resources selected to complement the fifty strategies as you put them to use in your classroom.

SAVING MY STUDENTS, SAVING MY SCHOOL

How can **Strategy #24: Create Reentry Opportunities for Expelled Students** be put to use in your classroom? What can you do to increase awareness and education among your group of colleagues?

_____

_____

_____

_____

_____

_____

_____

_____

_____

Share your thoughts with a colleague or group of colleagues.

10

Expect High Academic Performance

Well, looking back, it was really quite simple to explain how our school began to experience improved academic achievement for many of our at-risk students. We just started treating all of our kids as if they were gifted and talented. The rest is history.

—Teacher, Arkansas

Public education effectively teaches the top 20 or 30 percent of enrolled students. The challenge comes when high academic performance is expected of the other 70 percent. It is this group of students, many of whom are apathetic, bored, unmotivated, and often disruptive, that represents the greatest challenge for teachers and schools. The good news is that a growing number of schools nationwide have become increasingly successful with this demanding, often neglected majority. Even better,

---

FIND THE SOUTHERN REGIONAL EDUCATION BOARD'S "HIGH SCHOOLS THAT WORK" (HSTW) PROJECT ON THE WEB

- <www.sreb.org/programs/hstw/hstwindex.asp>

---

researchers have begun to document specific instructional approaches that can dramatically improve academic achievement. Students will live "up to" or "down to" our expectations. When students are taught through an aligned curriculum, personalized instruction, and a "can do" attitude from caring teachers, remarkable improvement can occur. The opposite is also true. If students are grouped into slow-learning tracks with low teacher expectations and boring instructional materials that fail to motivate them, they will often demonstrate low achievement. The difference between an individual student placed in either an applied mathematics course or a high school algebra course can be significant. Jaime Escalante, a professor and teacher of mathematics who gained renown for his work in Garfield High School, in the poor, Hispanic community of South Los Angeles, shocked his educational community by demonstrating that at-risk Hispanic students can be successful with advanced-placement calculus. The Southern Regional Education Board's High Schools That Work improvement initiative has proven repeatedly that if poor, at-risk, and minority students are placed in an algebra class and taught with high expectations, these students will learn algebra.

If schools are serious about all students achieving high academic standards, they must confront the destructive practices of tracking and retention that have so often characterized public education in the United States and have kept all students from pursuing a rigorous, challenging curriculum. Schools must address student needs, provide personalized instruction to capitalize on student abilities, and do everything possible to motivate the most needy students. For poor, at-risk, and other low-performing students, motivation is often the key to helping students becoming engaged, productive learners. The best way to generate student motivation is by using technology and engaging students in the real world outside of the artificial culture of schools. Especially for the poor and at-risk student, supplementing teacher-centered classroom learning that so typifies public education in the United States with the exciting world of technology and Internet-based learning and real-world experiences outside of school can have a remarkable, positive effect.

Using personalized, interactive technology, students are often able to catch up and accelerate their learning in a very short time. They also tend to be motivated by this turned-on approach to learning. The same is true of career-theme learning outside of the school. Students who have never responded positively to academics become active learners while participating in internships and practica in hospitals, television stations, courtrooms, banks, manufacturing centers, and police stations. Increasingly, school districts that have created focus programs or magnet schools in areas like law, health professions, radio and television broadcasting, performing arts, financial services, and technology discovered that students become academically revitalized because they can suddenly see relevance in their learning. A 1996 study comparing comprehensive high schools, private parochial schools, and career-theme magnet schools (which served the most diverse student population of the three types of schools), found that students in the career-theme schools were achieving the highest academic performance (Gamoran 1996b).

Two final observations are essential. Not only must students learn effectively and achieve acceptable academic standards, they must also prove successful on the high-stakes standardized tests that are increasingly being used to assess student achievement throughout the United States. Once again, schools and school districts across the country have demonstrated that they can help teach all students to be successful on these mandated tests. Finally, teachers can be successful with all students only if they have been provided detailed and ongoing professional development. The most effective professional development helps create teacher *learning communities* and leads directly to increased student achievement.

For all students to achieve and experience success, schools must help them become motivated learners, focus on their multiple intelligences, surround them with caring teachers with high expectations, provide them with relevant and challenging classrooms with effective teachers, offer them rich experiences in the real world of careers, and teach them to be successful on standardized tests and other assessments. This chapter presents six effective strategies that can ensure that all students achieve high academic standards.

Unconventional Wisdom

What Works for Experienced Teachers

Teachers become students for a day.

Last year, we established a new policy in our school that requires every teacher to become a student for a day. Teachers dress like students, ride the bus to school, complete an entire day of classes, eat in the lunchroom, and even ride the bus home. Like any other new students, the teachers are often teased and taunted by other students.

Nothing we have ever done in the way of professional development has had such a positive impact. The student-for-a-day experience dominates our discussion and faculty meetings. Even though we teachers are here in school every day, we have gained from experiencing our school from the students' perspective. If you want to improve your school, try the student-for-a-day program and see what happens.

—Teacher, Kentucky

Use mastery learning.

We do not have competition of any kind. The kids hate it. We do expect quality work. The students are encouraged to do work over and over until they can honestly tell us that they are proud of what they are turning in. The funny thing is that we have had several parents come in and say that their high school students have wanted them to post their schoolwork on the refrigerator again like they did in grade school. We all get a chuckle out of this.

—Teacher, Indiana

STRATEGY #25

Motivate Students

Well, it took me a long time, but I finally figured out the secret to effective teaching. It's not what I do that matters; it's what students are interested in and willing to do that counts. I have completely switched my approach. . . . Now I work day in and day out to get my students involved and engaged.

—Teacher, Wisconsin

Everyone has heard the old maxim that you can "lead a horse to water, but you can't make it drink." For classroom teachers, the reverse side of this maxim is unusually important: if a teacher can stimulate students' thirst for learning, students are likely to pursue learning on their own. The most significant contributor to learning is *motivation.* Although coaches have always known this, classroom teachers have too often focused on requirements, assessments, and tests rather than desire, determination, and motivation. There is a long history of athletic coaches who have taken players who are too small, too slow, and lacking in essential skills and motivated them to become champions. Their secret has been to focus their efforts—not on abilities, but on determination and skill development.

One classic story that has been told and retold revolves around a meeting with a student, a mother, and a principal. In the story, the principal is explaining that the student is so lacking in ability that he or she will have to be retained in a grade for another year. The mother, trembling with indignation, replies, "In our family we don't believe in ability." For teachers of at-risk students, it is not ability that is important; it is motivating students to desire to learn.

There has been considerable research on motivation that provides important insight into strategies for classroom teachers. First, teachers should not praise students for how smart they are or for their ability. Rather, teachers should focus their praise on student efforts and the strategies or processes that the students use in addressing problems or assignments. Teachers should focus on *effort,* not ability. The goal is to help students value their efforts—to relish a challenge—and for teachers to praise them for their attempts at addressing a problem. Teachers need to help students find satisfaction in tackling difficult tasks. Teachers also need to help students understand that their performance reflects their current skills and their current effort, not their intelligence. The overriding lesson for students must be that it is not intelligence that is important;

rather, effort, determination, and perseverance are important. Praising students for how smart they are is not effective. Praising students and reinforcing them for how hard they have tried is effective. Educators can significantly influence student self-esteem by showing students respect, ensuring that students feel the teacher cares for them, and putting students in charge of their own learning.

Learning for Learning's Sake?

For at-risk students, teachers must demonstrate the relevance of any learning assignment. At-risk students need more than simply learning for the sake of learning; they must see relevance and application. Teachers need to take highly complex, theoretical learning and break these tasks down into manageable learning assignments. Students find success in effectively completing one small problem after another. As they complete each small problem, they develop self-confidence in their abilities and subsequently increase their motivation. Another effective teaching strategy to foster motivation is to do everything possible to make students responsible for their own learning. Teachers should provide students with a variety of learning choices or options and should employ cooperative learning teams so that each student's multiple intelligences can flourish. Students should be encouraged to explore creative ways of completing assignments. Finally, throughout the day, teachers must maintain high academic standards and expectations.

The environment of the school and classroom is a critical influence on student motivation. The school and classroom should use multiple methods (symbols, awards, praise, ceremonies, rituals, etc.) to focus learning and behavior on high academic performance. Many alternative schools employ mastery learning, which requires that each student demonstrate an acceptable level of performance to progress. If students do less than acceptable work, the school provides afterschool homework assistance, personal tutorials, and a variety of other support mechanisms to help the student rework or make up academic assignments.

Teachers can also help develop intrinsic, short-term motivation by working with students to establish personal goals and then helping them develop a self-evaluation process to monitor their progress in achieving their goals. The use of progress charts, inventories, and progress reports helps students visually evaluate their progress toward goal fulfillment. Such support and self-evaluation can generate substantial motivation in students at risk.

Edward Hootstein's (1998) recommendations, or RISE model, for reaching unmotivated children are outlined in Figure 10.1 (page 198).

Motivate the Unmotivated

1. **Use relevant subject matter**:
   - Relate content to students' needs, interests, and expectations.
   - Communicate the value of the learning activity.

2. **Use interesting instruction**:
   - Attract students' curiosity by providing thought-provoking information.
   - Promote students' sense of control of the learning process.

3. **Satisfy the learner**: Provide rewards that motivate and capture attention.

4. **Expect success**: Emphasize that increased effort will lead to success.

Figure 10.1

SOURCE: From Hootstein (1998).

RESEARCH

- If students believe a classroom is a caring, supportive environment in which they feel a sense of belonging—one where all students are valued and respected—then students will develop trust, participate more fully, and invest a greater effort in learning.
- Student learning must be challenging, yet achievable.
- Relevance provides motivation by helping students see how learning connects their lives to the real world.
- Defining learning tasks into specific short-term, achievable goals encourages motivation.
- School and classroom policies and practices should stress mastery learning and student development rather than student intelligence.

TAKE ACTION

☑ **Focus on effort.** Focus on and praise effort and perseverance rather than ability or intelligence.

☑ **Emphasize school and classroom policies.** Work with other educators to ensure continuity between classrooms so that the entire school supports and encourages mastery learning, personal effort, and skill development.

☑ **Focus on manageable, short-term goals**. Organize instructional assignments into manageable, short-term learning goals that are achievable for students.

☑ **Make learning relevant.** Do everything possible to help students understand and connect the relevance and importance of classroom learning to their lives.

☑ **Place students in charge.** Encourage students to be creative in addressing problems and developing processes to achieve learning outcomes.

See the "50 Strategies Suggested Reading" section for a list of resources selected to complement the fifty strategies as you put them to use in your classroom.

SAVING MY STUDENTS, SAVING MY SCHOOL

How can **Strategy #25: Motivate Students** be put to use in your classroom? What can you do to increase awareness and education among your group of colleagues?

_____

_____

_____

_____

_____

_____

_____

_____

_____

Share your thoughts with a colleague or group of colleagues.

STRATEGY #26

Teach to Multiple Intelligences

We attended a great institute on multiple intelligences, and it changed our lives. It has also changed our school. We now address multiple intelligences across our curriculum, and we're seeing daily results in our students' performance.

—Teacher, Idaho

In 1983, Howard Gardner wrote the book *Frames of Mind*, in which he outlined a revolutionary theory regarding human intelligence. Rather than accepting the traditional unitary conception that intelligence could be described in a single quantifiable number, Gardner argued that intelligence was far more complex and should be defined as the ability to

- solve problems encountered in real life,
- generate new problems to solve, and
- make something or offer a service within one's culture.

Gardner believed that intelligence was not fixed—that it could be developed and exhibited in many ways. Rather than using intelligence to sort and group students, intelligence should be perceived as a way to understand and develop human capacity.

Gardner used this new conception of intelligence as a way to explain high achievement of the widest variety of people in different cultural settings: business leaders, doctors, dancers, religious leaders, surgeons, politicians, sculptors, musicians, teachers, researchers, and others. Out of this analysis, he defined seven distinct categories of multiple intelligence, and later, in 1995, he added an eighth category (see Figure 10.2 on page 202).

The theory of multiple intelligences provided a new basis for organizing classrooms and schools, managing classrooms, diversifying assignments, planning lessons, integrating teaching and learning styles, and encouraging excellence in all students—not just those students who tested as gifted and talented or who scored high on the PSAT, SAT, and other traditional standardized tests. Multiple intelligences proved to be a new way of perceiving students. It replaced the concept that some students were smart and others not with the belief that each and every student had the potential for unique and high-quality achievement. Rather than schools focusing narrowly on traditional academic

Gardner's Eight Intelligences	
Visual/Spatial	Images, graphics, drawings, sketches, maps, charts, doodles, pictures, spatial orientation, puzzles, designs, looks, appeal, mind's eye, imagination, visualization, dreams, nightmares, films, and videos
Logical/Mathematical	Reasoning, deductive and inductive logic, facts, data, information, spreadsheets, databases, sequencing, ranking, organizing, analyzing, proofs, conclusions, judging, evaluations, and assessments
Verbal/Linguistic	Words, wordsmiths, speaking, writing, listening, reading, papers, essays, poems, plays, narratives, lyrics, spelling, grammar, foreign languages, memos, bulletins, newsletters, newspapers, e-mail, faxes, speeches, talks, dialogues, and debates
Musical/Rhythmic	Music, rhythm, beat, melody, tunes, allegro, pacing, timbre, tenor, soprano, opera, baritone, symphony, choir, chorus, madrigals, rap, rock, rhythm and blues, jazz, classical, folk, ads and jingles
Bodily/Kinesthetic	Art, activity, action, experiential, hands-on, experiments, try, do, perform, play, drama, sports, throw, toss, catch, jump, twist, twirl, assemble, disassemble, form, re-form, manipulate, touch, feel, immerse, and participate
Interpersonal/Social	Interact, communicate, converse, share, understand, empathize, sympathize, reach out, care, talk, whisper, laugh, cry, shudder, socialize, meet, greet, lead, follow, gangs, clubs, charisma, crowds, gatherings, and twosomes
Intrapersonal/ Introspective	Self, solitude, meditate, think, create, brood, reflect, envision, journal, self-assess, set goals, plot, plan, dream, write, fiction, nonfiction, poetry, affirmations, lyrics, songs, screenplays, commentaries, introspection, and inspection
Naturalist	Nature, natural, environment, listen, watch, observe, classify, categorize, discern patterns, appreciate, hike, climb, fish, hunt, snorkel, photograph, trees, leaves, animals, living things, flora, fauna, ecosystem, sky, grass, mountains, lakes, and rivers

Figure 10.2

SOURCE: Adapted from *Problem-Based Learning and Other Curriculum Models for the Multiple Intelligences Classroom,* by Robin Fogarty. © 1997 Corwin Press. Used with permission.

achievement, teaching and learning could reflect a closer proximity to real life, where people with the widest possible skills and abilities could be valued for a wide range of services and products. This meant that every child could excel, contribute, and achieve high expectations. At the practical level, instruction emphasizing multiple intelligences matched quite appropriately with instruction based on participant teaching and learning styles. This confluence has provided new structure for teachers to employ in diversifying their classroom instruction, student assignments, and classroom management.

A growing number of public schools throughout the United States, like the Key Learning Community elementary and middle schools in Indianapolis, have employed multiple intelligences as a central theme for organizing instruction in the entire school.

FIND THE "KEY LEARNING COMMUNITY" ON THE WEB

- <www.616.ips.k12.in.us/Principal/default.aspx>

RESEARCH

- Human intelligence is not unitary and cannot be measured by a single test.
- The theory of multiple intelligences helps teachers meet the complex needs of diverse and at-risk students.
- Multiple intelligences offer opportunities for each student to demonstrate his or her unique strengths and abilities and leads to heightened self-esteem and more engaged participation and learning.
- Multiple intelligences enable students to demonstrate their understandings and mastery of concepts, content, and skills in a variety of different ways.
- Multiple-intelligences instruction is particularly effective for at-risk youth.

TAKE ACTION

☑ **Learn about multiple intelligences.** Participate in professional development on the use of multiple intelligences. Know your own personal intelligences and strengths and weaknesses and learn to construct lessons and assignments designed to develop the various intelligences in their diverse students.

☑ **Work with parents and other teachers.** Multiple intelligences provide an effective way to establish a common vision as well as a consistent philosophy of education to guide classroom instruction.

☑ **Use multiple intelligences in classroom instruction.**
Classroom lessons, student assignments, and assessments must
be diversified so that each student with various types of intelligences can choose appropriate lessons and achieve high expectations. Many schools emphasize a particular intelligence each
month and plan schoolwide events designed to recognize and celebrate student diversity and excellence.

See the "50 Strategies Suggested Reading" section for a list of
resources selected to complement the fifty strategies as you put them to
use in your classroom.

SAVING MY STUDENTS, SAVING MY SCHOOL

How can **Strategy #26: Teach to Multiple Intelligences** be put to use in your classroom? What can you do to increase awareness and education among your group of colleagues?

_____

_____

_____

_____

_____

_____

_____

_____

_____

Share your thoughts with a colleague or group of colleagues.

STRATEGY #27

Confront Tracking and Retention Practices

They placed me in the slow track at the end of the third grade, and I never got out. It was a nine-year sentence. I often wonder what I missed, what I could have learned.

—Student, Arizona

For at-risk students, two of the most debilitating and destructive approaches created by educators are *ability tracking* and *grade retention*. Few educational practices have been investigated so thoroughly. Far from supporting the poor, minority, and at-risk students they were designed to help, tracking and retention have had a vicious, negative impact on self-esteem, pride, motivation, and achievement. Neither of these practices has been shown to improve student achievement and help at-risk students accelerate their learning to catch up with their more advantaged classmates. Unfortunately, tracking and retention remain widely used and supported approaches, and today, with the widespread use of high-stakes testing for promotion and graduation, retention is being implemented frequently as a negative and ineffective motivational tool for learning.

Teachers, parents, school leaders, and school districts should

- confront tracking and retention,
- review the research and local data on the effectiveness of these practices with at-risk students, and
- work to establish school and districtwide policies that ban or restrict the use of these destructive practices.

Grade Retention

Few school practices are as detrimental to student development as retention. In one national survey of teenagers who had been retained at the early elementary grades, students reported that being retained was like "going blind" or having "your parents killed in an automobile accident" (Bracey 1989). Retention is also one of the four major factors (along with poverty, attending school with other poor children, and reading below grade level) that is a high-probability predictor of students in the third grade who will experience school failure and ultimately drop out. Retention is more likely to be used for boys, minorities, low-income students, and children rated low in social adjustment; yet it has not been proven to increase learning readiness, does not effectively increase academic achievement, has a negative effect on student self-concept, and leads directly to increased discipline problems.

Retention is a powerful force in students dropping out of school. School dropouts are five times more likely than high school graduates to have repeated a grade. Students who are retained twice face close to 100 percent probability of dropping out of school. Low-achieving students who are promoted tend to have greater achievement than similar students who are retained. Schools who continue to retain students do so despite more than thirty years of accumulative research that does not support this practice. Too often, teachers use retention to punish low-achieving students. Two prominent educational researchers concluded their review of research regarding retention with these chilling remarks: "Retained students are negatively affected academically, socially, and emotionally. As a strategy, retention FAILS" (Haberman and Dill 1993: 355).

Tracking

Despite more than three decades of research that documents the disastrous effects of ability tracking, the practice continues to be used in more than 95 percent of high schools and seems to be increasing at the elementary and middle school levels. Tracking is a highly popular and widely employed strategy for dealing with diverse student ability and achievement. Teachers almost everywhere believe that tracking makes teaching and learning more effective and more efficient. Unfortunately, tracking does not work and typically dooms students to less-experienced and often poor teachers, watered-down curricula, and low expectations. Few students assigned to low-achieving tracks ever get out.

Research has identified three major reasons why tracking has not been successful, especially for the students placed into the lower tracks. First, there is evidence that slower tracks receive fewer resources from the school. Often, these classes are large, housed in inadequate facilities, and limited by antiquated methods and equipment. Second, since teachers find these classes more demanding, both behaviorally and instructionally, the slower track typically does not attract the most experienced, effective teachers. Third, and even more disturbing, teachers tend to have significantly lower expectations for student learning in the slower tracks than for the students in the faster tracks. Frequently, students and teachers feel stigmatized by being in the slower tracks, and both share expectations of low achievement. The consequences of these factors for the lower-track students unfortunately include a less challenging curriculum, a slower instructional pace, test and homework assignments that are not as challenging, and few demands for higher-order thinking skills (see Figure 10.3).

The cumulative effects of tracking during a student's educational career can be devastating. Rather than helping students accelerate and catch up, tracking actually widens the achievement gap between the slower and more-advanced students. Rather than alleviating the problems of students with significant educational needs, tracking tends to exacerbate the problem.

Students tend to be tracked more by their socioeconomic status than by their academic ability. The higher-level academic track tends to enroll middle-class youth from educated families, and the lower track tends to enroll culturally diverse students, poor students, or students from homes with limited educational backgrounds. Unfortunately, once a child is assigned to the slow track, there is little hope of ever moving up to the advanced track. For students who are most at risk, tracking serves only to isolate, handicap, stigmatize, and actually prevent effective learning. For almost three decades, it has been known that if students were not slow learners when they are assigned to the slow track, they soon become so.

Inequities Inherent in the Slower Track

Fewer school resources

- Inadequate physical facilities
- Larger class sizes
- Antiquated equipment

Typically less-experienced and less-effective teachers

- Less-effective instructional strategies grounded in outmoded or ineffective pedagogy
- Low expectations
- Watered-down curriculum

Less-challenging curriculum based on low expectations of student achievement

- Slower instructional pace; less material covered
- Less demand for exercising and developing higher-level thinking skills
- Lack of exposure to models of academic achievement

Cumulative effect on tracked at-risk students

- Isolated
- Stigmatized
- Prevented from gaining life skills

Figure 10.3

RESEARCH

- The more times a student is retained, the greater the chances are of that child eventually dropping out of school.
- Retention and tracking do not increase learning readiness or improve student achievement.
- Retention and tracking can promote student disruptions and have negative effects on student self-concepts.
- Retention and tracking primarily impact the poor, culturally diverse, and other students rated low in social adjustment.
- Students assigned to low-achieving tracks almost never get out.
- Public high schools often hold low expectations for at-risk students and place them in general and vocational tracks. This process selects and sorts students whom teachers believe do not have the capacity to achieve high academic standards.

TAKE ACTION

- ☑ **Seek professional development.** Because of the widespread use of retention and tracking, educators need professional development to become aware of the voluminous research documenting the failure of these two practices. It is essential to learn about other, more effective approaches to addressing students who are low achievers.
- ☑ **Develop new policies.** School boards need to take urgent action to establish policies prohibiting the use of retention and tracking of at-risk students. Teachers and parents should be engaged in all phases of new policy development.
- ☑ **Educate the school community.** Inform parents and community stakeholders of the negative impact of retention and tracking. Many affluent parents and parents with gifted and talented children are extremely insistent that low-performing students be removed from regular classrooms so that they do not slow down the development of the higher-achieving students.
- ☑ **Assess and remediate.** Student skill development and academic achievement need to be assessed, carefully and constantly, to quickly identify students who fall behind. Intensive efforts need to be focused on these students to remediate and accelerate their learning so that they can catch up with their peers.
- ☑ **Help students catch up and accelerate.** Use a variety of approaches to help students who are falling behind catch up and accelerate their learning. Some schools use personalized

computer programs, like Plato or Nova Net. Extended-day as well as summer programs are especially effective.

See the "50 Strategies Suggested Reading" section for a list of resources selected to complement the fifty strategies as you put them to use in your classroom.

SAVING MY STUDENTS, SAVING MY SCHOOL

How can **Strategy #27: Confront Tracking and Retention Practices** be put to use in your classroom? What can you do to increase awareness and education among your group of colleagues?

_____

_____

_____

_____

_____

_____

_____

_____

_____

Share your thoughts with a colleague or group of colleagues.

STRATEGY #28

Initiate Targeted Professional Development

We have a good school. The teachers work so hard and give all they have to the kids. But we must get better. We know how to rescue kids and start them back on track. But these kids are so needy. How do we get better as a staff at helping a student move from dropout to competent graduate? How do we best accelerate the learning of a sixteen- or seventeen-year-old to catch up with peers, pass the state exit exam, and be academically prepared for college or other postsecondary learning? How do we do all of this?

—Principal, Alternative High School, Texas

Working on a team to focus on our most pressing needs and developing solutions that have provided immediate gains has been the best use of our professional development resources in the twenty-two years I've been teaching.

—Elementary Teacher, Colorado

"No child left behind," the phrase that drove the educational policy making of the 2002 federal government, set public education in America on a course previously charted by few districts and schools. To truly leave no child behind requires a fundamental shift in attitudes toward assistance to children from low-socioeconomic-status families. To truly leave no child behind requires core-level changes in classroom practice, school focus, and district policy making. To truly leave no child behind requires significant professional development of school leaders and classroom teachers to build the necessary capacity to accomplish this task.

For decades, small, focused alternative schools and, later, charter public schools have demonstrated dramatic success in developing common school visions and missions that have accelerated their success with student learning. The professional learning communities that have evolved in these public schools have emerged as models for targeted professional development today. These models share a set of common characteristics that drive their success (see Figure 10.4). These elements combine to provide what educators in these schools refer to as meaningful, immediate improvements through professional development.

Characteristics of Successful Learning Communities

- Common vision and mission
- Focus on student learning
- Attention to student needs
- Serious reliance on data
- Shared, cooperative decision making
- Commitment of necessary time and resources
- Teacher collaboration and study groups
- Ongoing, continuous assessment
- Targeted professional development

Figure 10.4

Targeted Professional Development

The approach to *professional development* outlined here stands in stark contrast to the standard staff development practice found in the vast majority of public schools today. Linda Darling-Hammond (1997), noted scholar from Stanford, refers to this common practice as "drive-by workshops." Darling-Hammond and a host of others continue to caution school leaders about the problems of this approach:

- Limited application of knowledge upon return to classrooms
- Expenses far outweigh results
- Low teacher buy-in
- Topics often at cross-purposes with real teacher needs
- Lack of focus on student learning
- Little teacher engagement in planning
- Limited follow-up to support continued improvement

Together, these challenges severely limit the value of this outdated approach and provide clear cause for educators to rally together to end these ineffective practices in favor of targeted professional development that works.

Fortunately, many national organizations, groups, and scholars and a growing number of school districts are changing their staff development approach to one that targets professional development. Figures 10.5 and 10.6 (page 216) reflect the specific actions and expected outcomes of a diametrically improved approach.

Coupled with the emergence of state standards and high-stakes tests, the teachers of our nation's schools are in need of immediate targeted professional development and resources to prepare them for the reality of a dramatically changed educational environment. For schools and teachers of at-risk students, this need is critical.

Professional Learning Communities

As mentioned previously, a number of alternative, magnet, charter, and other public schools have taken advantage of their small size, common vision, and collegiality to design professional development opportunities based on student needs. Rick DuFour and Bob Eaker (1998) chronicle how a school district can address these needs on a far larger scale. The Adlai Stevenson High School District 125 (of which DuFour was superintendent) in Lincolnshire, Illinois, has worked for two decades creating a professional learning community. The district's efforts are described in the critically acclaimed *Professional Learning Communities at Work: Best Practices for Enhancing Student Achievement.* This book describes the journey of a district toward developing a community of learning and achievement. Central to Stevenson's success has been the focus on the professional development of all staff. This approach, designed to address the content, process, and context of effective professional development, is summarized in Figure 10.7 (page 217).

Michael Fullan (2000), Dean of the School of Education at the University of Toronto and perhaps the most revered author and international speaker on school reform, vigorously embraces the creation of professional learning communities and the role of professional development reflective of DuFour and Eaker's work in Lincolnshire:

> School improvement happens when a school develops a professional learning community that focuses on student work and changes teaching . . . in order to do that, you need certain kinds of skills, capacities, and relationships. Those are what professional development can contribute . . . any school that is trying to improve has to think of professional development as a cornerstone strategy. (p. 276)

Teachers and leaders in successful schools for at-risk students work hard to create the time and place for collegial work, reflection, and needed

Improving Professional Development Research-Based Principles

- The content of professional development should focus on what students are to learn and how to address the different problems students may have in learning the material.

- Professional development should be based on analyses of the differences between (a) actual student performance and (b) goals and standards for student learning.

- Professional development should involve teachers in identifying what they need to learn and in developing the learning experiences in which they will be involved.

- Professional development should be primarily school based and built into the day-to-day work of teaching.

- Most professional development should be organized around collaborative problem solving.

- Professional development should be continuous and ongoing, involving follow-up and support for further learning—including support from sources external to the school that can provide necessary resources and new perspectives.

- Professional development should incorporate evaluation of multiple sources of information on (a) outcomes for students and (b) the instruction and other processes involved in implementing lessons learned through professional development.

- Professional development should provide opportunities to understand the theory underlying the knowledge and skills being learned.

- Professional development should be connected to a comprehensive change process focused on improving student learning.

Figure 10.5

Available at National Partnership for Excellence and Accountability in Teaching at http:// ed-web3.educ.msu.edu/npeat/

NOTE: These design principles reflect a synthesis of current research and are influenced by and mapped closely on similar propositions by the U.S. Department of Education and the National Staff Development Council, as well as other organizations concerned with professional development.

professional development. Many of these schools and programs have for decades reflected the recommended actions, concepts, and practices discussed here. Many of these schools operated as professional learning communities long before the term was coined.

Yet embracing the concepts of a professional learning community represents a commitment to a journey never completed: a mission of continuous improvement. For educators of at-risk students, the challenges

Promising Practices: New Ways to Improve Teaching Quality

A high-quality professional development program:

- Is focused on teachers as central to student learning, yet includes all other members of the school community.

- Is focused on individual, collegial, and organizational improvement.

- Respects and nurtures the intellectual and leadership capacities of teachers, principals, and others in the school community.

- Reflects the best available research and practice in teaching, learning, and leadership.

- Enables teachers to develop further expertise in subject content, teaching strategies, uses of technologies, and other essential elements in teaching to high standards.

- Promotes continuous inquiry and improvement in the daily life of schools.

- Is planned collaboratively by those who will participate in and facilitate that development.

- Requires substantial time and other resources.

- Is driven by a coherent and long-term plan.

- Is evaluated ultimately on the basis of its impact on teacher effectiveness and student learning, and this assessment guides subsequent professional development efforts.

Figure 10.6

From U.S. Department of Education (1998b).

of successfully meeting the needs of their students require continuous improvement of teaching based on the needs of the students. Targeted professional development is essential to support this necessity.

RESEARCH

- Targeted professional development is essential for educators of at-risk and low-performing students.
- A multitude of recent efforts confirms the necessity of creating professional learning communities to best support the professional development needs of educators.
- Teachers must "own" the process of professional development.
- Student learning and improving teaching practice must drive the process of professional development.
- Effective professional development is carefully informed and influenced by data.

Key Elements of Professional Learning Communities

Content of Professional Development

- Based on research.
- Focus on generic and discipline-specific teaching skills.
- Expand the repertoire of teachers to meet the needs of diverse students.

Process of Professional Development

- Attend to the tenets of good teaching.
- Provide the ongoing teaching that is critical to the mastery of new skills.
- Foster reflection in dialogue with all participants.
- Be sustained as an ongoing element of continuous improvement.
- Frequently evaluate progress and provide clear feedback, particularly on student achievement.

Context of Professional Development

- Be school focused and receive strong support from the central office.
- Embed professional development in daily work; do not implement it as separate program.

Figure 10.7

Used with permission. From *Professional Learning Communities at Work: Best Practices for Enhancing Student Achievement*, by Richard DuFour and Robert Eaker. Copyright 1998 by Solution Tree (formerly National Educational Service), 304 West Kirkwood Ave., Bloomington, IN 47404, 800–733–6786, www.solution-tree.com.

TAKE ACTION

- ☑ **Start with data.** Review key data on at-risk students to determine goals and priorities of professional development.
- ☑ **Focus on student learning and school success.** At-risk students require complex attention to learning needs and issues related to school success. Seek professional development plans that address both areas.
- ☑ **Garner district-level support.** Educators of at-risk students require different and unique resources, support, autonomy, and commitment from district-level administrators.
- ☑ **Create time and place.** Targeted professional development requires professional time and space. Schools and educators must have the support and autonomy needed to conduct their efforts.

☑ **Assess frequently and act on data.** Targeted professional development must be based on accurate data and be continuously assessed, monitored, and redirected as necessary.

See the "50 Strategies Suggested Reading" section for a list of resources selected to complement the fifty strategies as you put them to use in your classroom.

SAVING MY STUDENTS, SAVING MY SCHOOL

How can **Strategy #28: Initiate Targeted Professional Development** be put to use in your classroom? What can you do to increase awareness and education among your group of colleagues?

_____

_____

_____

_____

_____

_____

_____

_____

_____

_____

Share your thoughts with a colleague or group of colleagues.

STRATEGY #29

Create Career-Theme Schools and High School Academic Majors

It was a big gamble, but a gamble that really paid off. We accepted one of the school's most difficult students into our health professions magnet high school. The hospital where this student was placed gave him a white jacket with his name on it and assigned him to deliver the mail. Having real responsibilities, working with adults, and receiving praise for his work really made a difference. Here was a kid who had almost never come to school now coming in to help the hospital over the weekend because, as he said, "They needed me." His grades have improved, and he is going to graduate.

—Teacher, Michigan

Relating academic learning at the high school level to life outside the school has a positive impact. There are few factors in the teaching/learning process as important as relevance to real-world experiences. While relevance has a strong, positive effect on all learners, for the at-risk, unmotivated student, it can make a profound difference in academic success. Two unusually effective approaches to integrate academic learning with relevance outside the classroom are career-theme schools and the establishment of high school majors.

Career-Theme Schools

First used during the 1970s as an effective school desegregation strategy, career-theme magnet schools have grown into one of the most popular and effective approaches to public education for all types of students. First, school districts create a variety of optional focus schools, schools-within-schools, and/or programs that emphasize a particular career or profession. Next, students and their families voluntarily choose to participate in one of the specialized programs that relates to their particular interests. Career-theme schools, found throughout the United States, include a wide array of career and professional learning opportunities. School districts in Louisville, Houston, and Los Angeles have established hundreds such programs. Career-theme models include programs such as the following:

- Petrochemical engineering schools
- Radio and television broadcast schools
- Health profession schools
- Law and legal career schools
- Performing arts schools
- Science and technology schools
- International studies schools

Each of these schools includes all of the required courses for high school graduation, and the career theme is simultaneously integrated into each. These schools feature specialized courses and on-site internships in the professional workplace. While some of the schools serve only the gifted and talented, the majority are designed for all types of students. Students in law and legal career schools might be interested in careers ranging from practicing law to corrections police work, legal secretary or security work. Students in a health profession school may be pursuing a career that focuses on medicine, research, or technology.

Many at-risk students who have rarely exhibited an interest in academic studies often become highly motivated by their experiences in the world of work. Working with adults in responsible positions, these high school students are surrounded with new role models and develop new personal goals for their education and their lives. Many of these students stay in school and excel academically just to be able to participate in a career-based opportunity that links schooling to the real world.

High School Majors

The concept of high school majors was a natural outgrowth of the career-theme schools. So popular are career-theme schools that, unfortunately, there are almost always long waiting lists of students who are unable to participate in the specialized program. As a result, considerable pressure has grown for some type of career program to be available for all students. The Vancouver, British Columbia, school district began exploring high school majors after developing four career-theme magnet schools and experiencing their remarkable popularity. Interestingly, just as the grade point averages of college students usually increase once they reach their junior or senior years and move out of required core courses into courses in their chosen majors, high school students who select a career-theme or academic major likewise also appear to become more motivated and perform better. The high school majors concept works best when students are engaged in career explorations during their junior high or middle school years, followed by the selection of one or more careers to pursue during their high school years. Students participate in job shadowing, job visitation, career practica, and specialized elective courses.

In March 2006, the Florida House of Representatives passed legislation that requires high school students to declare a major in high school to better prepare for college and the workforce. South Carolina also started a similar program in 2005, requiring students to choose a "career cluster." A number of other school districts are exploring the idea of transforming the senior year into a community-college-like career immersion approach. Other schools have reorganized their weekday schedules to incorporate career-related activities during the school day.

Students in career-theme schools and high school major programs develop detailed post–high school plans for further education or employment. This act alone has a profound impact on an at-risk student's opportunity to complete school and transition into a productive life.

RESEARCH

- Establishing relevance between schoolwork and the outside world is critical to the school success of at-risk students.
- Supplementing high school graduation requirements with career-theme or academic majors has a powerful, motivating effect on students.
- Students in career-theme or academic majors programs see greater relevance in required academic coursework.
- Students in career-theme or academic majors programs tend to perform better than students in academic programs without career relationships.

TAKE ACTION

- ☑ **Gather information.** Contact school districts that are successfully implementing career-theme programs. Then, visit the programs of interest and begin developing a plan of development to establish career-theme schools and academic majors programs.
- ☑ **Work with local businesses and professionals**. Career-theme and academic majors programs represent an effective approach to building partnerships with local businesses and professions. Career-theme programs must be cooperatively developed with vocational and professional groups.
- ☑ **Start small.** Most school districts start by developing one or two career-theme or academic majors programs and add additional programs as interest develops.

☑ **Revise the school schedule.** Establishing career-theme and academic majors programs often serves as a catalyst for reorganizing the entire school schedule. Many schools have arranged academic coursework for four days a week and are using two-day block programs so that one day a week can be used exclusively for career-theme activities outside of school.

See the "50 Strategies Suggested Reading" section for a list of resources selected to complement the fifty strategies as you put them to use in your classroom.

SAVING MY STUDENTS, SAVING MY SCHOOL

How can **Strategy #29: Create Career-Theme Schools and High School Academic Majors** be put to use in your classroom? What can you do to increase awareness and education among your group of colleagues?

_____

_____

_____

_____

_____

_____

_____

_____

_____

Share your thoughts with a colleague or group of colleagues.

STRATEGY #30

Help At-Risk Students Pass High-Stakes Tests

My school assigned me to the lowest-performing students in the school, and I have a policy with the kids: We can never say, "I can't do this." We are always positive. I spend more time than a football coach trying to build self-confidence. We also work hard to prepare for the state tests. We develop rhymes, we sing songs, we chant together, we take simulated tests, and guess what? It all worked. Every one of my children passed the test!

—Teacher, Texas

With few exceptions, conversations with teachers, administrators, and parents everywhere in the United States tend to focus on the great challenge of helping at-risk students learn effectively, improve academic performance, and successfully pass the high-stakes achievement tests necessary in most states for grade promotion and graduation. Many of these students arrive at school from lives of poverty or limited-English-speaking backgrounds. Without significant intervention, most of these students fall behind; many are retained; and far too many ultimately drop out of school. These students are also traditionally poor test takers. As a result, schools face a dual and daunting challenge. Not only must they ensure that the students learn effectively, they must also help these students become effective test takers. Unfortunately, state-mandated tests often present students with a cultural bias, and, for many students, the tests are offered in a language in which the student may be less than fluent or confident.

The use of a single, standardized test for retention or promotion has been seriously criticized and has yet to be shown to be an effective incentive for learning; at its worst, the tests increase dropout rates, particularly for poor and minority students. High-stakes testing has also led to a growing number of teacher, parent, and student boycotts throughout the country, along with other types of civil disobedience. Yet, for good or bad, it appears that high-stakes tests are here to stay and that most families, educators, and students seem to be accepting them as a new way of life in school. Recent polls by Public Agenda (2002), a nonprofit polling organization, found that the great majority of middle and high school students are comfortable with increased testing in public schools. Eight out of ten students surveyed believed that standardized tests generally ask fair questions, and 78 percent said that their teachers did not emphasize the test at the expense of other important topics. Seven out of ten students, including poor and minority, said that most students do only the bare minimum to get by, and more than half acknowledged that they could try harder themselves.

The good news is that there are thousands of schools throughout the United States where students are successfully achieving both the challenging goals of learning effectively and passing the high-stakes tests. It is becoming increasingly common to hear teachers and principals of schools serving minority and low-income students stating unequivocally that all their students are learning effectively and passing the high-stakes tests. While there is little or no research regarding the most effective approaches to help at-risk students be successful with state-mandated tests, there is a growing body of information about how certain schools have become successful in having their students pass these exams. These approaches focus primarily on the role of teachers and the preparation of students for the tests.

Teachers can use a large number of techniques to help support and prepare their students for test taking, as well as for academic and lifelong success (see Figure 10.8).

The Role of Teachers

The importance of the individual teacher has been confirmed again and again. A single classroom teacher can have a profound positive effect on student learning, especially on poverty-level and other at-risk students, even though the school where the classroom teacher is working may be largely ineffective. Recent research has noted that individual classroom teachers have an even greater effect on student learning than previously believed, and, unfortunately, this effect can be negative as well as positive.

In a study of the Chicago public schools reported in 2001, two educational researchers once again documented the importance of individual teachers (Bracey, 2002). Of particular interest in their study was a review of student test scores in two similar schools in the same Chicago neighborhood. The test used was the Iowa Test of Basic Skills, and the school district threatened students with retention if they did not obtain satisfactory levels of scores on the test. At one of the schools, 53 percent of the students were perceived as "working hard in school," and over one-half of them achieved passing levels on the test and were promoted; another 36 percent were successful after summer school. In the other school, only 30 percent of the students were promoted on the basis of satisfactory test scores, and only an additional 15 percent succeeded after attending summer school. The researchers concluded that the teachers had made the difference in the two schools. One group of teachers "created an

---

Test Scores

T each for the test, not to the test.
Approach instruction as assessment; teach for conceptual understandings and life skills (what students know and are able to do); use big ideas; and stress transfer, application, and performance through a multiple intelligences approach.

E xpect the best; accept no less.
Set high expectations; use grade level or developmentally appropriate materials for all; enhance skill building with enrichment and acceleration as needed; use standards and benchmarks.

S tructure with cooperative learning.
Use small-group interactions to foster student-to-student dialogue and articulation; help students to hear what they and others are saying as they put ideas into their own words.

T each test-taking strategies explicitly.
Demonstrate techniques for true/false, multiple-choice, and essay questions; show how to outline or web ideas for quick reference and what students can do if they don't know the answers; use metacognitive reflections to anchor learning.

S tress prelearning strategies.
Emphasize prelearning strategies that tap into prior knowledge and background experience; create fertile mind-sets for learning.

C hunk the material for deep understanding.
Cluster ideas together into chunks that make sense; foster connection making and personal understanding of information; promote transfer through patterns and meaning.

O rganize with graphics.
Utilize graphic organizers to make student thinking visible; adapt advanced organizers as ways to gather information or as methods for reviewing material.

R eflect through mediation.
Foster reflective thinking and take time to make sense of things by mediating the learning with questions, logs, think-aloud partner dialogues, and other reflective tools.

E xpress ideas with mnemonic devices and visual cues.
Teach memory devices to aid in learning; use acronyms, rhymes, and other sound-alike devices; use visualization techniques of color, action, and exaggeration as well as metaphors to trigger short-term memory and to internalize for long-term retrieval.

S eek student choices in learning situations.
Allow freedom of choice within a given structure; capitalize on student interest and self-selection opportunities; create personally relevant learning; build in self-assessments and evaluation.

Figure 10.8

SOURCE: Fogarty, R. (1999). *How to Raise Test Scores.* Thousand Oaks, CA: Corwin Press. Reprinted by permission.

NOTE: Fogarty compiled findings by many other researchers to create this list. For a list of researchers Fogarty consulted, please see Fogarty (1999).

environment that was highly supportive of student learning. They acted as coaches, guiding students and structuring tasks in a way that demonstrated their own investment in having students . . . pass the exam" (Bracey 2002: 432). Students in this school "came to believe that reaching the test-score cutoffs was an obtainable and important goal" (p. 432). At the other school, students rarely talked with researchers about the role their teachers played in preparing them for the test, and they did not believe that they could pass the exam. And, like so many externally centered students of poverty, students in the second school reflected a nonchalant attitude of "If I don't pass, I don't pass; and if I do, I guess I'm just lucky" (Bracey 2002: 432).

This study demonstrated the power of teachers. Teachers can engage students, help motivate their efforts, reinforce a "can do" attitude, and help students come to believe in their abilities to succeed. They can also focus on their students' negative qualities, blame the students and their parents for their ineffectiveness, and largely destroy student motivation to succeed.

Preparing Students for Testing

In addition to encouraging and motivating students to do well on standardized tests, teachers, administrators, and parents can also employ a number of specific strategies that can have a significant, positive effect on students' scores (see Figure 10.9 and the discussion that follows).

Preparing Students for Testing

- Teachers, administrators, parents, and students must familiarize themselves with tests.

- Recognize that there is a great variance between tests.

- Align the curriculum with the state standards and teach for the test.

- Teach test-taking techniques.

- Allow for practice testing with sample questions.

- Schedule time for student development and practice.

- Use summer programs.

- Encourage students to take the test as soon and as often as possible.

- Be positive.

Figure 10.9

Teachers, Administrators, Parents, and Students Must Familiarize Themselves With Tests

All in the educational community need to thoroughly learn about state-mandated tests and the standards they measure. Wherever possible, teachers and parents should even take sample tests so that they understand exactly what is being tested and how the tests are constructed.

Recognize That There Is a Great Variance Between Tests

There is a great deal of variation in state-mandated tests. These differences are found between basic skills tests and content tests, between various types of subject matter tests, and between proficiency tests at different grade levels. Most agree that pencil-and-paper tests of basic skills (reading, writing, and mathematics) seem to be more realistic and straightforward. Tests of language arts, social studies, and science have proven to be more demanding and difficult for students, especially poverty-level students. But even basic skills tests may vary significantly with grade level. The content tested at one grade level may, in fact, vary considerably from what is tested at a different grade level.

Align the Curriculum With the State Standards and Teach for the Test

Educators become uneasy at the accusation that they are "teaching for the test." But if the test is an accurate reflection of the state standards and district curriculum goals, then that is exactly what all effective teachers do. Teachers of advanced-placement courses have never complained about focusing their instruction on the issues that are covered in the final exam. In fact, advanced-placement biology, history, and math teachers will explain that for their students to be successful, the teachers must help students complete the various experiments and assignments that are covered in the final exam. The same is true for the teacher-made tests in all courses. Concerns arise when someone external to the classroom and the school constructs the tests and emphasizes items that some teachers may not find particularly important or appropriate. Even worse, if an externally imposed test is poorly constructed or culturally biased, teachers are likely to object. Today, many teachers are choosing to either teach to the test, even if it is a poor test, practice civil disobedience (something an increasing number of teachers and students appear to be doing across the country), or work politically to improve the tests or change the policies. Teachers of poverty-level students who are successfully passing high-stakes tests openly discuss how they teach to the test.

Teach Test-Taking Techniques

Almost everyone who plans to take a standardized test in high school, college, or graduate school (whether the SAT, ACT, GRE, LSAT, or a host of others) either studies about test-taking strategies or actually takes a short course to learn how to increase the scores on the exam. Techniques such as recognizing key words on multiple-choice test questions (*always, never,* etc.) and key words used in questions regarding mathematics can greatly assist test takers, even young children. The Brazosport, Texas, school district created a help sheet for taking multiple-choice tests that was laminated and taped to every student's desk. Elementary teachers often use rhyming and music harmonics to teach young children to recognize words in math questions so that they know when to multiply and when to divide. English teachers use the same approaches regarding grammar and spelling.

Allow for Practice Testing With Sample Questions

Regardless of the test, students benefit by not only seeing sample questions from the test, but by actually taking pretests under simulated conditions. Such pretesting is useful in reducing the test anxiety that many at-risk students seem to experience.

Schedule Time for Student Development and Practice

Schools in many states have created supplemental courses taught by trained specialists to assist students in gaining essential skills. Almost all schools schedule daily if not weekly time to provide tutorial and group support to students in need of passing state tests.

Use Summer Programs

Many effective schools use summer programs with great success to focus intensively on one or more of the sections of the tests or to focus on a test section that the students have failed. Summer programs have proven to be unusually effective for both remediation and acceleration needs of at-risk and low-performing students.

Encourage Students to Take the Test as Soon and as Often as Possible

Most schools with significant populations of poverty-level and other at-risk students encourage their students to pass the required exams as early as possible. If possible, schools focus on the test in which their students have been most successful so that they can have the positive fulfillment of actually passing one area of the exam.

Be Positive

A critical factor in a district's effort to ensure the success of its students to pass state exams is positive leadership. Parents, teachers, administrators, and older students must all be as positive as possible with the younger students about the tests. The emphasis should be placed entirely on being positive, on the challenge, and on a "can do" attitude. Some schools convert basic skills concepts or subject matter content into slogans so that each day or each week, students are reminded of the skill or concept throughout the school building. Many schools have used this approach to help students and families prepare for such tests.

RESEARCH

- Individual classroom teachers can have a powerful effect on student learning and success on standardized tests even in an ineffective school.
- Students are more successful on standardized tests when teachers structure learning tasks in conjunction with the expectations of the tests.
- Teachers can motivate students to be successful on standardized tests and help them develop positive attitudes and confidence.

TAKE ACTION

- ☑ **Learn about the tests.** Teachers, administrators, and parents need to thoroughly understand the high-stakes tests they will be preparing their students to pass. It is important to know what is being tested, the different types of tests, and how those tests are administered, scored, and reported.
- ☑ **Seek professional development.** Learn how to align curriculum and instruction with the test and how to prepare students to take the exams.
- ☑ **Audit curriculum and its alignment.** Conduct curriculum audits to determine the degree to which curriculum and instruction aligns with required tests. When variance is found, plans to carefully realign curriculum and instruction with the tests should be developed.
- ☑ **Help students become better test takers.** There is a wide variety of excellent materials designed to help students learn

how to study and succeed with both objective and subjective tests. Access and use these resources.

 See the "50 Strategies Suggested Reading" section for a list of resources selected to complement the fifty strategies as you put them to use in your classroom.

SAVING MY STUDENTS, SAVING MY SCHOOL

How can **Strategy #30: Help At-Risk Students Pass High-Stakes Tests** be put to use in your classroom? What can you do to increase awareness and education among your group of colleagues?

_____

_____

_____

_____

_____

_____

_____

_____

_____

_____

_____

_____

Share your thoughts with a colleague or group of colleagues.

11

Teach All Students to Read

My principal really focused my attention on how important it is to teach every child to read. At the first of the school year, she visited my classroom and stopped to examine my bulletin boards that I had spent the week before school preparing. I was totally stunned when she said, "These bulletin boards are really attractive and so well-done, but I have a question. What do they do to teach reading?" I think I finally got the message that during the first grade, everything that we do must focus on reading instruction.

—Teacher, Idaho

Well, I just couldn't believe it. "In fact," the U.S. history teacher said, "I am embarrassed to say, I never even thought about it." This kid in my third-period history class came by after school and asked if he could talk to me. And look, the kid was doing okay in my class. Not great, but believe me, he was more than passing the course. He told me that he didn't know how to read. I thought he was teasing. It just blew me away. At the time I didn't even know what he meant, what he was talking about. Here I am with an eleventh-grade student with a C average and he is confiding in me that he doesn't know how to read? I was at a total loss. I told him I would see what was available and we would get him help. I immediately went to see the assistant principal and asked about a reading program. He gave me a blank look and said, "Don't students learn to read in the elementary schools?"

—High School Teacher, Connecticut

During the past decade, there has been a growing realization among researchers, political leaders, and teachers that reading is the key to all other learning. It is now recognized that reading is the foundational cornerstone of all public education. Former Secretary of Education Rod Paige stated bluntly that "reading is the civil right" of every child. Paige is joined by President George W. Bush, whose education policies emanate from the challenge of "leaving no child behind." Educators and researchers are increasingly voicing support for reading as the new civil right, the new entitlement of every child in the United States. As Robert Slavin, a leading scholar and founder of the widely implemented Success for All program has said, "If [reading] success is seen as an entitlement, educators must have methods that produce success for all nonretarded children regardless of home background, no matter how expensive these methods may be" (Wasik and Slavin 1993: 180).

Recognizing the importance of learning to read at an early age, an increasing number of elementary schools are reallocating

ESSENTIAL COMPONENTS IN EFFECTIVE READING PROGRAMS

Based on the 1999 National Reading Panel's conclusions regarding research on reading education, several specific components were identified that were considered essential to effective reading education as well as to the training of teachers and tutors. While controversial within the field of reading, these components are becoming widely accepted as the basis for effective teacher education. The panel concluded as follows:

- Phonemic awareness training of teachers resulted in student improvement in phonemic awareness, reading, and spelling.

- Systematic phonics instruction produced significant benefits for students in Grades K–6 and for those children having difficulty learning how to read.

- Impact on reading fluency was positive and significant with the use of guided, repeated oral reading procedures. The more children read, the better their fluency, vocabulary, and comprehension.

- Teaching a combination of reading comprehension techniques is necessary.

- Professional development of reading teachers that focused on current reading research produced significantly higher student achievement.

school resources from the upper grades (fourth, fifth, and sixth) to enrich the resources of the early grades. Public education now possesses the knowledge, methodology, and access to effective programs to achieve the goal of teaching every child to read. Implementing this knowledge and methodology into comprehensive, schoolwide programs represents the critical challenge public schools must confront if all children, particularly those at risk, are to succeed in school. While it is essential that all children learn to read well no later than the end of the third grade, it is equally important to teach older students how to read effectively. Before upper-elementary, middle-level, and high school students can achieve high academic performance, they must be equipped to read. Unfortunately, many districts and schools are unprepared to teach these older students to read.

Fortunately, as the social, political, economic, and educational significance of reading have been realized, there has been a corresponding development in research regarding effective approaches for reading instruction. Even the most prestigious universities and research centers agree that there is a definite process of teaching students to read and that all classroom teachers must learn this process. State after state has passed legislative initiatives or new standards that set a goal of all students reading at grade level by the end of the third grade. Many of these states are also requiring elementary teachers and administrators to participate in professional development toward achieving this goal.

In an age where literacy continues to be more and more critical to education and the workplace, it is still estimated that of the 53 million school-age children, 20 million have deficient reading skills. If a child does not learn to read and read well by the end of the third grade, the student will struggle with schoolwork and homework. Far too many students will fail their classes and will ultimately drop out and spend their lives

---

VISIT THE "SUCCESS FOR ALL FOUNDATION" ON THE WEB AT

- <www.successforall.net>

MAJOR DEVELOPMENTS IN TEACHING ALL STUDENTS TO READ

- *National Assessment of Educational Progress Report (1994).* Identified that 40 percent of the nation's eight-year-olds were at risk of reading failure.

- *America Reads Challenge Act (1997).* This was the first national commitment to the goal of every child reading at grade level by the end of the third grade.

- *Learning First Alliance (1998).* Representatives from twelve influential educational groups representing teachers, administrators, and families created a national consensus recommending that juried research be used in the design of all school-based reading programs and in the training of teachers and volunteers.

- *National Reading Panel (1999).* This panel was federally commissioned to bring the nation's top reading researchers together and synthesize research on reading. The panel concluded its work by identifying specific, research-based skills that were most effective in teaching reading.

- *No Child Left Behind Act (2001).* Federal legislation established requirements for implementing programs based on research, encouraged accountability in public schools, and promoted an increased focus on reading.

unemployed, underemployed, or unemployable. The result is sobering: more than half of the men and women in prison in the United States continue to be illiterate. A 2003 Bureau of Justice Statistics report (Harlow 2003), *Education and Correctional Populations,* estimated that in 1997, about 41 percent of inmates in the nation's state and federal prisons and local jails and 31 percent of probationers had not completed high school or its equivalent. We simply must teach all students to read.

Unconventional Wisdom

What Works for Experienced Teachers

Read to students.

High school students still love to be read to. Books on tape help a lot of students. Books on tape should not be thought of as "special education" only. Many alternative school students were never read to. I still read Dr. Seuss. (You have brains in your head. You have feet in your shoes. You can steer yourself any direction you choose.) I read children's classics, nursery rhymes, and other material they may have missed out on. We read the newspaper daily. In literature, I may read a chapter, then they read a chapter, and so on. I had a high school teacher at a conference ask me how we were improving reading skills by two grades or more every year. I told him I read to and with the kids frequently. He told me he was not going to be reading to high school kids. What a shame!

—Teacher, Indiana

Be careful when using silent, sustained reading.

Our school district requires silent, sustained reading. Even our middle school and high school students are required to read silently for twenty minutes every day. Was I ever shocked to learn from our state reading consultant that there is research on the negative effects of silent reading! And, it makes so much sense. I'm not sure why no one ever thought about it. Silent, sustained reading is very effective with students who read well, but for the poor readers, they are only "silent faking." To the poor reader, there is little or no value in silent, sustained reading. We're now in the process of changing our program for the lower-level readers.

—Teacher, Pennsylvania

STRATEGY #31

Guarantee That Every Child Learns to Read

At our school, we bit the bullet and announced to the entire community that we would "guarantee" parents that every child would learn to read to grade level by the end of the third grade . . . if the parents would help us. Wow, did that get all of us focused on what was important.

—Teacher, Washington

The good news is that research, evaluation, and long-term student follow-up assessments have made it dramatically clear that all students, with the exception of the seriously mentally impaired, can be taught to read. Today, there are a number of programs available to schools and communities that have well-documented track records of success in teaching all children, even those far behind, the skills necessary to read.

So compelling is current research and program development in reading that it is now possible to predict success or, as a growing number of schools are doing, to guarantee parents that their children will learn to read. This remarkable development in teaching and learning represents perhaps the most important advancement in schooling since public education was made available to all children. As reported earlier, reading deficiency is the most identified problem in research on at-risk children. The means now exist to correct this problem.

The time has come when schools must ensure that all children learn to read. Every parent should demand that local elementary schools provide assurances that their children will learn to read, and every parent should seek information regarding what they can do to assist in this process. This may require that certain expectations be established between the school and the home. Parents must assist their children by reading at home and monitoring homework for a specified amount of time each day. Parents must, if at all possible, keep the children in the same school for at least the first three or four years of school. With little more than these two assurances, schools should be able to teach all children to read.

In 1998, four California schools began a new 1,000 Days to Success program that was designed to ensure that all children

---

ENSURING THAT EVERY CHILD WILL LEARN TO READ

Parents must

- assist their children by reading at home and monitoring homework for a specified amount of time each day and

- keep the children in the same school for at least the first three or four years of school.

learn to read by the end of the second grade. One thousand days is roughly the equivalent of the number of days from kindergarten through the second grade. Each school in the 1,000 Days program spells out its commitment to teaching all students to read on a printed reading warranty card.

Guaranteeing that every middle-level and high school student can read is a far more complex and difficult task. In most schools, large numbers of children do not learn to read effectively during the early elementary grades and must be taught reading at the secondary level. For those who do learn to read, research has documented that without continued reinforcement, early gains may diminish. For high school students, in addition to continued, focused instruction on reading skill development, it is essential for reading instruction to occur across the curriculum. Reading instruction in the content areas provides the basis for enhanced reading comprehension. Recent research has recommended engaging students in a reading apprenticeship that employs problem solving, situational reading, and cognitive development. A reading apprenticeship is like working with a coach or a mentor on a day-to-day basis, constantly facilitating and drawing out the cognitive understanding of a text.

RESEARCH

- When schools establish a goal of teaching every student to read and carefully assessing student progress toward that goal, immediate, positive results will follow.
- Intensive efforts must be focused on those students with the greatest reading deficiencies and needs.
- Phonemic awareness, comprehension, and fluency skills must each be addressed in teaching or remediating reading.
- Comprehensive, schoolwide reading programs can dramatically improve early literacy.
- Secondary students' reading performance will accelerate quickly with appropriate intervention(s).
- Use of classroom secondary teachers as master readers to coach and assist the student apprentices in daily classroom academic work can help students increase their reading comprehension from very basic skill levels to an average ninth-grade level.

TAKE ACTION

☑ **Establish a goal.** Establish a goal of every student reading at grade level.

- ☑ **Commit resources.** Each district and school in the nation must accordingly reallocate or find other resources necessary to meet this goal.
- ☑ **Research best practices.** A multitude of research-driven best practices and programs to teach reading have been identified and are available. Visit model programs. Observing and creating networks will prove invaluable to a school's goal of all students reading at grade level.
- ☑ **Mobilize parents and other adults.** Work closely with parents to develop a guarantee that all students will learn to read. Parents play an essential role in teaching students to read. For secondary students, adult mentors or adult reading tutors may prove even more effective than parents.
- ☑ **Improve reading instruction.** Seek targeted professional development to help learn how to be an effective reading educator.
- ☑ **Use continuous assessment.** Establish an ongoing reading assessment program to document the success of students and identify those in need of extra effort.

 See the "50 Strategies Suggested Reading" section for a list of resources selected to complement the fifty strategies as you put them to use in your classroom.

SAVING MY STUDENTS, SAVING MY SCHOOL

How can **Strategy #31: Guarantee That Every Child Learns to Read** be put to use in your classroom? What can you do to increase awareness and education among your group of colleagues?

_____

_____

_____

_____

_____

_____

_____

_____

_____

_____

_____

Share your thoughts with a colleague or group of colleagues.

STRATEGY #32

Implement Effective Literacy Practices and Programs K–12

As teachers, I feel that we have entered a "brave new world." When we consider new textbooks, new instructional materials, professional development programs, or school improvement models, we have learned that there is only one thing that matters: does this program lead to higher student achievement? Whenever we're dealing with issues like this, our teachers now ask, "So what? Show us the evidence that this works."

—Teacher, Connecticut

A number of approaches and programs have been documented as highly successful in teaching at-risk children to read during the elementary years. Tutoring, extended-day programs, cooperative learning, and computer-assisted instruction each have been found to be especially effective in supporting the teaching of reading. When these components are blended into a comprehensive reading program, truly exceptional gains can occur with at-risk children.

Research and evaluation during the past decade has documented the impact of a number of comprehensive school improvement models and programs on the student achievement of at-risk students. As a result, it is now possible to identify those programs that have documented evidence of improving student achievement. Offering the impressive evidence of success for elementary youth at risk are Success for All, Reading Recovery, and Direct Instruction. A number of other programs show promising evidence of improving student achievement as well.

Success for All

Robert Slavin and other scholars at Johns Hopkins University developed the Success for All (SFA) model. The SFA school concept was originally started two decades ago in seven schools in three of the most disadvantaged urban and rural school districts in the country. By 1997, SFA had been implemented in more than 750 schools in 37 states. Today, there are more than 1,800 SFA schools in 48 states and five other countries. The SFA approach prescribes a schoolwide effort that successfully integrates Chapter 1 funds to enrich the entire school student body. The SFA approach is grounded in a strong foundational knowledge base and has demonstrated exceptional success in improving at-risk youth achievement. SFA is perhaps the most widely recognized and implemented model showing evidence of successfully improving student achievement for elementary youth at risk.

The SFA schools emphasize the importance of early intervention, while believing in the need to retain young children's positivity and enthusiasm. As a result of this belief, SFA has developed four major goals (see Figure 11.1). Research has documented that the SFA program has been successful in achieving each of these goals (Slavin and Fashola 1998).

SFA employs four major components:

- Reading tutors
- Cross-age reading groups
- Family-support team
- Advisory committees

Success for All

- Ensure that every student will perform at grade level in reading, writing, and mathematics by the end of the third grade.

- Reduce the number of students referred to special education classes.

- Reduce the number of children who are held back a grade.

- Increase attendance.

Figure 11.1

SOURCE: From Slavin and Fashola (1998).

The SFA program also assesses student reading levels at eight-week intervals to re-level students and ensure that all students are being served appropriately. Each component of the program works with the other components to deliver the results that have established SFA as a highly effective program.

Reading Recovery

The tutoring approach that has been thoroughly researched most carefully over time is Reading Recovery. This early intervention approach, originally designed by Marie Clay, a New Zealand child psychologist, focuses on intensive, one-on-one tutoring. Following initial success, the program was moved to Ohio State University and has emerged as one of the most successful approaches for teaching reading to the poorest readers in the school. Today, Reading Recovery is being used in more than 10,000 schools in forty-nine states.

The program relies on the use of certified teachers who have been trained in the Reading Recovery approach. (The certification program is approximately one year in length and requires an internship.) The program is implemented in elementary schools and focuses on the lowest-achieving students in the first grade. In addition to classroom reading instruction, these students are provided supplemental, intensive, one-to-one tutoring for thirty minutes each day for approximately sixteen weeks. The Reading Recovery teacher tutors each child to become an independent reader. When the goal is attained, the tutoring is discontinued and the next-lowest-level reader takes his or her place in the program.

After years of study, the research and evaluation on the Reading Recovery approach concluded that "regardless of sex, socioeconomic status, or social linguistic group, the lowest achieving children make accelerated progress in the program and continue to make satisfactory progress after release from the program" (Pinnell et al. 1994: 19). Fewer than 1 percent of the students who completed the program needed further referral. Comparative studies in Ohio found that Reading Recovery children "achieved at higher levels than did children who received other compensatory treatments" (Pinnell 1990: 19).

Direct Instruction

Created to extend the gains that low-income students made in the federally funded Head Start Program into the early elementary school years, Direct Instruction was originally referred to as "Project Follow Through." Developed by Siegfried Englemann and his colleagues at the University of Illinois, Champaign, and later at the University of Oregon, Direct Instruction was employed primarily as a basal reading intervention for remedial students. More recently, Direct Instruction has demonstrated success as a comprehensive school reform model. The Direct Instruction program currently serves Grades K–6 in 150 schools and several thousand classrooms nationwide. While it was developed primarily for low-performing schools in high-poverty areas, Direct Instruction has been used successfully with all students.

Direct Instruction teachers follow highly specific instructions regarding how to teach the prepared units as well as what units should be taught. Students begin Direct Instruction at the kindergarten or first-grade level. Students participating in the program have been evaluated positively on academic performance using both criterion-referenced and norm-referenced measures.

Effective Elementary Programs

The National Institutes of Health have researched and identified programs that successfully aid in the instruction of basic reading skills as well as prevent and remediate reading deficiencies (see Figure 11.2).

Effective Secondary Reading Programs

Reading levels at the middle and high school grades are cause for concern. Data from the 2004 National Assessment for Educational Progress (NAEP) (Perie, Moran, and Lutkus 2004) indicate the following: students at age thirteen show no significant improvement in recent years, although most reporting metrics indicate that performance in 2004 was higher than in 1971. At age seventeen, no measurable differences in performance were found between 1971 and 2004 for any reporting metric.

Beginning Reading Programs That Work*

- Accelerated Reader/Reading Renaissance (Developer: Judi and Terry Paul; distributed by Renaissance Learning, Inc.) <www.renlearn.com/reading.htm>

- ClassWide Peer Tutoring (Developer: Juniper Gardens Children's Project; CWPT manual and charts are distributed under the name "Together We Can," by Sopris West™)

- DaisyQuest (Developer: Gina C. Erickson) <www.whatworks.ed.gov/InterventionReportLinks.asp?iid=211&tid=01>

- Early Intervention in Reading (EIR) (Developer: Dr. Barbara Taylor; distributed by the Early Intervention in Reading Program)

- Kaplan SpellRead (Developer: Kaplan, Inc., Kaplan K12 Learning Services Division)

- Peer-Assisted Learning Strategies (PALS) (Developer: Lynn and Doug Fuchs; distributed by Vanderbilt Kennedy Center for Research on Human Development) <www.kc.vanderbilt.edu/pals/>

- Reading Recovery (Developer: Dr. Marie M. Clay, University of Auckland, New Zealand; distributed through the Reading Recovery® Council of North America, RRCNA)

- Start Making a Reader Today (SMART) (Developer: Oregon Children's Foundation, Start Making a Reader Today®; SMART® is self-distributed)

- Stepping Stones to Literacy (Developer: J. Ron Nelson, Penny Cooper, and Jorge Gonzalez; distributed by Sopris West)

Figure 11.2

NOTE: As determined by What Works Clearinghouse. (2007). 2277 Research Boulevard, MS 5M, Rockville, MD 20850, <www.whatworks.ed.gov>

This, of course, may not be surprising given the technological culture of teenagers today. Teenagers are almost constantly "plugged in" to audio, video, or digital mediums, not print. For huge blocks of time, teenagers talk on their cell phones, use instant messaging or e-mail, surf the Net, play video games, or use their headphones to listen to the latest music. Too often, they are not reading.

Programs that have been documented as positively affecting student achievement in reading and math at the middle grades include Exemplary Center for Reading Instruction, Grades 1–10; Reciprocal Teaching, Grades 1–8; Profile Approach to Writing, Grades 3–12; and Multicultural Reading and Thinking, Grades 3–8 (Barr and Parrett 2001; Slavin and Fashola 1998). Other effective secondary reading programs include those outlined in Figure 11.3.

Reading Programs That Work for Teenagers

Decoding

LANGUAGE!

Developed by Jane Fell Green and published by Sopris West, 4093 Specialty Place, Longmont, CO 80504, (303) 651-2829, (800) 547-6747, <www.sopriswest.com>

Fluency

Read Naturally

Read Naturally combines three research-proven strategies into a powerful program to develop the reading fluency of special education, ELL, Title I, as well as mainstreamed students. Read Naturally, 750 S. Plaza Drive 100, Saint Paul, MN 55120, (651) 452-4085, (800) 788-4085, <www.readnaturally.com>

Edformation

Edformation provides support through its AIMSweb Continuous Improvement System, a formative assessment approach to guide instruction. Edformation, Inc., 6420 Flying Cloud Drive, Suite 204, Eden Prairie, MN 55344, (888) 944-1882, <www.edformation.com>

Comprehension

READ 180

Authored by Dr. Ted Hasselbring, William T. Bryan Professor and Endowed Chair in Special Education Technology at the University of Kentucky. <www.teacher.scholastic.com/products/read180/overview/> Published by Scholastic, (877) 234-READ.

Figure 11.3

RESEARCH

- Every school in the United States can teach all students to read at grade level.
- Schools must assess student reading needs and target intervention with evidence of proven success.
- Early reading success must be continually reinforced at the upper-elementary, middle, and high school level.

TAKE ACTION

☑ **Carefully select reading approaches and programs.** In selecting reading materials and schoolwide instructional approaches, carefully review reports that have assessed the effectiveness of these approaches and programs.

☑ **Seek external funding and support.** The Comprehensive School Reform Demonstration Program (CSRD) offers three-year awards of $50,000 annually each to school districts throughout the country. Contact your state department of education for details.

☑ **Monitor progress and continuously adjust for better results.** Even the most effective programs require adjustment to local needs. Any reading intervention should be carefully monitored for needed improvements.

 See the "50 Strategies Suggested Reading" section for a list of resources selected to complement the fifty strategies as you put them to use in your classroom.

SAVING MY STUDENTS, SAVING MY SCHOOL

How can **Strategy #32: Implement Effective Literacy Practices and Programs K–12** be put to use in your classroom? What can you do to increase awareness and education among your group of colleagues?

_____

_____

_____

_____

_____

_____

_____

_____

_____

Share your thoughts with a colleague or group of colleagues.

STRATEGY #33

Employ One-on-One Tutoring

We learned a very important lesson over the past year: Nothing works better in teaching reading than one-on-one tutoring. Last summer, we heard about the effectiveness of this approach in our summer program, but this year, we saw it happen in our own classrooms.

—Teacher, New Hampshire

Most researchers agree that one-on-one tutoring is the most effective form of instruction. One-on-one tutoring offers immense potential for use in the early grades to ensure that all children without serious learning disabilities can learn to read, especially when the tutor is a trained professional. Research and evaluation of one-on-one tutoring using trained professionals has demonstrated the dramatic effectiveness of this educational approach, especially with at-risk youth.

Early success in reading has a long-term impact. Students completing Reading Recovery (a tutoring program) were found to read material three levels above comparison children. Ninety percent of the Reading Recovery children met or exceeded the average range in reading. An Ohio follow-up study of Reading Recovery graduates found that by the third grade, these children could read material one grade level above comparison children, and 69 percent met or exceeded the average range of reading ability of their fellow students. The research clearly indicates that Reading Recovery has immediate as well as long-term positive results. Reading Recovery teaches low-achieving children to read and write and helps them to progress rapidly to the levels of success experienced by their classmates (Pinnell et al. 1994; Wasik and Slavin 1993).

A number of other highly successful one-on-one reading tutorial programs have accumulated impressive research and evaluation data. They include Success for All (described in Strategy #32), Prevention of Learning Disabilities (which uses certified teachers), Wallach Tutorial Program (paraprofessional tutors in both inner-city and rural locations), and Programmed Tutorial Reading materials (paraprofessionals tutors in both urban and rural areas).

One-on-one tutoring can also be effective when using peer tutors. Research demonstrates the positive effects of peer tutoring on the tutor as well as the tutee. In a landmark peer tutoring study, tutees were able to read faster and make fewer errors. When a mistake was made, it was more often self-corrected. This study concluded that one-on-one peer tutoring not only taught children to read but also made them more self-confident in their reading (Winter 1986).

The use of professional, paraprofessional, and peer tutoring to help at-risk youth overcome reading deficiency in the early grades represents a practice that works and should be available in every elementary school. The peer tutoring model shown in Figure 11.4 presents an example of one effective approach.

Model Peer Tutoring Program

Reading together:

1. Read aloud with your partner, letting her set the pace and share her book.

2. If your partner hesitates or makes a mistake, tell her the correct word, and make her repeat it before continuing.

Reading alone:

1. If your partner signals that he wants to read alone, then stop reading aloud and follow the story.

2. If your partner hesitates or makes a mistake while reading alone, tell him the correct word, make him repeat it, and then read aloud with him until he next signals.

3. Whenever your partner reads a difficult word or sentence, corrects his own mistake, or signals he can read on his own, then praise him.

Figure 11.4

SOURCE: From Winter (1986: 103).

RESEARCH

- One-on-one tutoring is the most effective form of instruction. One-on-one tutoring offers immense potential for teaching children with serious learning difficulties to read.
- The best tutor is a trained reading teacher, but regular classroom teachers can be extremely effective and so, too, can any adult volunteer, older student, or peer, who has been trained.
- The use of professional, paraprofessional, cross-age, and peer tutoring to help at-risk youth to overcome reading deficiencies in the early grades is a practice that works and should be available in every elementary school.

- Cross-age tutoring has been documented as an effective instructional tool. Cross-age tutoring benefits both the student being tutored and the student doing the tutoring.

TAKE ACTION

☑ **Organize reading instruction to include tutoring.** Organize reading instruction to maximize teacher, paraprofessional, volunteer, or peer one-on-one tutoring assistance.

☑ **Establish a cross-age tutoring program.** Every elementary school should establish a cross-age tutoring program.

☑ **Establish a tutoring program that utilizes adult volunteers.** Every elementary school should establish an adult volunteer tutoring program.

☑ **Establish reading partners (peer tutoring).** Match a reading partner with a student who is struggling. This combination of peers can help both students with the development of needed reading skills.

☑ **Provide ongoing training for tutors.** Adult and cross-age tutors need continual training and support to realize their maximum effectiveness.

 See the "50 Strategies Suggested Reading" section for a list of resources selected to complement the fifty strategies as you put them to use in your classroom.

SAVING MY STUDENTS, SAVING MY SCHOOL

How can **Strategy #33: Employ One-on-One Tutoring** be put to use in your classroom? What can you do to increase awareness and education among your group of colleagues?

_____

_____

_____

_____

_____

_____

_____

_____

_____

_____

Share your thoughts with a colleague or group of colleagues.

STRATEGY #34

Start Early

At the time, we didn't think that starting a Head Start program and expanding kindergarten to a full day was a big deal. But what a positive difference it has made in our students! Kids are now arriving to school at the first grade ready to learn.

—Teacher, Oklahoma

Our preschool program used to consist of playing together, having fun, and learning the alphabet. Now, we know we have a very essential responsibility . . . to get kids ready for reading. We still have fun, but we understand now how important it is to get kids started on reading very early.

—Teacher, Colorado

There is a narrow window of opportunity to maximize the teaching of reading. While virtually anyone of any age can be taught to read, from age three through Grade 3 is a time of natural development when children can best learn to read. Research has documented the power and positive influence of high-quality child care and preschools with developmentally appropriate curriculum. Both programs have long-lasting positive effects on the growth, education, and development of children.

Head Start

One of the most successful federal programs for providing assistance to preschool youth is Head Start. Started in 1965 as an intensive summer program during President Lyndon Johnson's "war on poverty," the federal program continues to serve more than 900,000 disadvantaged preschool youth with an allocation of more than $6 billion per year (Head Start 2007). A wide variety of research has documented that the Head Start Program has had strong positive effects on language development and IQ scores (Schorr and Schorr 1989).

Unfortunately, research has also documented that the early positive effects of Head Start can diminish rapidly with each subsequent year until, for the most part, they are undetectable by the end of the second or third grade. This result has led to a variety of follow-through programs that attempt to maintain and continue educational enrichment gains from preschool and early elementary years. With these continued programs, Head Start children sustain long-term positive gains, as evidenced by their high school graduation rates and lack of delinquency (Schorr and Schorr 1989).

Kindergarten

Almost everyone has come to agree on the value of kindergarten, and in most states, kindergarten is now required. As of 2003, kindergarten enrollment is the fastest-growing area of public education. Research comparing full-day kindergarten to half-day programs and studies of available curricula have found the effect of all-day kindergarten to be similar to the effects of preschool programs: initial positive results are likely to diminish quickly without continued program support (Schorr and Schorr 1989). Like preschool, kindergarten is not sufficient to ensure lasting educational success, but it provides an essential foundation to later success.

The debate over the most appropriate, most effective kindergarten curriculum continues. This debate centers on whether or not kindergartens should be highly academic or nonacademic and how to balance these two positions. Some feel that the first-grade curriculum should be simply moved down to the kindergarten level, while others believe that too much academic pressure on young children is debilitating to their development.

Increasingly, research has begun to identify those aspects of the kindergarten curriculum that are most significant. While it is important to have extended- or all-day kindergarten, how the kindergarten students spend their time appears to be equally as important as the amount of time spent in kindergarten. Early childhood curriculum experts believe that the kindergarten curriculum should offer a variety of balanced activities that are provided in the context of project work. These activities might include investigating real objects or events. Examples of a quality kindergarten curriculum are listed in Figure 11.5.

Quality Kindergarten Curriculum

- Integrated topic studies, rather than whole-group instruction in isolated skills
- Opportunities for children to learn by observing and experimenting with real objects
- A balance of child- and teacher-initiated activities
- Opportunities for spontaneous play and teacher-facilitated activities
- Group projects in which cooperation can occur naturally

Figure 11.5

SOURCE: From ERIC Clearinghouse on Elementary and Early Childhood (1993: 1).

RESEARCH

- High-quality child care and preschool programs can have lifelong positive effects, as evidenced by their high school graduation rates and lack of delinquency, but follow-up support during Grades K–3 is essential.
- Head Start has been studied more than any other federally funded program, and this research has documented that it is the most successful federal program ever developed for providing assistance to preschool youth.
- All-day kindergarten is one of the most effective approaches for preparing poor, at-risk children for the first grade.

TAKE ACTION

☑ **Review research.** Review the research on the long-term positive effects of quality child care, preschool, Head Start, and all-day kindergarten.

☑ **Champion early childhood education.** Work to convince state legislatures, local school boards, and taxpayers of the value in high-quality early childhood and preschool programs as well as all-day kindergarten.

☑ **Support Head Start.** The Head Start Program has been identified as one of the most effective educational programs ever supported by the federal government. Do everything possible to ensure that Head Start is available in your area.

☑ **Reallocate resources.** These programs are so important to poor children that public schools and government funds should be reallocated to support child care, preschool, and all-day kindergarten.

☑ **Seek external funding and support.** Districts should access state, federal, and private funds to supplement current efforts to effectively intervene with any child in need.

See the "50 Strategies Suggested Reading" section for a list of resources selected to complement the fifty strategies as you put them to use in your classroom.

SAVING MY STUDENTS, SAVING MY SCHOOL

How can **Strategy #34: Start Early** be put to use in your classroom? What can you do to increase awareness and education among your group of colleagues?

_____

_____

_____

_____

_____

_____

_____

_____

_____

_____

Share your thoughts with a colleague or group of colleagues.

STRATEGY #35

Redesign Grades K–3

*After our summer inservice, I asked our school district reading coordina-
tor a question: "If reading is so important, shouldn't we emphasize it twice
a day?" She replied, "Yes, of course. We must do anything and everything
to teach reading, even if it means restructuring our school day." I know
reading is important, but what about the things I lose if I have to focus
more time on reading?*

—Teacher, South Carolina

Because of the importance of teaching young children to read, there is a
growing understanding that the early grades need to be redesigned and
the curriculum and instruction aligned with the important instructional
standards being established at the state and national levels. More and
more evidence is accumulating that many teachers for these early grades
are inadequately prepared. New teacher education programs and certification programs are emerging that address the critical need for and
importance of highly trained teachers at the early elementary levels.

The redesign of the early grades must focus on teaching all children to
read. This may mean allocating more of the school day to reading, and it
may demand that teachers be increasingly held responsible for teaching
all of their children to read. Because of the essential nature of teaching
reading, some schools are moving instructional aides from intermediate
grades and clustering them in the first three grades. Other schools are
offering *looping*, a practice in which a teacher stays with the same group
of students through the first two or three years of school. Other school districts are providing "extended-day weekends" and intensive summer
programs that focus on students who are reading below grade level.

A growing body of research supports two effective concepts: looping
and multiage classrooms. Both of these concepts are rooted in the traditional, one-room schools of an earlier era.

Looping

Looping dramatically reduces the time required to establish
teacher/student relationships and allows teachers to provide needed extra
time for new "mobile" students or others in need. Participating teachers
report substantial gains in learning due to building and maintaining
a community of learners that dramatically increases instructional time

because of a greatly enhanced knowledge base and relationship between parents, teachers, and students.

Multiage Classrooms

The concept of multiage classrooms is as old as public schooling and is increasingly being used in today's schools. In typical schools today, age-grouped grade-level classrooms consist of students performing at multiple levels. This makes it possible to individualize instruction so that developmentally appropriate learning can take place. For example, students in Grades 1–3 can be organized for instruction into appropriate levels, with older students helping younger students. The goal of a multiage classroom is to ensure that all students achieve the goal of reading at grade level by the end of the third grade. Multiage classrooms, coupled with developmentally appropriate instruction, eliminate the need for retention in the early grades and replace it with a positive, successful instructional approach.

Together, looping and multiage instruction hold considerable promise for at-risk students.

RESEARCH

- Holding a single teacher accountable for teaching a group of children to read over a two- to three-year period holds great promise as an effective strategy.
- Students in multiage classrooms are less likely to be identified as or labeled slow learners.
- Cross-age tutoring benefits both the older and younger student.

TAKE ACTION

- ☑ **Review research.** Review research on looping and multi-age grouping of students and consider establishing looping and multi-age classrooms as effective strategies.
- ☑ **Visit multiage and looped classrooms.** For teachers who have always taught in age-grouped classrooms, observations and clinical experiences in a school organized around looping or multiage classrooms are essential.
- ☑ **Work closely with parents.** Provide careful orientation and information regarding multiage grouping in order to gain parental support.
- ☑ **Consider a school-within-a-school.** Establish multiage classrooms as an option, and let parents select the type of classroom in which they place their children.

See the "50 Strategies Suggested Reading" section for a list of resources selected to complement the fifty strategies as you put them to use in your classroom.

SAVING MY STUDENTS, SAVING MY SCHOOL

How can **Strategy #35: Redesign Grades K–3** be put to use in your classroom? What can you do to increase awareness and education among your group of colleagues?

_____

_____

_____

_____

_____

_____

_____

_____

_____

_____

Share your thoughts with a colleague or group of colleagues.

STRATEGY #36

Continuously Assess Reading Progress

IDAHO READING INITIATIVE

In 1998, Idaho became the first state in the nation to legislate a mandate to put in place a comprehensive program designed to ensure all elementary students were reading at grade level by the end of the third grade. This initiative included these components:

- The reading level of all K–3 students was assessed three times each year. The state implemented the Idaho Reading Indicator as a short, diagnostic instrument for assessing student reading progress and grade-level equivalence.

- Funds were provided to schools for mandatory extended-day and extended-year programs for the remediation of low-performing students.

- All K–8 teachers were required to complete an approved research-based reading course that focused on phonetic awareness, comprehension, and assessment.

- All preservice teachers were required to pass a reading assessment with a performance component before they could be certified to teach in the state.

- When the legislation was first passed, approximately 50 percent of Idaho's K–3 children were reading at grade level. By the fall of 2001, that number had increased to 53 percent, and in 2002, it reached 63 percent. Today, more than 70 percent of the state's K–3 students are reading at or above grade level.

SOURCE: Glasser (2002).

The teacher was really being resistant.

She said, "I have been an effective first-grade teacher for twenty years, and now you are suggesting that I change everything that I have been doing."

I asked her one question: "How do you know you have been effective?"

She just gave me a blank stare, and I didn't hear any more questions from her.

—Reading Specialist, Idaho

The key to ensuring that no child is left behind and that all students learn to read effectively is continuous assessment for Grades K–3. K–3 teachers who understand that the primary, overarching goal is to teach all students to read realize they must work closely together to monitor student achievement, provide intensive support for those students who are behind, and explore new approaches as needed.

Teachers of K–3 students must carefully review the reading standards and reading assessments at the school, district, state, and federal levels. Increasingly, these standards are being aligned across all of those levels so that parents and teachers can clearly understand the expected performance level of children age three through eight. Teachers at every grade level, or in multiage classrooms K–3, must establish specific goals for each school year. But to be effective, schools and teachers cannot wait until the school year is over to assess effectiveness. Teachers at each grade level must assess student reading performance every two to four weeks with simple assessments that teachers themselves develop and all agree to use. Teachers at each grade level should also agree to meet for at least thirty to forty-five minutes each month to review the assessment of their students. When something is not working, a revision or change should be considered immediately. Assessments should focus attention on the students who are not achieving and lead to individualized instructional programs for each of these students to help them accelerate their learning.

It is also essential that reading assessment not end at the elementary level. Early reading success must be continually supported, maintained, and improved or initial success in reading can diminish. Assessment must continue during the middle and high school years to ensure continued growth and improvement. All states now employ reading assessment through high school toward the goal that 100 percent of all high school students will read by 2014. A system that aligns curriculum and instruction with established goals and standards, assesses achievement monthly, and engages teachers in frequent meetings to review student progress can have an immediate effect on student performance. More than a dozen studies that contributed to the effective school research base (Cotton 2000) have been synthesized into a recommended monitoring and assessing system (see Figure 11.6).

Monitoring and Assessing Student Performance

- Collect and review student performance data to ensure early identification and support for students with learning difficulties.

- Establish and use procedures for collecting, summarizing, and reporting student achievement information; use aggregated data to determine overall performance and trends and disaggregated data to review the performance of specific student groups.

- Review test results, grade reports, attendance records, and other materials to identify problems and take action based on findings.

- Review assessment instruments and methods for their suitability to the students being evaluated, and make changes as needed (e.g., for students whose native language is not English).

- Make summaries of student performance available to all staff for their use in planning; make periodic reports to parents and community members.

- Use assessment methods beyond standardized achievement tests (e.g., performance assessments, portfolios) to enrich teachers' understanding of students' progress.

- Align classroom assessments of student performance with the written curriculum and actual instruction.

- Routinely check students' understanding by conducting recitations, checking students' work during seatwork periods, assigning and checking homework, administering quizzes, and reviewing student performance data.

Figure 11.6

SOURCE: From *The Schooling Practices That Matter Most,* by Kathleen Cotton. © 2000 Northwest Regional Educational Laboratory. Used with permission.

RESEARCH

- When teachers work together to establish measurable goals, monitor students' progress, and assess instructional effectiveness, remarkable gains in achievement occur.
- Schools and teachers must not wait until the end of the year to assess student performance. Assessment must be frequent and ongoing. Continuously assessing progress leads to immediate, dramatic improvement in student performance.
- Monitoring student progress and assessing instructional effectiveness also encourages teachers to examine and test new ideas, methods, and instructional materials.
- Careful attention to student performance provides the necessary framework to successfully intervene with at-risk students.

TAKE ACTION

- ☑ **Explore continuous assessments.** Study the process of goal setting, aligning curriculum and instruction with goals and standards, and assessing student performance every two to four weeks.
- ☑ **Establish an assessment system.** Establish a system to monitor student performance and assess instructional effectiveness and agree to meet monthly to review data.
- ☑ **Consider data retreats.** Conduct and/or attend data retreats to learn what student information is available and explore ways to best use data to improve student performance.
- ☑ **Seek professional development.** Assessment of student performance is an area where most teachers need training. Professional development on assessment techniques can be remarkably beneficial.

 See the "50 Strategies Suggested Reading" section for a list of resources selected to complement the fifty strategies as you put them to use in your classroom.

SAVING MY STUDENTS, SAVING MY SCHOOL

How can Strategy **#36: Continuously Assess Reading Progress** be put to use in your classroom? What can you do to increase awareness and education among your group of colleagues?

_____

_____

_____

_____

_____

_____

_____

_____

_____

_____

Share your thoughts with a colleague or group of colleagues.

Select Results-Driven Instructional and Assessment Practices

Strategy #37
Personalize Instruction

Strategy #38
Recognize the Critical Importance of an Aligned Curriculum

Strategy #39
Select Research-Based Instructional Practices

Strategy #40
Use Homework Effectively

Strategy #41
Require Student Portfolios, Projects, and Performance Exhibitions

Strategy #42
Incorporate Technology Across the Curriculum

Strategy #43
Create Assessment-Literate Classrooms

It took me a decade of teaching and attending yearly inservices to arrive at a sobering reality: it was me, and what I did in my class-room with each individual student that determined how well they would perform academically. Sure, the continual onset of new school programs, services, and instructional leadership from above can and does help some of my kids . . . but the one who can help all of my kids, particularly those at greatest risk of failure is ME.

—Teacher, Idaho

Teachers and classroom instructional practices don't make a difference in student achievement; teachers and classroom practices make *the* difference.

Over three decades ago, James Coleman and his colleagues assured us through their widely acclaimed work that only a small portion (10 percent) of a student's academic improvement could be attributed to the school: ninety percent was the result of the influence of a student's "natural ability, socioeconomic status, or the home environment." In short, schools and teachers could do little to help a poor student from a poor home, particularly if he or she had limited "natural ability" (Coleman et al. 1966). Today, we know Coleman and his colleagues were wrong.

Studies carefully designed and conducted by Good and Brophy (2002); Teddlie and Stringfield (1993); Wright, Horn, and Sanders (1997); Marzano (1998); and Marzano, Pickering, and Pollock (2001) have clearly served to end the long-accepted and harmful conclusions of Coleman and his colleagues. Despite the fact that research has proven beyond a doubt that a quality school and an effective teacher can significantly improve the achievement of at-risk students, our nation's schools and classrooms continue to demonstrate an alarming rate of failure to raise the achievement of these students.

Schools and classrooms that succeed with at-risk students don't simply get lucky or have a good year; they

- align curriculum,
- implement research-based instructional and assessment practices, and
- endeavor to personalize instruction and schooling.

The seven strategies discussed in this chapter have demonstrated significant effectiveness with underachieving and at-risk students. The degree to which a school and teacher implement them appropriately will make the difference.

Unconventional Wisdom

What Works for Experienced Teachers

Use appropriate instructional approaches.

The teachers at our alternative school have discovered that we should abandon the normal way we are taught to teach regular kids. We have found that by combining what teachers do in special education and gifted education works. Now we know teachers like their niches and this will upset some people, but we have found this to be very effective. Others will think there is no way you can blend the two. In special education, you make educational adaptations for students, such as repeating and simplifying instructions; using computer-assisted instruction; allowing longer testing time; supplementing verbal instructions with visual instructions; adjusting class schedules; using tape recorders; using books on tape; using auditory, visual, and tactile approaches to learning; using modified textbooks; and so on. This helps all kids.

. . . In gifted education, you provide numerous open-ended learning experiences, decision making, reflection, self-assessment, observation, exploration, and outlets and audiences for their creative products. You compact curriculum, test out of material, provide learning contracts, provide alternative learning activities, accelerate learning, customize curriculum, do problem-solving activities and independent study, use extended learning activities, give many choices in reading and projects, use Socratic seminars, use learning centers, and so on. These too are good for all kids.

. . . We have found that by combining these strategies, you get a pretty healthy classroom and some motivated students. We have created a course syllabus for every class that we teach (with help from our students). We provide many choices for our students in what they read and do and for projects.

. . . This is the first teaching experience that I have ever had where I actually asked students to slow down just a little bit so I could keep up. What a great feeling!

—Teacher, Indiana

Reorganize courses into short modules.

I have been trying to teach pre-algebra to at-risk students for years and years, but kids who are not very good students have such a block when it comes to mathematics. I finally tried a completely different approach. Last summer, I took that huge textbook that has always been so intimidating to my students and broke it down into 184 short learning modules. Rather than facing that entire textbook, the student only saw one small assignment at a time. Once they finished a module, I would check out their work, quiz them to make sure they had the concept, and then they would proceed on to the next module. Rather than trying to keep the entire class together on the same lesson, suddenly every student was progressing through the course at their own pace. Some students quickly completed the modules and actually moved on to algebra, but all students made progress exceedingly well. If one student was having trouble, another student who had completed that particular module would be able to give them help. This system has taken a little work and organization, but it really works.

—Teacher, Indiana

Teach with technology.

I have been teaching for sixteen years. When I went to college, technology meant the overhead projector, filmstrips, and how to use 16 mm film. So when computer technology overwhelmed the schools, I was frustrated and frightened. But guess what? Today my classroom has a Web site that keeps parents and students updated regarding assignments, tests, and upcoming classroom events. My daily e-mail is packed with conversations with parents. What an incredible tool for communication between the home and the school. It's hard to believe, but I have become technology literate.

—Teacher, Nevada

STRATEGY #37

Personalize Instruction

Next fall, I'll graduate and will be going to the community college. I can't believe it! Two years ago, my life was trashed. My mom moved back to Illinois, and I decided to stay . . . for one reason . . . this school. Even working my two jobs can fit here thanks to the high school and Jean, Bob, Charlie, and Karen. These teachers have helped me get my life back. They believed in me and are always here for me. If it weren't for them, I wouldn't be in school, let alone graduating. I never thought I could make it.

—Student, Alternative School, Idaho

I could not help my students if I didn't know them on an individual level— their families and out-of-school lives, their individual needs. Only after I establish a trusting relationship with a student can I construct an academic plan that has a likelihood of working.

—Teacher, Alternative School, Indiana

Teachers who care deeply for students do more than educate. For at-risk kids, they may mean the difference between a life of struggle or productivity, between detriment or contribution to society, and sometimes between life or death. Yet caring alone will not reverse the downward spiral of many of our children's lives. These students require academic skills and the capacity to process and apply knowledge and information. Effective teachers deeply care for and hold high expectations for the academic growth of their students.

Ask any successful teacher of at-risk students or other low-performing kids how he or she succeeds where so many other teachers have failed. Successful teachers will tell you that they get to know the students and their individual circumstances and help them where they most need help, being a "constant" in their lives.

Successful schools and programs for at-risk youth have always implemented some form of individualized instruction as a key strategy that works best when the elements of a trusting relationship are joined by a clear understanding of the student's academic and social needs, a plan to address those needs, continuous reviews of the student's progress, and interventions followed by adjustments and midcourse corrections.

Why wouldn't any school have these services and approaches available to their at-risk students? Linda Darling-Hammond (1997), noted scholar and school improvement advocate, eloquently addresses this issue in her book *The Right to Learn.* Darling-Hammond urges all schools to create and offer students the structures described in Figure 12.1.

Structures for Schools and Students

- Caring and serious learning that enables teachers to know their students and intensively work with them
- Shared exhibitions of student work that demonstrate the clarity of school values and how the students are doing
- Teacher teams that collaborate and focus on student learning
- Shared decision making and dialogue about teaching and learning with other teachers, parents, and students

---

Figure 12.1

SOURCE: From Darling-Hammond (1997).

Ensuring that these structures are in place and supported will dramatically change the opportunities for success any student at risk faces in a conventional school. These practices also mirror the structural components of effective alternative schools—many with more than thirty years of successful operation. These structures further support what so many of our students need most: a personalized approach to schooling and learning.

Keefe and Jenkins, in their February 2002 article, "Personalized Instruction," identify six basic elements that characterize the content and associated culture of an effective personalized instructional environment (see Figure 12.2).

Six Basic Elements of Personalized Instruction

- Teachers perform dual roles of coach and advisor.
- Programs are based on a diagnosis of student learning characteristics.
- Cultures of collegiality and collaboration are supported and embraced.
- Interactive learning environments are fostered.
- Schedules are flexible and instruction is appropriately paced.
- Assessment is authentic.

Figure 12.2

SOURCE: From Keefe and Jenkins (2002).

This formula for personalizing instruction will guide a school's efforts toward meeting the needs of at-risk students. However, the larger the school, the more difficult and challenging successful implementation can be. A lingering controversy persists over which of these two approaches should be used to reach every student:

- Continue to force the child (every child) to fit the current large-scale, impersonal structure, or
- Change the structure to a personalized approach—an approach with decades of evidence demonstrating effectiveness.

RESEARCH

- Personalized learning enhances academic achievement.
- Personalized instruction can be implemented in any school.
- Individualized, personalized instruction is necessary for at-risk students.
- Smaller learning environments provide greater opportunities for success for students at risk.
- Parents, students, and other stakeholders strongly support the merits of a personalized approach to teaching and learning.

TAKE ACTION

☑ **Assess the needs.** Assess the academic and social needs of each student.

☑ **Explore strategies.** Explore strategies for creating smaller, more personalized learning environments.

☑ **Create structures.** Create structures that promote collaboration among teachers, school leaders, parents, and students to better focus on student learning.

☑ **Consider proven models.** Do not reinvent the wheel. Customize proven models to local circumstances.

☑ **Assess progress.** Frequently assess progress and provide opportunities for needed midcourse corrections.

See the "50 Strategies Suggested Reading" section for a list of resources selected to complement the fifty strategies as you put them to use in your classroom.

SAVING MY STUDENTS, SAVING MY SCHOOL

How can **Strategy #37: Personalize Instruction** be put to use in your classroom? What can you do to increase awareness and education among your group of colleagues?

_____

_____

_____

_____

_____

_____

_____

_____

Share your thoughts with a colleague or group of colleagues.

STRATEGY #38

Recognize the Critical Importance of an Aligned Curriculum

I can hardly hold my high-risk students accountable for low scores on our state tests. Until recently, the curriculum we have is basically from text-books. How can these kids be expected to do well when we probably haven't taught them what's on the tests?

—Teacher, Idaho

We're now in our third year of having an aligned K–12 curriculum. It took state content standards, testing, and a good bit of money to get us here, but let me tell you, it's working. Never before had our elementary teachers talked to our middle school teachers about what they were teaching and vice versa. And I know the high school staff rarely even talked to each other about content, let alone teachers at the other levels. Now we have all agreed on what to teach and when—and our scores have risen.

—District Superintendent, Illinois

Students at risk need targets. They need to understand what is expected of them and how and why it connects with their lives. Sitting in a classroom or working independently on an assignment just because a teacher says "Do this" often isn't enough of an incentive to gain the desired result from any student, particularly one who has struggled in school. To increase the school performance of these kids, schools and teachers must make every effort to establish an aligned curriculum that carefully addresses the state and local standards of learning and meets required assessments. An aligned curriculum allows a teacher to help every student progress toward meeting the expectations of school. This is also an important step that enables an at-risk student to connect classroom and school learning with the realities of her or his life.

Fenwick K. English, a noted curriculum scholar, believes that the alignment of curriculum is as important as anything a district can do to improve learning and student performance (English 1992). Long considered a good strategy, aligning curriculum has been completed in most districts. Today, most of our nation's 15,000-plus school districts are being confronted with this serious question: "Is what we're teaching meeting state standards and assessments?" Thus the need to monitor and manage a written curriculum that aligns with state and local standards is, in reality, no longer an option for local school boards.

What Is an Aligned Curriculum?

What we teach in schools has evolved from multiple origins into an intertwined patchwork of courses and content. The "three R's" focus of our early common schools has grown to include a wide array of courses and subjects unique to the districts in which they are taught. While most of the developed nations in the world long ago decided that a national curriculum locally delivered was most advantageous to student learning, the United States has continued to use a local control model. Now that the state legislators across the country (and the federal government) have begun to require standards-based assessments from all states and public districts, it is critical to ensure that what is tested is taught. For the students at risk, this new expectation can provide severe consequences for years of not accumulating requisite knowledge to succeed on standardized assessments. Despite this challenge, the positive side of the recent assessment movement is that for the first time, teachers of at-risk youth must clearly address specific content as opposed to creating what they think is the best approach for the student. At-risk students will learn and reach their goals only when they can see the targets.

For perhaps the first time, an aligned curriculum provides teachers of at-risk students with a level playing field. If a district's K–12 curriculum is aligned to state standards, resources must be targeted, first, toward the materials necessary to support the curriculum and, second, toward enhancing the instructional capacity of the school and classroom to deliver results. If any component of the district remains out of alignment, assessment data should immediately identify the discrepancy and point to needed intervention that becomes the subsequent priority.

If a district is committed to an aligned curriculum and to the proposition that every child can learn and achieve, interventions for low-performing and at-risk students must occur. Aligning curriculum alone will not ensure that these students achieve, yet this process is a vital, integral component of helping these students.

RESEARCH

- An aligned curriculum helps to provide a level playing field for at-risk students.
- Aligning curriculum must occur to ensure that the curriculum on which students are tested is being taught.

- An aligned curriculum does not ensure quality teaching; instructional leadership does.
- Aligning the curriculum and managing its implementation in a district will focus attention on the needs of at-risk students.

TAKE ACTION

☑ **Hold high expectations.** Every educator should seek to increase the achievement of at-risk youth and provide the needed resources to accomplish success.

☑ **Initiate district-level action.** Each district should provide resources to assess the current alignment of approved K–12 curriculum to state standards and all required assessments.

☑ **Ensure that teachers have the resources to deliver the curriculum.** Make certain that an aligned curriculum is available to teachers of at-risk youth.

☑ **Provide targeted professional development.** Teachers of at-risk youth require specific support for their unique professional development needs.

☑ **Create a curriculum management team.** All schools need to have ownership of an aligned curriculum and must actively work to adapt the curriculum to local needs. Monitor progress, review data, and design midcourse corrections.

See the "50 Strategies Suggested Reading" section for a list of resources selected to complement the fifty strategies as you put them to use in your classroom.

SAVING MY STUDENTS, SAVING MY SCHOOL

How can **Strategy #38: Recognize the Critical Importance of an Aligned Curriculum** be put to use in your classroom? What can you do to increase awareness and education among your group of colleagues?

_____

_____

_____

_____

_____

_____

_____

_____

_____

Share your thoughts with a colleague or group of colleagues.

STRATEGY #39

Select Research-Based Instructional Practices

I have been taking education courses to improve my reading for years and years. I have completed a master's degree in education, and I have endured hours of inservice courses. Now, it seems we have real evidence documenting effective instructional strategies and programs. It appears that we are (sort of) moving toward a science of teaching and learning. I really think that we are getting closer to knowing what needs to be done and how to do it.

—Teacher, Michigan

In 1998, Bob Marzano, a senior research fellow at the Mid-continent Research for Education and Learning (McREL) in Colorado, concluded and published a landmark study. *A Theory-Based Meta-Analysis of Research on Instruction* for the first time presented classroom teachers and educators with nine instructional practices that vividly demonstrate substantial achievement gain with all students when deployed effectively. Marzano next joined colleagues Debra Pickering and Jane Pollock in authoring *Classroom Instruction That Works*, a 2001 publication designed to synthesize Marzano's meta-analysis into a practical, teacher-friendly approach and guide to implementing the nine identified practices (see Figure 12.3).

Each of these practices, whether implemented individually or in combination, will impact the academic achievement of at-risk students. The research of Marzano and others illustrates the key components of each of the nine strategies. An overview of this research follows.

Research-Based Strategies for Increasing Student Achievement

- Identifying similarities and differences
- Summarizing and note taking
- Reinforcing effort and providing recognition
- Homework and practice
- Nonlinguistic representations
- Cooperative learning
- Setting objectives and providing feedback
- Generating and testing hypotheses
- Cues, questions, and advance organizers

Figure 12.3

SOURCE: Adapted with permission from R. J. Marzano, D. Pickering, and J. Pollock. *Classroom Instruction That Works,* © 2001, ASCD.

Identifying Similarities and Differences

Many believe the capacity to identify differences and similarities to be fundamental to all learning. Teachers should engage their students in the following ways to develop competence in identifying similarities and differences:

1. Present students with explicit guidance in how to identify similarities and differences.

2. Blend teacher-directed activities with independent, student-initiated efforts.

3. Take the time necessary to represent similarities and differences in symbolic and/or graphic visual forms.

4. Implement the use of comparisons, classifications, and/or creation of metaphors and analogies.

Summarizing and Note Taking

These practices have long accompanied formal classroom instruction. Research suggests that teachers focus on these practices to enhance students' abilities to summarize:

1. Students must be taught to delete, keep, and substitute information to effectively summarize.

2. Students must learn to analyze information thoroughly to learn how to effectively delete, retain, and substitute,

3. Students must become aware of the explicit structure of information.

Note taking is central to effective summarizing. Teacher-prepared notes, student-generated notes, or a combination of a note-taking technique that employs Internet surfing can help students to formally process information. Teachers should consider the following in teaching students to effectively take notes:

1. Verbatim note taking is the least effective method.

2. Always consider note taking a work in progress.

3. Teach students to use their notes to study for tests.

4. More is better; students cannot take too many notes.

Summarizing and note-taking skills empower students to understand and learn.

Reinforcing Effort and Providing Recognition

These practices support students' attitudes and beliefs about learning. It is critical that teachers help students understand the importance of believing that their efforts "pay off" and that they can, if necessary, develop understanding of how their efforts contribute to their learning. Teachers should recognize the relationship between student effort and success. It is equally important that teachers and students monitor progress. In effectively recognizing gain, teachers should remember the following:

1. Rewards don't dampen intrinsic motivation.

2. Rewards work best when closely connected with the accomplishment of specific work or tasks.

3. Symbolic recognition is more effective than tangible rewards.

Recognition of effort should be highly personalized, occur as frequently as appropriate, and be in the form of both verbal and concrete forms of appreciation. Appropriate recognition both encourages learning and fosters motivation.

Homework and Practice

When used effectively, homework can have immediate and lasting positive effects on learning. Marzano and others recommend four principles to assist teachers:

1. As the value of homework increases with age, the amount assigned should be increased.

2. Parents should facilitate homework for their children, but they should be cautioned not to solve problems for them.

3. Teachers should clearly explain the purpose of the homework.

4. All homework assigned must be reviewed and responded to by the teacher.

Any teacher or school assigning homework should provide students and their families with a clearly stated homework policy. The policy should clearly explain the purpose and expected outcome and that teachers will vary their methods of responding to and providing feedback on homework.

Homework can be a powerful tool to extend the school day learning of children. However, it must be noted that if home support and an adequate environment are limited or unavailable, the value of homework may diminish dramatically. (For more information about homework, see Strategy #40.)

Nonlinguistic Representations

Nonlinguistic representations are images that accompany a learner's linguistic representations (actual language statements) and are used to remember and recall information. Marzano's and others' work concludes that a variety of activities, such as creating graphic representations, making physical models, operating mental pictures, drawing pictures and pictographs, and engaging in kinesthetic activities, contribute to a student being able to form clear pictures or images of information beyond the linguistic or written, language-based representation. This activity is particularly important for at-risk students as so many of them possess limited language skills and are often susceptible to distraction.

Cooperative Learning

Cooperative learning is a popular practice found in most schools. Designed to work in heterogeneous classrooms, this practice can have powerful learning effects on all students, particularly those at risk. Johnson and Johnson (1999) recommend five practices that should drive the effective implementation of cooperative learning (see Figure 12.4).

The Defining Elements of Cooperative Learning

- Positive interdependence (a sense of sink or swim together)

- Face-to-face promotive interaction (helping each other learn, applauding success and effort)

- Individual and group accountability (each of us has to contribute to the group achieving its goals)

- Interpersonal and small-group skills (communication, trust, leadership, decision making, and conflict resolution)

- Group processing (reflecting on how well the team is functioning and how to function even better)

Figure 12.4

SOURCE: From Johnson and Johnson 1999, as adapted by R. J. Marzano, D. Pickering, and J. Pollock. *Classroom Instruction That Works*, © 2001, ASCD.

Research on cooperative learning indicates substantial gain for students when the strategy is appropriately implemented. Teachers using the practice should limit the use of ability-level grouping, as this appears to negatively affect low-performing students. Teachers should also keep groups small, in the range of three or four students, and should work to systematically and consistently use the strategy as a tool when appropriate, not as the predominant focus of all instruction. For students at risk, cooperative learning can accelerate performance and enhance achievement.

Setting Objectives and Providing Feedback

Students at risk often lack goals or successful school experiences in effective goal setting. Marzano and his colleagues recommend that a teacher (a) use goal setting to clearly define and narrow a student's focus; (b) be specific, but not too specific; and (c) encourage all students to personalize each goal. This practice is critical to youth at risk because if used effectively, it will also positively impact their lives outside of school.

Research on providing feedback is equally clear. When providing feedback, teachers should use it for corrective purposes, apply it as immediately as possible, relate it to specific criteria, and encourage students to apply their own feedback. Rubrics provide a most effective tool for both teacher-generated and student-initiated feedback.

Teaching at-risk students through the use of clearly stated objectives and immediate feedback will encourage them to perform. For too many students, classwork has been confusing at best, all too often characterized by limited or absent feedback on their progress and efforts.

Generating and Testing Hypotheses

Long a standard practice within the sciences, generating and testing hypotheses has been found to have powerful effects on learning. Because of its active nature, students at risk often perform quite well when asked to participate in this strategy. This practice can draw out the inductive and deductive skills in a student provided the teacher has clearly defined the hypothesis to be tested or has asked students to clearly define the hypothesis. Marzano and his colleagues recommend that teachers use this practice to accomplish the following six tasks:

- *Systems analysis*—The study of the multitude of systems students encounter as part of the study of various content areas across the curriculum

- *Problem solving*—Obstacles and constraints confronting students
- *Historical investigations*—Constructing and proving their own explanations and theories
- *Invention*—Creating new systems and structures based on standards
- *Experimental inquiry*—Conducting experiments to test "hypothesized" solutions
- *Decision making*—Getting to appropriate or correct solutions

For low-performing students and other at-risk students, each of these tasks can provide an active and engaging opportunity to learn.

Cues, Questions, and Advance Organizers

These techniques assist students in recalling learned information. For students at risk, it is critical that teachers follow Marzano and his colleagues' four recommendations from the research on cues and questions:

1. Focus on the important as opposed to the unusual.

2. Use high-order questions to produce deeper learning.

3. Employ wait-time to elicit increased quality and depth of student response.

4. Use analytic questions to begin as well as conclude a lesson.

Advance organizers also provide essential assistance to low-performing and other at-risk learners. Advance organizers prepare students for effective learning and promote efficiency in the work of studying and acquiring knowledge. Advance organizers may be of several types, including the following:

- Expository (to give an explicit description of forthcoming content)
- Narrative (to address the topic in a story format)
- Skimming (to gain an initial overview of forthcoming content)
- Graphic representations (to present a visual image of the forthcoming content)

Cues, questions, and advance organizers help students increase learning when used appropriately. For at-risk students, these practices are essential as teachers prepare and assist them in learning.

RESEARCH

- Instructional practices have a powerful effect on student learning.
- While classroom instruction for years has been the discretional property of individual teachers, recent research dictates that all classroom instruction be focused on proven strategies.

TAKE ACTION

☑ **Seek professional development.** Every school should seek to equip its educators with research-based knowledge of proven instructional practices.

☑ **Improve teacher preparation programs.** Every teacher preparation program in the nation should require its preservice teachers to be competent in proven instructional practices.

☑ **Improve teaching methods.** Implement research-based instructional practices for at-risk students.

☑ **Directly link practices.** Link specific instructional practices to aligned curricular and learning standards.

 See the "50 Strategies Suggested Reading" section for a list of resources selected to complement the fifty strategies as you put them to use in your classroom.

SAVING MY STUDENTS, SAVING MY SCHOOL

How can **Strategy #39: Select Research-Based Instructional Practices** be put to use in your classroom? What can you do to increase awareness and education among your group of colleagues?

_____

_____

_____

_____

_____

_____

_____

_____

_____

Share your thoughts with a colleague or group of colleagues.

STRATEGY #40

Use Homework Effectively

How can you assign homework to poor kids who live in homes with no paper, no pencils, no books, no encyclopedias, and no computers? So many of my students live in such dysfunctional situations, they have no quiet place even to work. We do homework in our class, and we do it every day, but we do it while the students are at school.

—Teacher, Oklahoma

Few issues in public education are as controversial and complex as homework. One indication of the complex controversy is the fact that for more than 100 years, public attitudes toward homework have cycled back and forth between supporting the use of homework and opposing it. Even more frustrating, a large body of research conducted on the effects of homework is also relatively inconclusive.

Proponents of homework maintain that the practice leads to better retention of knowledge, increased understanding, better study habits, better self-discipline, and better time management. Opponents of homework express concern regarding fatigue, lack of academic satisfaction, and loss of interest. Concerns also focus on inappropriate parental influence and even cheating.

For poor, at-risk, and other low-performing students, concerns regarding homework are often even more intense. A primary reason for students' failure in a traditional school, dropping out, or transferring to alternative schools is often related to a failure to complete homework. All jokes aside regarding the age-old excuse "The dog ate my homework," students coming from poor or dysfunctional families may truly find it impossible to complete their assignments at home. Visits to impoverished homes often reveal few assets to support and enrich school learning, provide adequate space, or provide assistance in completing school assignments. These are the children and youth on the "far side" of the digital divide. Students living in the stress-filled, emotionally charged environment of a dysfunctional family may find it difficult to even find a quiet place to work, let alone a place to complete homework in a timely, purposeful manner. Teachers must be sensitive to the challenging family situations of these students and make appropriate adjustments.

The approaches to homework that work for poor and at-risk students are listed in Figure 12.5 and described fully in the following text.

**Whole-School Programs That Attend to the Need
to Complete Homework**

- Before- and afterschool programs

- Supervised in-school study

- Extended periods and blocked programs

- Homework hotline

- Long-term homework projects

- Mentors and homework helpers

Figure 12.5

Before-, During-, and AfterSchool Programs

For students who live in homes where school instruction may not be enriched or supported, it is essential that they have time while at school to work on their assignments and have additional support to assist them. Before-, during-, and afterschool programs can offer a safe, supervised, and supportive environment. These programs are especially effective with young children and can provide opportunities for nutrition and recreation as well as homework support. For at-risk students, completing their assignments will often lead to a boost in self-confidence and self-esteem.

Extended Periods and Blocked Programs

Organizing the school schedule into extended 90-minute periods or into 2 × 2 block programs can allow sufficient time for instruction as well as individual work on assignments while the teacher is available to provide support.

Homework Hotline

With the help of volunteers or university students, many schools have established homework hotlines or Web sites to provide assistance to students while they complete their assignments. Unfortunately, this practice works only for families that have telephones or computers.

Long-Term Homework Projects

Low-performing and other at-risk students often respond positively to extended, out-of-school projects. Projects such as interviewing and taping parents, grandparents, and veterans on their life experiences or conducting career exploration projects have proven highly effective.

Mentors and Homework Helpers

Research has clearly documented the positive influence of adult role models serving as mentors. Working with homework magnifies the mentor's positive contribution to the student. Marzano and his coauthors offer recommendations based on their study of homework as an effective practice (see Figures 12.6 and 12.7).

Guidance From Research About Using Homework

- The amount of homework assigned to students should be different from elementary to middle to high school.

- Parent involvement in homework should be kept to a minimum.

- The purpose of homework should be carefully identified and articulated.

- If homework is assigned, the teacher should comment on it.

Figure 12.6

SOURCE: Adapted with permission from R. J. Marzano, D. Pickering, and J. Pollock. *Classroom Instruction That Works,* © 2001, ASCD.

Effective Classroom Practice in Assigning Homework

- Establish and communicate a homework policy.

- Design homework assignments that clearly articulate the purpose and outcome.

- Vary the approaches to providing feedback.

What the research says:

- Mastering a skill requires a fair amount of focused practice.

- While practicing, students should adapt and shape what they have learned.

Figure 12.7

SOURCE: Adapted with permission from R. J. Marzano, D. Pickering, and J. Pollock. *Classroom Instruction That Works,* © 2001, ASCD.

RESEARCH

- The majority of research studies have documented the positive impact of homework.
- The positive effects of homework vary with grade level and subject matter. The overall effect of homework has been found to be twice as high for high school students as for middle school students and twice as high for middle school students as for elementary school students. Homework has the largest positive effect in science and social studies. Homework has the smallest effect on mathematics.
- There is a relationship between the amount of homework assigned and completed during a week and related student achievement, especially for middle and high school students.
- Out-of-class assignments for students living in poverty or dysfunctional families must be carefully planned and individualized.
- Students should be provided a variety of opportunities during the school day to complete school assignments.

TAKE ACTION

- ☑ **Develop a school and classroom homework policy.** Have focused discussions regarding the role of homework in school. Develop, implement, and monitor a homework policy throughout the school.
- ☑ **Establish before-, during-, and afterschool programs.** Many children need to complete most of their homework and class assignments while they are at school. These opportunities can be scheduled before and after school or at special times during the school day. It is also important that children have opportunities to utilize libraries and computers to complete their assignments.
- ☑ **Consider a modified academic week.** Reorganize the weekly schedule to allow one day or a half day for students who need special assistance for their class assignments.

See the "50 Strategies Suggested Reading" section for a list of resources selected to complement the fifty strategies as you put them to use in your classroom.

SAVING MY STUDENTS, SAVING MY SCHOOL

How can **Strategy #40: Use Homework Effectively** be put to use in your classroom? What can you do to increase awareness and education among your group of colleagues?

_____

_____

_____

_____

_____

_____

_____

_____

_____

Share your thoughts with a colleague or group of colleagues.

STRATEGY #41

Require Student Portfolios, Projects, and Performance Exhibitions

I was invited to be part of an assessment panel with the responsibility of evaluating high school students during their high school graduation performance exhibitions. In my entire life, I have never seen anything like this in a public school. It was like a graduate comprehensive and oral examination all rolled into one. Students presented "portfolios of evidence" to our panel for evaluation. The portfolios included annotated reading lists, descriptions of service learning experience, descriptions of courses completed at community colleges, research papers, long-term projects, letters of reference documenting their work. . . . It was absolutely amazing. I never dreamed high school students could accomplish such high-quality work.

—Lawyer, Minnesota

The idea of using student portfolios, projects, and performance exhibitions to motivate students to achieve remarkable accomplishments has been used effectively in the American public schools since the time of John Dewey and the Progressive educators of the early 1900s. Unfortunately, historically, this approach to teaching and learning has been focused primarily on students considered gifted and talented. Since the late 1960s, a growing interest has emerged in the use and value of portfolios and project learning for students of all abilities and all ages, as well as in using student performance exhibits as an alternative (sometimes required) approach to graduation requirements in public schools. Three developments have generated renewed interest and more widespread application of these models to teaching and learning (see Figure 12.8 on page 292 and the discussion that follows).

First, the development of the concept of multiple intelligences helped educators better understand the wide range of talents that all students possess and how few are stimulated and developed through the exclusive use of teacher-led classroom learning. Recognizing the concept of multiple intelligences has helped educators at all levels to try to develop learning activities that permit students to demonstrate and develop a wide array of their unique abilities and talents.

Catalysts for Using Student Portfolios, Projects, and Performance Exhibitions

- Recognition of multiple intelligences
- National assessment movement, high-stakes testing, and the need for authentic assessments
- Renewed focus on portfolios, projects, and performance tasks

Figure 12.8

Second, the national testing movement has generated a growing search for ways to supplement standardized testing by assessing students in more authentic ways. This effort has led to the focus on performance assessment rather than limiting assessment to pencil-and-paper-examinations. Many of the most provocative and promising developments in public education have been in schools where students are demonstrating graduation competencies through some type of performance or exhibits. A few schools like the St. Paul Open School in Minnesota, Central Park East in New York City, and a number of other Coalition of Essential Schools member schools have used performance assessment to transform the entire school curriculum and environment by replacing traditional course graduation requirements with a set of performance competencies or exhibits.

Third, portfolios, projects, and performance exhibits have become the focus of those endeavoring to reinvent the high school and senior year experiences. Recent research documenting a phenomenon educators have historically called "the twelfth-grade problem"—alarming drop-offs in the academic achievement of high school seniors—has spawned a new label: "the senior slump" (National Commission on the High School Senior Year 2001). Other national and international achievement tests have also documented this significant decline, reporting that one-third of the college students in the United States take remedial courses; one-fourth of high school seniors who go to college do not graduate; and high school seniors find their culminating year boring, lacking in academic challenge, and largely a waste of time. One promising antidote for the senior slump has been the senior project or culminating experience.

Regardless of the grade level or the academic content, high-quality portfolios, projects, and performance exhibits almost always share a number of basic characteristics but are often presented in a variety of different formats. These basic characteristics are listed in Figure 12.9.

Common Characteristics of High-Quality Portfolios, Projects, and Performance Exhibits

- Empowers the student by focusing on an area of personal interest in which the student chooses to work.

- Uses an interdisciplinary approach.

- Requires active inquiry and investigation.

- Promotes in-depth learning rather than content coverage.

- Allows for student creativity.

- Includes academic learning, out-of-school experiences, and group activities.

- Material is selected to showcase and document student development and growth over time.

- A final project is completed.

- A final project culmination, performance assessment, or exhibit is presented before an audience of peers, teachers, or other adults.

Figure 12.9

SOURCE: Adapted from Bransford (1999), Osher (2001), and Wagner (2002).

One of the most widely used descriptions of the characteristics of high-quality, project-based learning includes the following characteristics:

- Builds on previous work
- Integrates speaking, listening, reading, and writing skills
- Incorporates collaborative teamwork, problem solving, negotiating, and other interpersonal skills
- Requires learners to engage in independent work
- Challenges learners to use English in new and different contexts outside the class
- Involves learners in choosing the focus of the project and in the planning process
- Leads to clear outcomes
- Incorporates self-evaluation, peer evaluation, and teacher evaluation

Portfolios

Portfolios represent the building blocks of all long-term student projects and performance exhibits and a tried-and-true approach to authentic assessment. In its simplest form, a *portfolio* is a collection and presentation of student work, usually over time. A portfolio can be a collection of work selected by the teacher, or it can be a collection of a student's best achievements chosen by the student. Portfolios are unique to the student developer and might include such content as a table of contents, a "Dear Reader" introduction to research reports, personal reflections, an annotated list or log of experiences, activities or readings, visual aides, interviews, artwork, original writing or poems, and so on. Three types of portfolios include showcase portfolios, growth portfolios, and limited portfolios.

- *Showcase portfolios* are often culminating or final products. Students select their work and add pictures, dialogue, design pages, and often video or PowerPoint presentations to document and showcase their work.
- *Growth portfolios* reflect what the term implies. They provide students with an opportunity to select consecutive pieces of their work that documents their improved achievement over time.
- *Limited portfolios* are more highly focused on a particular assignment or special report. Often, limited portfolios display one type of assignment for a group or even an entire class.

Students invariably enjoy preparing and showcasing their work and usually keep copies of their portfolios for later reference.

Student Projects

There are numerous excellent examples of schools using student projects and, in particular, senior projects. One of the most highly acclaimed senior projects is used in the North and South High Schools in Medford, Oregon. These schools have established a senior project as a graduation requirement, which has been acknowledged by the National Education Association and *Redbook* magazine as one of the nation's most innovative and successful high school programs. Senior projects in Medford comprise three aspects:

THE MEDFORD PUBLIC SCHOOLS

The Medford Public Schools (Oregon) have developed a detailed "how to do it manual that includes everything you need to know about creating an effective senior project program." (Contact Medford Public Schools, 500 Monroe St., Medford, OR 97501. Phone: [541] 776-8608.)

- An in-depth research paper on an issue of the student's choosing
- A project related to the research paper that allows the student to apply the knowledge learned during the investigation
- A presentation and portfolio that is presented to a senior board

A senior board, composed of school faculty as well as selected community members with special interests or expertise, serves as an evaluation panel. Students present their research, their project activities, the lessons they have learned from their efforts, and the problems they encountered during their work. Following the student presentation, the panel quizzes the student during an oral examination. Examples of senior projects include research on the question of why so many Hispanic students drop out of school, followed by a volunteer experience in an elementary school with a significant Hispanic population; research on real estate procedures, followed by securing a loan; an investigation of the origins of theatrical choreography, followed by choreographing a high school musical; an investigation of the assassination of John F. Kennedy, followed by planning and conducting a mock trial.

At the elementary and middle school levels, student projects focus on interdisciplinary themes and engage students in testing area streams for water quality, conducting scientific investigations dealing with the weather, preparing presentations of creative writing, and completing studies of World War II and the Great Depression. All projects involve library research as well as interviews with older veterans and senior citizens.

Performance Exhibitions

The Coalition of Essential Schools (CES) (<www.essentialschools.org>) has established "Graduation by Exhibition" as a requirement of completing school. This approach combines portfolio development, project learning, and performance assessment. One of the most widely recognized CES models may be observed at Central Park East, an alternative high school in New York City that enrolls 90 percent minority youth from economically impoverished homes. Students prepare for graduation by entering a senior institute at the start of the eleventh grade and begin work on achieving a number of merit badges by developing fourteen portfolios and completing exhibits or presentations in four major subject areas. Most students begin preparing their portfolios as early as the ninth grade. The fourteen requisite portfolio entries include those shown in Figure 12.10 on page 296.

For students at risk, the opportunity to engage in authentic academic experiences and to demonstrate their learning through portfolios, projects, and exhibitions is invaluable to their success in school. These experiences work exceptionally well for these students and should be a part of every school.

**Graduation Portfolio Requirements at Central Park
East Secondary School**

- Postgraduate plan
- Autobiography
- School/community service and internship
- Ethics and social issues
- Fine arts and aesthetics
- Mass media
- Practical skills
- Geography
- Second language and/or dual language
- Science and technology
- Mathematics
- Literature
- History
- Physics challenge

Figure 12.10

SOURCE: From Wagner (2002).

RESEARCH

- Students report great motivation and personal satisfaction in completing portfolios, projects, and performance exhibitions.
- Senior students report that project work improved their ability to work together as a collaborative team, enhanced interdisciplinary skills, and improved their professional development.
- Successfully completing projects and portfolios draws on a variety of talents and skills associated with multiple intelligences.
- Senior projects provide students with in-depth learning in an area of interest, combine academic research with experiences outside of school, and require the students to defend their learning in a presentation or oral examination.
- Performance exhibits provide students an opportunity to document their growth, development, and achievement and to be evaluated by a panel of experts.

TAKE ACTION

- ☑ **Learn about portfolios, projects, and performance exhibitions.** A number of school districts have developed extensive information on how to establish portfolios, senior projects, and graduation exhibits.

- ☑ **Seek professional development.** The Coalition of Essential Schools, the National Association of Secondary Schools, and the Association for Supervision and Curriculum Development provide professional development opportunities on portfolios, senior projects, and graduation performance exhibits. Professional development is also available through multiple-intelligences workshops.

- ☑ **Visit schools.** The best way to plan a major emphasis on portfolio development, project learning, multiple intelligences, senior projects, or performance exhibits is to visit schools that have established high-quality programs. The Coalition of Essential Schools can provide a list of schools in your region that use graduation exhibits.

- ☑ **Establish performance graduation requirements.** Implement a senior project/graduation requirement program with a more ambitious performance exhibition to reduce the "senior slump" in achievement, to increase motivation, and to synthesize and integrate course-based learning.

 See the "50 Strategies Suggested Reading" section for a list of resources selected to complement the fifty strategies as you put them to use in your classroom.

SAVING MY STUDENTS, SAVING MY SCHOOL

How can Strategy **#41: Require Student Portfolios, Projects, and Performance Exhibitions** be put to use in your classroom? What can you do to increase awareness and education among your group of colleagues?

_____

_____

_____

_____

_____

_____

_____

_____

_____

Share your thoughts with a colleague or group of colleagues.

STRATEGY #42

Incorporate Technology Across the Curriculum

Five years ago, almost all our teachers were technologically illiterate. Other than overhead projectors, VCRs, and copy machines, there was simply no advanced technology in our school. The checkout person at the local grocery store had more technology at their fingertips than we did as teachers. Today, we have all been retrained. Now, we have three to five computers in each classroom, a good computer technician, and most of our teachers have their own Web sites. Welcome to tomorrow.

—Teacher, Iowa

For poor and at-risk students who too often live in homes with little or no education support (few books, encyclopedias, computers, or other educational enrichments), it is essential that schools systematically work to teach these students essential technology skills; help them understand the variety of computer-related educational tools and skills; show them how to use technology to pursue independent, self-paced learning; and give them ample time to access computer technology.

Technology Can Benefit At-Risk Students

The aspects of technology that relate directly to the needs of at-risk students are listed in Figure 12.11 with discussion following.

Self-Paced Learning

Computer technology can be unusually effective in helping at-risk students catch up on and accelerate their learning. When elementary

---

Benefits of Using Technology

- Self-paced learning
- Internet interactive courses
- Learning technology skills
- Vocational technology training
- Teacher professional development

Figure 12.11

students arrive at school less-than-ready to succeed, software programs like Wiggle Works and Waterford provide effective tools to help students catch up and learn to read. For middle and high school students, programs such as Read 180, Nova Net, and Plato have documented evidence of their effectiveness. Many students who fail traditional classroom courses are able to use technology-based programs to acquire academic skills and catch up with their peers.

Internet Interactive Courses

There has been a sudden and expanding development of high-quality Internet K–12 courses. Some of these courses are available through private vendors; others have been developed by and for public education. One of the first virtual schools, the Florida Virtual High School, was started initially to serve two counties; today it is the state's largest high school. Students can earn individual course credit or pursue an entire high school diploma through the school. The development of Internet-based K–12 courses represents a significant advancement in traditional correspondence coursework. These courses are self-paced and interactive and usually enable students to continue their education while they work full- or part-time. Students who have been suspended from school programs or incarcerated in juvenile detention centers are also benefiting greatly from these opportunities.

Learning Technology Skills

Because at-risk students may have little or no access to technology in their home, they represent a classic example of the "digital divide" that has emerged as a growing national concern. Public schools must ensure that at-risk students gain the technology skills that too often separate them from their more advantaged peers. During recent years, the essential skills that are necessary to become fluent in technology have been identified, and a number of established models exist that provide a comprehensive technology curriculum. The technology curriculum for K–12 students has emerged, expanded, and rapidly become integrated throughout the schools. Today, there exists a growing agreement on the essential technology skills that all K–12 students need to be effective in school and in later life. The International Society of Technology in Education offers a list of essential skills (see Figure 12.12).

Vocational Technology Training

Because technology skills can lead to direct employment opportunities for students, K–12 public schools should provide opportunities for students

---

Essential Technical Skills

- Databases
- Word processing
- CD-ROM searches
- Use of e-libraries
- Online maps
- Spreadsheets
- Internet searching
- Desktop publishing
- Presentation and hypermedia software
- E-mail

Figure 12.12

SOURCE: From Eisenberg and Johnson (2000).

to pursue certification in vocational and technical training programs. One of the most direct avenues into good jobs is via technology certification programs. High school students who complete Novell Network, Att, Mons, or other certifications can immediately access job opportunities in business, industries, and often in the districts and schools they attend.

Teacher Professional Development

Most of today's teaching force was prepared prior to the computer revolution. As a result, most experienced teachers need training in technology skills and how to integrate technology into their daily classroom practice. Schools likewise have matured in their understanding of technology. Initially, schools placed computers in laboratories but more recently have begun to move technology into each classroom. Such an infusion into classrooms demands that teachers modify their instructional approach to accommodate the opportunity provided by computers and Internet access.

Some schools have integrated technology to such an extent in their teaching and learning that it has led to dramatic reorganization of the school curriculum and master schedule, even the redesign of school buildings. The Vancouver, Washington, public schools have recently completed a new high school that provides space for traditional classroom learning for only one-third of the student body at any one time. The school has small technology centers for group investigations that accommodate an additional third of the students, and individual technology-learning carrels for the other third.

RESEARCH

- Low-performing and at-risk students benefit directly from opportunities to use technology in their learning.
- Students with essential technology skills gain great power in accessing information, enhancing their ability to learn on their own.
- To maximize the integration of technology, both teachers and students need extensive professional development.

TAKE ACTION

- ☑ **Integrate technology into classroom instruction.** Integrate technology into the classroom, making every effort to engage low-performing and at-risk youth.
- ☑ **Enrich classrooms through technology.** Regardless of the state or community, schools must be enriched with technology. Voters in many school districts have passed "technology bonds" that have enabled schools to purchase technology; others have successfully lobbied legislators for designated technology funds. Some have even outfitted schools with donated computers.
- ☑ **Provide technology curriculum.** Using national or state-recommended curriculum standards, identify essential technology skills and integrate these skills into the classroom and library/media center.
- ☑ **Seek effective training.** Seek professional development training in technology.
- ☑ **Provide career exploration opportunities.** Provide K–12 students with effective career education programs related to technology. Students need to learn about the importance of computer technology in the workplace and explore the vast array of technology-related jobs available in business, industry, and the public sector.

 See the "50 Strategies Suggested Reading" section for a list of resources selected to complement the fifty strategies as you put them to use in your classroom.

SAVING MY STUDENTS, SAVING MY SCHOOL

How can **Strategy #42: Incorporate Technology Across the Curriculum** be put to use in your classroom? What can you do to increase awareness and education among your group of colleagues?

_____

_____

_____

_____

_____

_____

_____

_____

_____

_____

Share your thoughts with a colleague or group of colleagues.

STRATEGY #43

Create Assessment-Literate Classrooms

The tests are a drag. I really enjoy my time with Bart [her teacher]. I learn a lot from him, but then I work to do the tests. They suck; it's just memorizing facts that I'll never use.

—High School Student, Alternative School

After each unit, the computer makes us pass a test before we can go on to the next unit. They're stupid. I can just guess, and if I miss, I get a second chance that is even easier. This is just a game.

—High School Student, Alternative School

Most students have little regard for testing and assessment. Unfortunately, for students at risk, this reality may be chronic. Years of marginal success (at best) in schools has left most low-performing and other at-risk students with an absence of interest in what they consider the "hoops" of traditional schools—taking the tests and completing homework and assignments.

In fact, the disinterest held by at-risk students in assessment may not be all that different from that of students who are succeeding or making it through conventional schools. More concerning is the present combination of apathy, confusion, and anger held by far too many educators, which has been ignited by a recent decade of standards and accompanying mandated state and local high-stakes assessments.

Lorna Earl (2002), of the Ontario Institute for Studies in Education, adds two additional challenges beyond what she labels the "standards stew" that seriously impact the classroom teachers' capacity to improve assessments: competing purposes of assessment and the presence of assessment illiteracy in many teachers. Earl cites the work of a variety of scholars who have found many different purposes for classroom assessments that drive teachers (see Figure 12.13).

Compounding this disparity of purpose, Earl suggests that the nation's teaching force is fundamentally illiterate in the tools and processes of effective classroom assessment. This illiteracy has resulted from the failure of teacher preparation and professional development to focus on effective training in meaningful and relevant assessment practices and theory.

Competing Purposes of Teacher-Led Assessments

- Grading
- Reporting to parents
- Diagnosing learning
- Setting expectations
- Assessing prior knowledge
- Motivating students
- Controlling behavior
- Planning instruction
- Grouping students

Figure 12.13

SOURCE: Adapted from Earl (2002).

For students at risk (or any student for that matter), a general lack of regard for and apprehension of assessments coupled with a classroom atmosphere characterized by teacher frustration with the demand for assessment presents a challenging atmosphere for learning. The combination of a lack of teacher assessment knowledge, competing purposes, uses of local assessments, and mandated high-stakes tests combine to paint a dreary portrait of the likelihood of improvement. Yet as our nation's attention and educational policy increasingly focus on required state assessments of learning, it is critical, for the sake of our children, that we endeavor to improve our assessment practices. Fortunately, an approach exists to build teacher capacity that holds considerable promise. This approach focuses on the creation of assessment-literate classroom educators through a collaborative learning team process.

Rick Stiggins, noted assessment scholar and founder of the Assessment Training Institute, has created this approach for classroom teachers to acquire the skills of assessment literacy. He begins with the goal that it is the teacher's job to "take your students to a place where they no longer need you to tell them whether they have done well—to a place where they know in their minds and hearts how they have performed because they know the meaning of success. We seek classrooms where there are no surprises and no excuses" (Stiggins 2001: 17).

To accomplish this goal of assessment literacy, Stiggins offers a model of guiding principles (see Figures 12.14 and the discussion that follows). Driving this model are four guiding principles best described in Stiggins's own words:

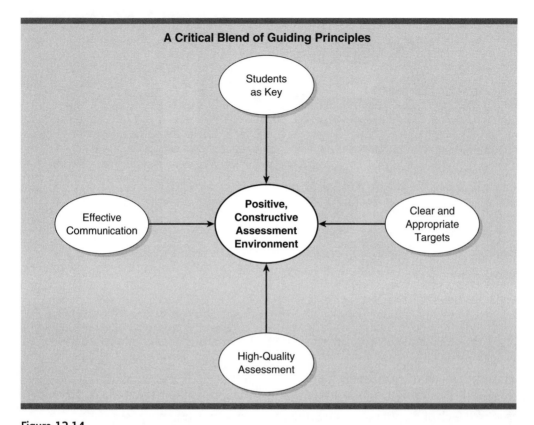

Figure 12.14

SOURCE: Stiggins, R., (2001). *Student Involved Classroom Assessment,* 3rd Edition. Reprinted by permission of Pearson Education, Inc., Upper Saddle River, NJ.

1. **Students are the key assessment users**. "Right from the time students arrive at school, they look to their teachers for guidance of their success. If that early evidence suggests that they are succeeding, what begins to grow in them is a sense of hopefulness and an expectation of more success in the future. This in turn fuels the motivation to try, which fuels even more success. . . . However, when the evidence suggests to students that they are not successful . . . what can begin to grow in them is a sense of hopelessness and an expectation of more failure in the future. . . . This can rob them of the motivation to try, which in turn can lead to more failure. Students decide how high to aim based on their sense of the probability of future success based on their record of past successes as reflected in their prior classroom assessment experience. No single decision or combination of decisions made by any other party exerts greater influence on student success."

2. **Clear and appropriate targets are essential**. "From the outset, any assessment's quality is reliant upon its clear and appropriate

definition of the expected activity. Be it a musical performance, a set of mathematical problems, a book review, or an explanation of cell biology, each assessment must clearly communicate its intended target. Teacher confidence in understanding the key concepts of the assessment and what it means to achieve success are key to communicating to students the clear target."

3. **Accurate assessment is a must**. Stiggins insists that a high-quality or sound assessment must contain five critical elements: "clear targets, focused purpose, proper method, sound sampling, and be accurate and free from bias and distortion. All assessments must meet all standards. No exceptions can be tolerated because to violate any of them is to risk inaccuracy, placing student academic well-being in jeopardy." Figure 12.15 (page 308) further illustrates the meaning of quality assessment.

4. **Sound assessments must be accompanied by effective communications**. For many, assessment has meant numbers, scores, and percentiles. Yet all educators inherently know that "words, pictures, illustrations, examples, and other means can far better explain a child's mastery of conceptual knowledge and content. Further, whatever the symbols chosen to communicate achievement and success . . . they are only as meaningful and useful as the definitions of achievement that underpin them and the quality of the assessments used to produce them. Assessment-literate educators are constantly asking, 'precisely what is being assessed here and how do I know what the results mean?'

SOURCE: Richard Stiggins, *Student-Involved Classroom Assessment*, 3rd Edition, © 2001, pp. 17–23. Reprinted by permission of Pearson Education, Inc., Upper Saddle River, NJ.

Assessment Literacy Learning Teams

To become assessment literate and create an assessment-literate classroom requires targeted professional development. Stiggins and the Assessment Training Institute (ATI) have created and successfully implemented a collaborative model of teacher-directed learning to accomplish this task. Thousands of classroom teachers, school leaders, and district administrators from every type of school have participated in this process over the past decade. The result? Today, a growing number of America's children are being assessed through the process of clear, guiding principles and effective assessment practices. (Contact ATI for further information and resources: <www.assessmentinst .com>, [800] 480-3060.)

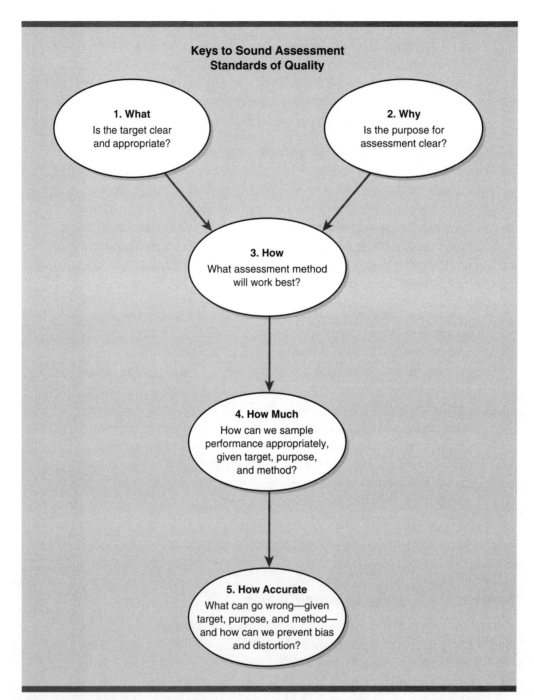

Figure 12.15

SOURCE: Stiggins, R., (2001). *Student Involved Classroom Assessment,* 3rd Edition. Reprinted by permission of Pearson Education, Inc., Upper Saddle River, NJ.

For students at risk, success in school is imperative to their future success as productive members of society. Success on mandated and other assessments must be achieved. Teachers of these students must create assessment-literate classrooms and teach the skills necessary for their students to be both confident in the assessment of their learning and capable of success.

RESEARCH

- Classroom assessment practices and results improve with targeted professional development.
- At-risk students have likely experienced a series of negative assessment experiences in prior classrooms.
- Many at-risk as well as more successful students see little value in testing and are disconnected from the assessment process.
- Formative (process) assessment can provide in-depth information to students, parents, and other stakeholders about student and school success.

TAKE ACTION

☑ **Set classroom and school goals of assessment literacy.** Every school should target professional development on improving assessment literacy in every classroom.

☑ **Seek help.** Use recent research and practice as a model for enhancing assessment literacy.

☑ **Engage students, parents, and stakeholders.** Every effort should be made to engage all participants—the recipients and consumers of assessment data—in improving the assessment process.

☑ **Target schools and teachers that serve at-risk and other low-performing students for immediate intervention.** These students, their teachers, and schools need immediate help.

See the "50 Strategies Suggested Reading" section for a list of resources selected to complement the fifty strategies as you put them to use in your classroom.

SAVING MY STUDENTS, SAVING MY SCHOOL

How can **Strategy #43: Create Assessment-Literate Classrooms** be put to use in your classroom? What can you do to increase awareness and education among your group of colleagues?

_____

_____

_____

_____

_____

_____

_____

_____

Share your thoughts with a colleague or group of colleagues.

Support Social and Emotional Growth

13

I never dreamed what a fulfilling experience it would be to serve as a mentor to this kid. Three years later, I am no longer just a mentor. I am not exactly sure what I am. Maybe I am now a godparent. Our relationship has grown, and we have become such close friends. I can see what an impact that I have had on this boy, but I never anticipated what an impact he would have on me.

—Volunteer, Kansas

Compared with earlier generations, today's youth seem to have stepped through the looking glass into a strange, new, and sometimes violent land. In fact, the world of today does not look much like the one most adults grew up in. Public education as well has been confronted by a dramatic change in student demographics and likely will never be the same. The American Academy of Child and Adolescent Psychiatry (2002) has voiced the following concerns about television violence and its powerful influence in developing value systems and shaping behavior:

- Children may become "immune" or numb to the horror of violence.
- Children may gradually accept violence as a way to solve problems.
- Children may imitate violence they observe on television.
- Children may identify with certain characters, victims, and/or victimizers.

With the disintegration of the family unit; with television, music, movies, and video games surrounding youth with violent images; and with too many children growing up with negative attitudes and often worse behavior, there is little wonder that today's youth have become aggressive and even violent. The question remains: what can schools do?

Increasingly, schools have been forced to fill a role that earlier generations perceived as exclusively belonging to the family. If children and youth are to learn personal respect and responsibility and if they are to develop strong self-concepts and personal pride in accomplishments, more and more communities are concluding that schools must assume a share of the responsibility for the education of these essential traits.

Some call for character, citizenship, or values education, others for resiliency training or "the other curriculum." The Association for Supervision and Curriculum and Development (ASCD) labels this need "social and emotional learning." Many feel that this area represents a critical missing piece of public education today. While this emerging area of curriculum is still rather ill defined, there is universal agreement that for at-risk youth, especially violent youth, this missing piece of the curriculum is absolutely essential. Many predict that through addressing these needs, schools will graduate students who are more tolerant and more responsible and possess an increased awareness and sense of personal honor and integrity.

The goal is to help students develop more positive attitudes, behaviors, and cognitions. It is to help students become healthy and confident. In Alexandria, Virginia, a character development partnership has established a long-term goal of character development that emphasizes the following: "knowing, caring about, and acting upon core ethical values such as fairness, honesty, compassion, responsibility, and respect for self and others." The National Association of Secondary School Principals has endorsed and recommended character education for all schools. A new mandate for character education has been established in the states of Florida and Louisiana.

Character education, as this area of curriculum is often called, is meant to teach our students to be good citizens with positive values and to interact and behave positively. The challenge for educators is to clarify the educational methods that most successfully contribute to these outcomes (something educators have been attempting to do since the seven cardinal principles of education were proposed at the beginning of the twentieth century). Today, there exists a growing research base that supports the need to enhance the character of our nation's youth through mentoring, service learning, peer mediation, and student leadership activities and opportunities.

Unconventional Wisdom

What Works for Experienced Teachers

Mentor a needy student.

In my own small way, I decided to single out one of my neediest students and to become her personal mentor. I invite her to attend special weekend and afterschool activities. We go to a movie and get an inexpensive meal. We go for hikes, ball games, and sometimes just hang out in a shopping mall. My personal mentoring program has resulted in a lifelong friend. . . . If every teacher could take on just one needy student, think of how many kids could be transformed in a truly remarkable way.

—Teacher, Connecticut

Get kids involved in Meals on Wheels.

We could never get many of our at-risk high school kids to participate in service learning. But one day, I asked three of the students to join me after school in my own personal volunteer work. The students rode around the neighborhoods with me and delivered Meals on Wheels to the elderly. I asked the kids to help carry the food and go into the elderly people's homes and apartments, and the students responded positively to the thanks and praise of the elderly. While this type of service learning is not for every student, I find that a few of my most difficult students liked the experience. Two of the students now use their own cars and have their own Meals on Wheels routes. Our students are much better kids because of this little program.

—Teacher, Michigan

STRATEGY #44

Create Student Mentoring Programs

Becoming a Big Brother for Darin, a poor elementary child, turned out to be the most challenging and satisfying experience that I have ever had. Looking back, I understand why we were required to complete a training program and commit to three years of participation. If you're not willing to work with these children over the long haul, don't even start. The one thing these kids don't need is to see another adult come and go in their life.

—Business Owner, Illinois

One of the most effective programs for at-risk students is mentoring. One caring adult can, indeed, make a dramatic difference in a young person's life. Yet many at-risk youth have never experienced a positive, personal relationship with an adult. The positive benefits of developing a mentor program for elementary, middle, and high school at-risk students are clear.

Mentors can be teachers who are willing to develop a new and different relationship with students, volunteers from business and industry, senior citizens, university students, and a host of others. The important consideration is that regardless of who the mentor might be, it is essential that each be screened, trained, and taught to work as part of an established program. With the increasing incidence of sexual abuse perpetrated by adults, screening the histories of potential mentors is awkward but extremely important and must be done.

Successful mentor programs involve far more than simply matching an adult with an at-risk youth. Considerable research has been conducted during the past decade on developing and evaluating mentor programs for a wide variety of different organizations. The National Dropout Prevention Center recommends a process to guide the development of a mentor program (see Figure 13.1 on page 316).

MENTOR PROGRAMS AND PROJECTS COME IN A VARIETY OF FORMATS

Examples of national mentor programs:

- Big Brothers/Big Sisters
- I Have a Dream Foundation
- Summer Training and Education Program (STEP)
- Sponsor a Scholar
- One Plus One

Examples of local business programs:

- Project Step Up
- Adopt-a-Student

Examples of university-based programs:

- Campus Contact
- Linking UP
- Career Beginnings

How to Start a Mentoring Program

1. Establish the need.

2. Secure a commitment of building and district leadership.

3. Identify and select program staff.

4. Establish program goals and objectives.

5. Prescribe activities and procedures.

6. Identify students.

7. Promote program and recruit mentors.

8. Train mentors and students.

9. Match mentors and students.

10. Monitor the mentoring process.

11. Evaluate ongoing and terminated cases.

12. Revise program and repeat steps.

Figure 13.1

SOURCE: Adapted from *Mentoring Programs for At-Risk Youth,* by the National Dropout Prevention Center. © 1990 The National Dropout Prevention Center, Clemson University, Clemson, SC.

RESEARCH

- The National Dropout Prevention Center identifies mentoring programs as one of the most effective strategies available that has a positive impact on the dropout rate.
- Because many poor and at-risk youth have had few, if any, positive adult role models, adult mentoring programs that provide students with an ongoing experience with a caring supportive adult can have impressive positive results.
- The longer a mentor maintains an active relationship with a student, the greater the influence for positive change.
- The Adopt-A-Student program in Atlanta reports great success in mentoring eleventh- and twelfth-grade students in the bottom quarter of their class. Researchers at Georgia State University report that students participating in the Adopt-A-Student program had a 92 percent high school graduation rate, with a 93 percent rate of job placement or enrollment in higher education.

TAKE ACTION

☑ **Find existing mentoring programs.** Almost every community has existing mentoring programs like Big Brothers/Big Sisters. Other programs are often available through Boys and Girls Clubs, YMCA/YWCA, and professional service clubs. School districts and universities often coordinate mentoring programs as a part of service learning efforts.

☑ **Connect students to mentoring programs.** Few outside the family know students' challenges and problems better than teachers. Recognize the need of a particular student for an adult mentor. Encourage students to participate in mentoring programs. Include parents in the process so that they will understand the program and be supportive.

☑ **Select an approach that fits.** With the abundance of effective mentoring programs available, it is critical that a school select the best match to ensure the longevity of the program. Starting and stopping mentor programs may actually be worse for at-risk students than having no program.

☑ **Monitor the effectiveness of the program frequently.** It is likely that any program will need regular "adjustment." Frequently monitor the program's effectiveness to address any issues.

☑ **Use teachers as mentors.** Integrate teachers into mentor programs. Because of the extended student contact and academic tutorial assistance as well as social and emotional support they can provide, teachers are often very effective mentors.

☑ **Select mentors carefully.** When an adult mentor drops out of the program after developing a positive relationship with a student, it can have a crushing effect on student trust. Every potential mentor should be carefully reviewed and assessed for the prospect of a long-term commitment.

See the "50 Strategies Suggested Reading" section for a list of resources selected to complement the fifty strategies as you put them to use in your classroom.

SAVING MY STUDENTS, SAVING MY SCHOOL

How can **Strategy #44: Create Student Mentoring Programs** be put to use in your classroom? What can you do to increase awareness and education among your group of colleagues?

_____

_____

_____

_____

_____

_____

_____

_____

_____

_____

Share your thoughts with a colleague or group of colleagues.

STRATEGY #45

Establish Service Learning Programs

We get our elementary kids to participate in Paint the Town, Rake Up the Parks, Earth Day, and every other community service activity we can find. We want our kids working with adults, contributing to the community, and building strong values. What's so great is that kids love these activities.

—Teacher, Ohio

A particularly effective means of developing personal responsibility is to provide at-risk students with opportunities to be responsible and to be held accountable for their actions. When students work in retirement centers or hospitals or participate in Paint the Town or Habitat for Humanity projects, they learn responsibility, which transfers over to their personal lives. Through tutoring younger children, serving on school governance boards and committees, being involved in the cooperative development of rules and regulations for their schools, participating in youth courses, or mediating student conflicts, they also learn and grow. Learning experiences such as these place students in real-world situations where they must learn to act responsibly and to contribute. The subsequent personal learning that occurs for students is often quite remarkable.

Service learning is one of the most effective strategies for reducing school dropout rates and has far-reaching implications for schools and communities. As an intervention, service learning

- helps students learn and develop by participating in thoughtfully organized service that is conducted in and meets the needs of a community,
- can bring together caring adults from colleges and universities or the community with children in elementary or secondary schools
- fosters a sense of civic responsibility,
- integrates and enhances the curriculum by using skills in a real-world context, and
- provides structured time for students or other participants to reflect on the service experience (Schargel and Smink 2001).

In the past decade, service learning programs have spread throughout the country. Research on these programs continues to build a growing body of evidence regarding the positive effects of this approach for students. Author Shelley Billig outlines attributes and outcomes of a successful service learning program (see Figure 13.2).

To effectively implement a service learning program, essential elements should be in place (see Figure 13.3).

Service Learning Works

- Service learning has a positive effect on the personal development of public school youths.

- Students who participate in service learning are less likely to engage in risky behaviors.

- Service learning has a positive effect on students' interpersonal development and the ability to relate to culturally diverse groups.

- Service learning helps develop students' sense of civic and social responsibility and their citizenship skills.

- Service learning provides an avenue for students to become active, positive contributors to society.

- Service learning helps students acquire academic skills and knowledge.

- Students who participate in service learning are more engaged in their studies and more motivated to learn.

- Service learning is associated with increased student attendance.

- Service learning helps students become more knowledgeable and realistic about careers.

- Service learning results in greater mutual respect between teachers and students.

- Service learning improves the overall school climate.

- Engaging in service learning leads to discussions of teaching and learning and of the best ways for students to learn.

- Service learning leads to more positive perceptions of schools and youth on the part of community members.

Figure 13.2

SOURCE: From Billig (2000).

Essential Elements of Service Learning

The following elements are necessary for effective service learning:

1. There are clear educational goals that require the application of concepts, content, and skills from the academic disciplines and involve students in the construction of their own knowledge.

2. Students are engaged in tasks that challenge and stretch them cognitively and developmentally.

3. Assessment is used to enhance student learning as well as to document and evaluate how well students have met content and skill standards.

4. Students are engaged in service tasks that have clear goals, meet genuine needs in the school or community, and have significant consequences for themselves and others.

5. Formative and summative evaluations are employed in a systematic evaluation of the service effort and its outcome.

6. Student voice is maximized in selecting, designing, implementing, and evaluating the service project.

7. Diversity is valued as demonstrated by the participants, the practice, and the outcomes of the service learning activity.

8. Communication and interaction with the community are promoted, and partnerships and collaboration are encouraged.

9. Students are prepared for all aspects of their service work. They possess a clear understanding of tasks and roles, as well as the skills and information required by the tasks, awareness of safety precautions, and knowledge about and sensitivity to the people with whom they will be working.

10. Student reflection takes place before, during, and after service, uses multiple methods that encourage critical thinking, and is a central force in the design and fulfillment of curricular objectives.

11. Multiple methods are designed to acknowledge, celebrate, and further validate students' service work.

Figure 13.3

SOURCE: From Toole (1999).

RESEARCH

- The National Dropout Prevention Center has identified service learning as one of the top three most successful programs for reducing dropout rates.

- Service learning has an enormous, positive effect on the social and emotional development of K–12 as well as college students.
- Service learning leads to greater mutual respect among students and teachers.

RESOURCES FOR ESTABLISHING
A HIGH-QUALITY SERVICE
LEARNING PROGRAM

- Corporation for National and Community Service, Learn and Serve America, 1201 New York Ave. NW, Washington, DC 20525, (202) 606-5000, <www.nationalservice.org>
- National Service-Learning Clearinghouse, ETR Associates, 4 Carbonero Way, Scotts Valley, CA 95066, toll-free, TTY accessible phone: (866) 245-SERV (7378), <www.servicelearning.org>
- National Youth Leadership Council (NYLC), 1667 Snelling Ave. N., Suite 300, St. Paul, MN 55108, (651) 631-3672, <www.nylc.org>
- National Service-Learning Exchange, (877) 572-3924, <www.nslexchange.org>
- Learning in Deed: Making a Difference Through Service Learning, National Service-Learning Partnership, Academy for Educational Development, 100 Fifth Avenue, New York, NY 10011, (212) 367-4570, <www.service-learningpartnership.org>

Take Action

☑ **Establish service learning opportunities.** Engage students of all ages in some type of service learning.

☑ **Identify service learning programs.** An impressive number of organizations exist that offer help in establishing a high-quality service learning program.

☑ **Follow established guidelines.** Because of the extensive research on service learning, essential guidelines have been identified for effective programs. Become familiar with these guidelines and use them as a checklist in developing service programs.

☑ **Frequently monitor the effectiveness of the program.** It is likely that any program will need regular adjustment. Frequent monitoring of the program's effectiveness will address these issues.

See the "50 Strategies Suggested Reading" section for a list of resources selected to complement the fifty strategies as you put them to use in your classroom.

SAVING MY STUDENTS, SAVING MY SCHOOL

How can **Strategy #45: Establish Service Learning Programs** be put to use in your classroom? What can you do to increase awareness and education among your group of colleagues?

_____

_____

_____

_____

_____

_____

_____

_____

_____

_____

Share your thoughts with a colleague or group of colleagues.

STRATEGY #46

Teach Peer Mediation

As a principal, I used to spend the majority of my time dealing with student discipline problems. Since we have trained our students in peer mediation, the students themselves work out many of the issues. Our students have learned skills that they will use throughout their lifetimes.

—Principal, Pennsylvania

Conflict is an integral component of our contemporary society. International conflicts characterized by intense and often vicious ethnic, religious, and cultural conflict; issue-oriented conflicts over the environment, economy, energy, and abortion; and ever-present personal conflicts represent examples of the pervasive reality of conflict. Contemporary media saturate youth with conflict in violent movies, television series, and computer games. Even the evening news seems at times to be little more than talking heads, posturing and criticizing one another from antithetical points of view.

Children and youth in the United States grow up with conflict—everything from playground disputes to prejudice over ethnic backgrounds or sexual preferences to racism. If the research is accurate, almost all children are bullied, taunted, or teased at one time or another, and many kids are the perpetrators of such bullying. It is just these rather typical daily events of taunting between teenage cliques that seem to have been instrumental in leading to violent acts of murder at Columbine High School, in Colorado; Thurston High School, in Oregon; and other school buildings across the nation.

Unfortunately, until recently, public schools have not engaged students in addressing and dealing effectively with their own conflicts. When conflicts have occurred, teachers or administrators have too often reviewed the situation, determined who was to blame, and decided on appropriate punishment. Student conflicts have typically led to detention, suspension, and expulsion. But more and more districts and communities have begun to wonder whether there might be other alternatives to conflicts that might prove more educationally effective.

Many schools have created student support groups, counseling groups, student courts, and anger management programs to address the needs of students in conflict. Peer mediation is another highly successful approach. By learning techniques of mediation and a process of mediating conflicts, students not only come to resolve their own disputes but also learn strategies that can be used throughout their lives.

Conflict is a typical and normal part of everyday life. Without training, most students react to conflict with defensiveness, aggressiveness, or withdrawal. Such approaches have potential negative effects. Research has shown that both the bully and the student being bullied can suffer long-term negative effects. Teaching students mediation strategies offers a different, far more positive approach to conflict and disputes among children and youth.

Peer mediation is a method of conflict resolution that helps students involved in disputes reach mutually acceptable agreements with the help of another student who serves as a neutral mediator. Peer mediation becomes a win-win strategy. Peer mediation is a simple process that can easily be taught to students as young as third or fourth grade.

The peer mediation process involves only the students involved in a dispute and a peer mediator. No adults are involved. The process of mediation follows a series of basic steps (see Figure 13.4).

To create an appropriate peer mediation program model, use the process outlined in Figure 13.5 on page 326.

The Peer Mediation Process

1. Mediator arranges for a mediation session for two participants and asks each participant to adhere to certain rules:
   - Try to solve the problem.
   - Do not interrupt others.
   - Do not use put-downs or threaten the other while telling each side of what happened.
   - Be honest.
2. Mediator asks one participant what happened.
3. Participant responds.
4. Mediator summarizes what was said.
5. Mediator asks the other participant what happened.
6. Participant responds.
7. Mediator summarizes what was said.
8. Feelings of both participants are discussed.
9. Mediator asks participants to think of ways to solve the problem.
10. Alternatives are discussed and some eliminated.
11. A solution that both disputants can agree to is reached.

Figure 13.4

SOURCE: Adapted from *Resolving Conflict Through Peer Mediation. A Series of Solutions and Strategies,* No. 9, by Marie Rogers. © 1994 The National Dropout Prevention Center, Clemson University, Clemson, SC.

Steps to Implement a Peer Mediation Program

1. Form an advisory council that includes
   - students,
   - parents,
   - teachers,
   - administrators,
   - counselors, and
   - community stakeholders.

2. Send representatives to be trained, or bring in a professional mediator to train staff members on site. Training can occur during several inservice sessions. All teachers, parents, administrators, and counselors should be invited to attend.

3. Purchase or write a program manual including your purpose, procedures, and plan (with timetable). Establish goals, and make modifications along the way as needs are revealed.

4. Select the students to be trained as mediators. This can be done through various means:
   - teacher recommendation,
   - student interest application,
   - student body elections,
   - student body sample (appointed), or
   - conflict mediator club participants.

5. Train the student mediators by first analyzing the alternatives to violence, exposing them to the simple mediation process (establish rules, hear each student's side of the conflict, summarize, and suggest possible solutions to the problem), and, finally, placing them in many impromptu role-playing situations in which students take turns being the mediator.

6. Make sure the student body is made aware of the purpose and availability of the peer mediation program.

7. Keep the program going by holding monthly or bimonthly meetings with the advisory council and the student mediators. Discuss happenings, problems, and successes and offer encouragement and feedback to all involved.

Figure 13.5

SOURCE: Adapted from *Resolving Conflict Through Peer Mediation: A Series of Solutions and Strategies*, No. 9, by Marie Rogers. © 1994 The National Dropout Prevention Center, Clemson University, Clemson, SC.

RESEARCH

- Students engaged in peer mediation demonstrate less physical violence in classrooms and on playgrounds. There is less taunting, teasing, and bullying and, over time, more caring behavior emerges.
- Peer mediation leads to more willingness to cooperate, and students become sensitive to other points of view.
- Peer mediation leads to student-initiated problem solving.
- Peer mediation not only helps students resolve disputes but also helps them learn strategies that can be used throughout their lives.

TAKE ACTION

- ☑ **Learn about peer mediation programs.** There are many excellent books and articles on peer mediation and a number of organizations that can help school districts develop programs. Organize a team of interested educators and parents to visit another school or district that is operating an effective program.
- ☑ **Select a model for implementation.** Carefully consider possible options and present a choice of effective programs to stakeholders for selection.
- ☑ **Monitor the effectiveness of the program frequently.** It is likely that any program will need regular adjustment, and frequent monitoring of the program's effectiveness will address these issues.
- ☑ **Develop schoolwide consensus.** Effective peer mediation programs should be established as a schoolwide effort. It is essential that parents, teachers, and administrators understand peer mediation and support the program.
- ☑ **Train students, teachers, and parents.** Schools utilizing peer mediation need to ensure that everyone understands the program and is trained for his or her specific role or can train others.

See the "50 Strategies Suggested Reading" section for a list of resources selected to complement the fifty strategies as you put them to use in your classroom.

SAVING MY STUDENTS, SAVING MY SCHOOL

How can **Strategy #46: Teach Peer Mediation** be put to use in your classroom? What can you do to increase awareness and education among your group of colleagues?

_____

_____

_____

_____

_____

_____

_____

_____

_____

_____

_____

Share your thoughts with a colleague or group of colleagues.

STRATEGY #47

Build Self-Esteem and Respect Through Student Leadership

You cannot build pride and respect through textbooks. If you want to build character, you employ proven strategies that have to focus on the shared societal and cultural values that make us good people. It doesn't just happen.

—Teacher, Connecticut

Because at-risk students often have low self-esteem, some schools, especially alternative schools, have had great success in developing specific programs designed to build pride and self-worth through engaging students in leadership roles. Research has shown that when at-risk students are placed in positions of responsibility and provided sufficient support to ensure success, highly positive outcomes can occur. Placing students in positions of responsibility sends a loud message to students who have a tradition of failure. Many schools have been unusually creative in designing programs that place students in responsible leadership roles.

Students in Positions of Responsibility

Examples of programs that promote student responsibility are listed in Figure 13.6 (page 330) with discussion following.

Greenbelt Guides

At Meridian Academy, in Idaho, at-risk students choose to enroll in a class called "Greenbelt Guides." The students study the biology and ecology of the Boise River's greenbelt bike trails. After thorough study and demonstrations of their abilities, the at-risk high school students conduct half-day field studies along the Boise River for fourth-grade students. The program's success is exemplified by large waiting lists for fourth-grade classrooms and increased competition at Meridian Academy to enroll in the class.

Science Circus

Because of the seasonal limitations of the Greenbelt Guides program, Meridian Academy established a second program, "Science Circus." Students in this program plan and conduct a hands-on scientific laboratory

---

Programs That Promote Student Responsibility

- Greenbelt Guides
- Science Circus
- Juvenile Justice Student Court
- School Disciplinary Committees
- Student Entrepreneurship
- Student Internships
- Cross-Age Tutors
- Teacher Selection Committees

Figure 13.6

lesson in fourth-grade classrooms throughout the area. Just as in the Greenbelt Guides, the at-risk high school students complete extensive preparation and must present the lesson to peers and adults at the Academy prior to conducting the lessons in elementary classrooms.

Juvenile Justice Student Court

Many communities recruit, train, and use high school students to serve as jurors in juvenile justice courtrooms. Law enforcement officers and juvenile justice judges agree that the students take this work very seriously and are often more forceful in their recommended punishment than adult jurors.

School Disciplinary Committees

Many schools have created disciplinary committees composed entirely of students. Carefully developed guidelines identify students who must go before the committee, and the guidelines also establish a process to guide the student reviewers in their decisions. Often, students who are referred to the committee must be accompanied by their parents and/or a friend. The student and the teacher involved present their cases and are cross-examined by the students on the disciplinary committee, which, in turn, recommends action to the principal.

Student Entrepreneurship

Students at the St. Paul Open School established a classic student-run business. Their consumer protection service, Nathan's Raiders (named after a teacher), advertised widely in the St. Paul/Minneapolis area and investigated complaints brought by area consumers. If the students found that a consumer had been mistreated or cheated and was unable to mediate or resolve the dispute, they turned the case over to the local authorities and/or the Better Business Bureau. The Raiders enjoyed an impressive satisfactory resolution record and were recognized by the community. A host of other models, such as food service, craft business, small-engine repair, and student bookstores characterize this approach.

Student Internships

Many schools are offering credit opportunities by arranging student internships with lawyers, judges, architects, engineers, stockbrokers, doctors, nurses, bankers, and a variety of other business and professional leaders. These students are often assigned real-life responsibilities that they are expected to perform. The internships usually last one semester and closely relate to student career interests and focus on area businesses and industries.

Cross-Age Tutors

Older students can benefit greatly by tutoring younger children. Research has clearly shown that tutoring helps both the tutor and the tutee. Many middle and high school programs for at-risk youth employ valuable services and programs.

Teacher Selection Committees

Many schools use students as part of selection committees to interview prospective new teachers, administrators, and student teachers. Some schools require the candidate to first pass the student selection process before being considered further.

The list of possible student leadership programs is limited only by the imagination. But in every case, students functioning in responsible leadership roles inevitably feel better about themselves, experience a sense of pride, and learn skills essential to life in a democratic society. The process described in Figure 13.7 (page 332) is recommended for establishing leadership programs.

National Centers for Student Leadership

- Center for Civic Education, 5145 Douglas Fir Rd., Calabasas, CA 91302, (818) 591-9321, <www.civiced.org>

- Educators for Social Responsibility, 23 Garden St., Cambridge, MA 02138, (617) 492-1764, <www.esrnational.org>

- Learn and Serve America, Corporation for National Service, 1201 New York Ave., NW, Washington DC 20525, (202) 606-5000, www.learnandserve.org

---

Educating for Democratic Life

- Expand opportunities for young people and adults to become more involved in meaningful service with neighborhood and community organizations by making service learning an integral part of the educational experience.

- Encourage students to explore the twin issues of character development and responsible participation in the civil society by integrating service learning, character education, and citizenship education opportunities into the classroom.

- Weave the historical legacy and values of the civil society into a broad range of curriculums and community programs.

- Extend the values of democracy and community to the classroom by engaging students in the design of their own learning experiences.

- Elicit more direct involvement among community organizations, civic associations, businesses, local schools, colleges, and universities.

- Ensure that faculty, students, staff, families, and community organizations have a genuine voice in school, college, and university policy making.

- Make every effort to ensure that the human, financial, and community resources needed to accomplish these goals are made available.

Figure 13.7

SOURCE: Partnering Initiative on Education and Civil Society, Washington, DC.

RESEARCH

- Children and youth live "up to" or "down to" the expectations of the significant adults in their lives. The higher the adult expectations, coupled with adequate support, the better the attitudes, behavior, self-concepts, and performance of students.
- Students learn respect and responsibility by being placed in positions of leadership with genuine, significant goals to accomplish.
- At-risk youth often suffer from low self-esteem. Placing at-risk students in responsible leadership roles has a significant, long-term positive impact on their self-esteem.

TAKE ACTION

☑ **Explore programs.** Explore programs that place students in positions of responsibility. In almost every community, such programs can be found in either schools or the community.

☑ **Seek information.** Contact one or more national centers for additional information (see sidebar).

☑ **Create programs and engage students.** Engage students in exploring possible programs, gaining training and experience, and then planning a new program. Programs engaging students in positions of responsibility are long-term projects and must be sufficiently planned and implemented to ensure effective longevity.

☑ **Include students in planning.** Involve students early in the planning process to design, develop, and implement programs of student responsibility.

☑ **Monitor the effectiveness of the program.** It is likely that any program will need regular adjustment, and frequent monitoring of the program's effectiveness will identify issues that need to be addressed.

See the "50 Strategies Suggested Reading" section for a list of resources selected to complement the fifty strategies as you put them to use in your classroom.

SAVING MY STUDENTS, SAVING MY SCHOOL

How can **Strategy #47: Build Self-Esteem and Respect Through Student Leadership** be put to use in your classroom? What can you do to increase awareness and education among your group of colleagues?

_____

_____

_____

_____

_____

_____

_____

_____

_____

_____

Share your thoughts with a colleague or group of colleagues.

14

Use Community Resources and Services

The principal laughed and shook his head. Do you remember the good old days when we had parent conferences? Well, let me tell you, the world has changed. Last week, I asked the secretary to schedule a meeting with this really screwed up fifteen-year-old kid and everyone who had some type of responsibility for him. When I walked into the conference room I nearly fell over because the room was packed. There was the kid, his probation officer, his mother, his grandmother, his foster parents, his attorney, his caseworker from Health and Welfare, and God knows who else. There must have been a dozen people in the room. Let me tell you, so many of these kids are just a mess. When you really find out what's going on in their lives, the really remarkable thing is not that they drop out of school, but that they ever bother to come to school at all.

—Superintendent, Oregon

No school is an island. In fact, schools are the reflection of the social, economic, and political communities in which they exist. The more schools expand their curricula and instruction outside the school walls, the more students become engaged in learning, the more relevance they see in learning, and the more motivated they become. John Dewey, in his 1916 educational classic, *Democracy and Education*, summarized the concept of community-based learning with the phrase "learning by doing." Decades of educational research and experience have validated his claim that students must be actively engaged in real-life issues, situations, and experiences to magnify their learning and deepen their understanding. If the goal of public education in America is to prepare all students for active participation in our democracy, students must be provided opportunities to interact with the real world outside of schools. This opportunity is particularly important for at-risk youth. Learning by doing often provides the exact intervention needed to positively redirect a struggling child's life toward successful outcomes.

Students engaged in service activities in hospitals; day care centers; retirement centers; or research projects, such as testing water samples, voting patterns, or climatic changes, learn by doing and so do students who develop and operate small businesses or participate in cultural exchange programs. Such experiences transform learning from pencils and paper and desks and books into relevant, often vivid learning experiences that can profoundly impact student interest, future careers, and even values and attitudes.

The communities outside of schools do far more than provide an exciting laboratory for learning; communities are filled with resources, expertise, and services that schools usually cannot provide. Research at the Search Institute in Minneapolis has documented how assets in the home, community, and school can influence student behavior, values, and academic performance. More and more health clinics as well as drug and alcohol abuse programs are being located in high schools. *Full-service schools*, a relatively new concept, are becoming increasingly popular as intervention agencies and schools work to coordinate efforts.

Unconventional Wisdom

What Works for Experienced Teachers

Stretch the school day.

For poor kids who come from families with little educational enrichment or support, our school decided to stretch the school day with before- and afterschool programs. We staff these programs with teachers, parents, grandparents, and other volunteers. We work hard on tutoring these at-risk kids as well as providing a nutritional snack whenever we meet.

—Teacher, Wyoming

STRATEGY #48

Embrace the Community as a Classroom

Why do we isolate kids from the real world? If you want students to grow up to become good citizens, you better get them learning outside of your classroom and your school!

—Teacher, North Carolina

While schools have always used the surrounding community for field trips, outings, and guest classroom appearances, the recognition of the importance of the community in relevant student learning began to emerge in the late 1960s. Vocational programs have always utilized apprenticeships and on-the-job training, but similar developments in relation to a school's core academic curriculum have only recently come into being. Students today are learning in banks, museums, courtrooms, hospitals, businesses, and zoos, as well as in the forests, wetlands, and urban areas of their communities. Over thirty years of research has documented and demonstrated how powerful these experiences can be on the understanding of academic concepts as well as on building personal self-esteem, responsibility, and positive attitudes. Community learning may engage students in interviewing veterans of notable events such as the following:

- Pearl Harbor
- D-Day or the Bataan Death March
- Korean or Vietnam Wars
- Desert Storm
- The destruction of NYC's World Trade Center towers on September 11, 2001
- Wars in Afghanistan or Iraq

Other activities could include

- participating in the stock market game,
- playing a part in a mock United Nations or Economic Summit,
- taking part in social or career internships,
- conducting Foxfire-type community interviews, and
- carrying out student-initiated research outside the school.

At-risk students appear to benefit greatly from these experiences. Relevance to their lives is particularly motivating and is often a requirement for productive classroom participation. For these students, out-of-school learning is not a luxury, but a necessity.

Research has helped identify a wide variety of legitimate out-of-school learning experiences in both rural and urban areas and has also identified the elements of effective internships and service learning programs. In addition to providing real-world, hands-on experiences, these programs, especially service learning, also lead to social and emotional growth, particularly in the areas of responsibility and respect. Examples of real-world experience programs are listed in Figure 14.1 and discussed below.

Facilitating Real-World Experiences

- Service learning
- Entrepreneurism
- Folklore collection
- School-to-work
- Schools without walls
- Career-theme magnet programs
- Adventure-based education

Figure 14.1

Service Learning

Both high schools and colleges have embraced service learning in the community. These programs include students providing service in retirement centers, health centers, hospitals, and a wide variety of community cleaning, painting, and fix-up projects. Such service learning activities build positive attitudes and help students learn the important lesson of responsibility.

Entrepreneurism

There is a growing movement throughout the country to assist students in becoming business owners. Originally started as part of vocational education and Junior Achievement, the concept of student operated and managed businesses has greatly expanded during recent years. Students have started small companies to sell school supplies, hardware,

RURAL ENTREPRENEURSHIP
THROUGH ACTION LEARNING (REAL)

115 Market St., Suite #320, Durham, NC 27701, (800) 798-0643, <www.ncreal.org>

crafts, and jewelry. They fix small engines, run bakeries, and operate import/export businesses. A national project in North Carolina focuses on rural entrepreneurism found throughout the country (see sidebar).

Folklore Collection

One of the nation's most recognized entrepreneurial efforts has been Foxfire, Inc., a multimillion-dollar, student-owned business selling books and newsletters documenting Appalachian and American folklore. While national interest in students collecting regional or cultural folklore started with Foxfire, the concept has expanded throughout the country to include a wide variety of rural and urban ethnic experiences. Foxfire was established in a poor, rural area in Georgia where many students traditionally dropped out of school and went to work in the region's textile mills. Based on the rather simple idea of collecting and publishing the folklore of their region, students traveled throughout the countryside interviewing parents, grandparents, and mountain people about subjects ranging from how to make homemade soap to dowsing for water to building log cabins.

School-to-Work

Through the U.S. Department of Labor's school-to-work program, students throughout the country have participated in a variety of real-world learning experiences in business and industry. These experiences ranged from short-term orientations and career fairs to internships and summer employment with area corporations and small businesses. While federal school-to-work funding has now expired, a multitude of effective programs continue to operate and positively influence many students throughout the nation's school districts.

Schools Without Walls

Ever since the Philadelphia Parkway School was created as a "school without walls," many cities have created programs to move learning experiences out of school buildings and into museums, aquariums, government offices, banks, and businesses. Students attend classes in a number of venues and are taught by professionals in a wide variety of occupations. Hundreds of these schools continue to thrive across the country.

Career-Theme Magnet Programs

During the past twenty years, there has been a dramatic increase in career-theme magnet programs, in which students choose to voluntarily participate in a career area in which they have a strong personal interest. Examples of magnet schools include such diverse themes as performing arts, law and legal professions, design and architecture, science and technology, analytical studies, and health professions. Participating students are dramatically influenced by the opportunity to learn in the real world from practicing professionals. The result is high academic performance.

Adventure-Based Education

Educational programs for at-risk students that are built around wilderness adventure and adventure-based education programs have proven to be increasingly successful. Programs that place students in "neutral" wilderness settings have proven instrumental in helping students develop self-esteem, more positive attitudes, and more self-confidence. One of the oldest established adventure-based programs is Outward Bound USA. This program operates through regional centers across the United States and for decades has provided students with a variety of adventure-based activities. This program has been studied more than any other outdoor education program, and its success, particularly with at-risk students, has been clearly demonstrated. Outward Bound courses include rock climbing, sailing, river adventure, hiking, and other trust- and responsibility-building experiences that help students discover their own limits and inner resources. Activities such as these, especially for students with little or no success in their schools or communities, have proven to be powerful in building self-concept, self-respect, and motivation for learning.

In the early 1990s, Outward Bound USA developed Expeditionary Learning, a comprehensive K–12 school improvement program that is based on two fundamental ideas: that students learn better by doing than by listening and that the development of character, high expectations, and a sense of community are just as important as developing academic skills and knowledge. Outward Bound's Expeditionary Learning approach includes the following core practices (Godfrey 1980):

- **Learning Expeditions**: Long-term, multidisciplinary projects combine academic, service, and physical education.
- **Reflection and Critique**: Teachers work with each other to expand their own instruction and students' worth.
- **Cultivating School Culture**: The school culture emphasizes community and collaboration, high expectations for all students, service, and cultural diversity.
- **Improving School Structure**: The school reorganizes to include shared decision making among teachers and administrators and to develop positive relationships among staff, students, parents, and the community.

More than 120 schools throughout the country are currently using the approach, and, even though the program is relatively new, a significant amount of research has indicated significant gains, particularly for at-risk youth (Herman 1999; Ulichny 2000).

RESEARCH

- Community-based learning greatly benefits the academic success of at-risk students.
- Community learning, especially service learning and adventure-based education, can have a profound impact on the academic, social, and emotional growth of students, especially at-risk students with limited life successes.
- Engaging students in out-of-school learning in the community or in outdoor settings is very influential in the development of students' positive self-concepts, motivation, attitudes, behavior, and academic concepts, as well as career choices.

TAKE ACTION

- ☑ **Add a community-based component to any class.** No matter what the curriculum content of a class, help enrich and motivate students by adding a "non-book" community component to their courses.
- ☑ **Establish service learning or academic and career internships.** Work with other educators to provide service learning opportunities for every student. Students at the middle and high school levels should be provided not only with service learning opportunities but also with opportunities to participate in short-term career explorations and job shadowing. Many will also be ready for and benefit from extended internships.
- ☑ **Learn about community-based learning.** Participate in professional development experiences to learn effective approaches and models for community-based learning.
- ☑ **Frequently monitor the effectiveness of the program.** It is likely that any program will need regular adjustment, and frequent monitoring of the program's effectiveness will provide valuable insight into addressing these issues.

See the "50 Strategies Suggested Reading" section for a list of resources selected to complement the fifty strategies as you put them to use in your classroom.

SAVING MY STUDENTS, SAVING MY SCHOOL

How can **Strategy #48: Embrace the Community as a Classroom** be put to use in your classroom? What can you do to increase awareness and education among your group of colleagues?

_____

_____

_____

_____

_____

_____

_____

_____

_____

Share your thoughts with a colleague or group of colleagues.

STRATEGY #49

Develop Communitywide, Extended-Day Programs

After I started visiting the homes and neighborhoods of my students, I suddenly realized how important it was for the kids to have a safe place to be after school. Our little latchkey program has grown and expanded to include recreation, tutoring, a nutritional snack, and a lot of fun. Of course, it is also a safe, supervised environment. You know, I believe our afterschool programs are as important as our school program.

—Teacher, Wyoming

Because so many at-risk students arrive at school with learning needs that must be remediated, live in impoverished home situations where it is often difficult to complete homework assignments, and are too often left alone and unsupervised for hours at the end of the school day, schools have become more and more forceful in developing programs to supplement the "regular" academic school day. For years, research has documented the negative impact of pullout remediation programs that deny an uninterrupted school day to those students who need it most. As a result, extended-day programs and various approaches to reorganize the school day have been developed and are proving to be far more effective than pullout programs.

Millions of children and youth in the United States have little positive support in their lives other than what they receive from school. Consequently, schools are developing extended days designed to provide at-risk students the support they need to catch up and accelerate their learning, to participate in supervised recreation, and to help assist students with daily homework assignments.

Teasing, bullying, vandalism, and other types of youth crime increase during a particular time of day—from approximately 3 p.m. to 7 p.m., when most adults are at work. This is also the time when most teenagers experiment with sex, access pornographic Web sites, experiment with drugs and alcohol, and get pregnant. If ever an entire community needs to come together to raise a child, it is certainly in the afterschool hours. Few other educational issues lend themselves so productively as communitywide collaboration in offering afterschool programs.

At-risk children and youth living in dysfunctional family situations are not lacking in intelligence or in their ability to learn. What often places these students at such a disadvantage is that too often, their home situations do not enrich school learning because they fail to provide adequate support to maintain and enhance the learning that occurs at school. To be effective with at-risk students, schools must develop extended-day programs and enrichments to support academic learning without interrupting classroom teaching and learning.

Schools alone cannot adequately address the diverse and complex needs of students. To have the range of services and the needed resources to assist students in the afterschool hours, when young people so often find themselves unsupervised and with time on their hands, schools must work to partner with the following entities:

- Public libraries
- Boys/Girls Clubs
- YMCA/YWCA
- 4-H clubs
- Big Brothers/Big Sisters of America programs
- Police athletic leagues
- Parks and recreation
- Boy Scouts, Girls Scouts, and Campfire Girl programs
- Faith-based organizations
- Law enforcement agencies

Dr. Olatokunbo S. Fashola, senior research scientist with the American Institutes for Research and adjunct research scientist with Johns Hopkins University, in her book *Building Effective Afterschool Programs* (2002), recognizes the need for schools to work closely with community-based, afterschool programs such as those listed above. She cautions, however, that afterschool programs should never be used to replace daily instruction, but instead should be used to supplement what children learn during the day.

Many schools that are successful with at-risk youth consider extended-day programs vital to their programs. A number of these schools attract working parents from great distances. For decades, one of the most popular magnet schools in Houston, Texas, has had the extended-day program, in part because of the advantages it offers to both parents and students. For parents who leave for work before the traditional school day begins and do not finish their workdays until after school is over, these programs offer a welcome alternative to a number of undesirable options that working parents regularly encounter. In Springfield, Virginia, public schools at all levels use before- and afterschool programs for student enrichment. Extended-day programs often offer gymnastics, intramural sports, chess, art, and music enrichment programs, in addition to academic activities. Many schools now offer free breakfast and nutritionally sound afterschool snacks. Every school should seriously consider the valuable advantages of before- and afterschool programs.

For at-risk students, such programs provide additional time for tutoring, homework, and cultural enrichment. Extended-day programs help at-risk youth to catch up and accelerate their learning without pulling them out of their regular classes. Extended-day programs may be staffed with teacher aides, student teachers, parents, or other volunteers. Before- and afterschool enrichment programs also provide a wonderful means to solicit and gain community, business, and volunteer support. Many community service clubs support these programs, and many schools use these programs to mobilize parent and other community volunteers. If a college or university is nearby, before- and afterschool programs can be largely staffed with older students serving as cross-age tutors to help younger students.

Before- and afterschool programs can also include supervised playtime and personal development activities, while simultaneously saving children from lonely time at home in an unsupervised situation. Many programs develop one-on-one tutoring programs for children who need reading assistance. They provide students with a supportive place to complete their homework, to get tutorial assistance from other students or from adults, and to have library and computer resources available for their work.

The federal government is now supporting afterschool and summer programs at 3,600 rural and urban public schools in 903 communities through the 21st Century Community Learning Centers Program. This effort, initiated by a partnership between the Charles Stuart Mott Foundation and the U.S. Department of Education, is demonstrating a remarkable, positive impact on at-risk students.

Another recent development in enrichment is the extension of these afterschool programs to the regular school day. For at-risk students, opportunities to catch up and accelerate their learning cannot be left for volunteer programs before and after school that are often at the mercy of bus schedules, dwindling budgets, or parental whims. The Brazosport, Texas, School District, along with a growing number of other districts, has reorganized the entire school day to provide one hour, 2:30 p.m. to 3:30 p.m., of intensive tutorials for students in need of acceleration to catch up and enrichment programs for those students already performing well academically.

MAKING AFTERSCHOOL TIME COUNT

Periodic newsletter of the Charles Stewart Mott Foundation, no longer published. Archives available at http://www.mott.org/publications.aspx

---

RESEARCH

- Remedial pullout programs that disrupt a student's daily academic schedule show little evidence of effectiveness.
- Inability to complete homework has been identified as one of the primary factors in students' decisions to drop out of school.
- Homework assignments can actually punish children and youth living in poverty or in dysfunctional families because these students often have little or no support or resources for completing their assignments outside of school.
- Children of poverty may often be deprived of the cultural, recreational, and academic experiences that are so essential to success in learning.
- Most teenage crime and risky behavior occur during the unsupervised time between 3 p.m. and 7 p.m., when there are few adults in the home and neighborhood.

TAKE ACTION

☑ **Develop before- and afterschool programs.** Provide resources, services, recreation, and academic enrichment before and after school. Find volunteers in the community and among colleagues to staff these programs.

☑ **Reorganize the school day.** Extend each class period so that students can complete their homework assignments while teachers are available to provide assistance. Reorganize the school day to provide direct enrichment to needy students without pulling them out of regular classes.

☑ **Seek allies.** Many schools staff before- and afterschool programs with older students and university students. Cooperative programs with the YMCA/YWCA, Boys and Girls Clubs, and other organizations can fill this gap in the afterschool time.

☑ **Frequently monitor the effectiveness of the program.** Rich data on student gain should characterize the program. It is likely that any program will need regular adjustment, and frequent monitoring of the program's effectiveness will identify issues that need to be addressed.

See the "50 Strategies Suggested Reading" section for a list of resources selected to complement the fifty strategies as you put them to use in your classroom.

SAVING MY STUDENTS, SAVING MY SCHOOL

How can **Strategy #49: Develop Communitywide, Extended-Day Programs** be put to use in your classroom? What can you do to increase awareness and education among your group of colleagues?

Share your thoughts with a colleague or group of colleagues.

STRATEGY #50

Become a Full-Service School

What a storm we caused when we established a small health center in our high school! But we weathered the storm because we knew that none of these kids' families had health insurance and that the students were participating in some of the most reckless behaviors that were placing their health and well-being at risk. While these tough kids would not listen to teachers or follow our advice, it's remarkable how much attention they give to the nurses.

—School Counselor, Georgia

The more that is known about at-risk students, the more it is recognized that schools deal with only a very small part of the problem. It is increasingly obvious how significant a student's family situation, socioeconomic level, and a wide variety of risky student behaviors (including tobacco, drug, and alcohol abuse; and community violence) can all but overwhelm even the best efforts of high school programs. Every day, of the 40 million children and youth who arrive at school, one in four—10 million elementary and secondary students—are at high risk of school failure. In many communities, almost every student has some level of serious social, emotional, or health issue. Some have compared these school and community situations to life in a developing country, in which people are isolated and abandoned by the mainstream society.

Joy Dryfoos, author of *Full-Service Schools* (1998), maintains that schools today must

- feed children;
- provide psychological support services;
- offer health services;
- offer health screening;
- establish referral networks related to substance abuse, child welfare, and sexual abuse;
- cooperate with the local police and probation officers;
- add curricula for prevention of substance abuse, teen pregnancies, suicide, and violence; and
- actively promote social skills, good nutrition, safety, and general health. (p. 5)

Can schools do all this and still provide high-quality education? Recent incidents of school violence have further increased the pressure on schools to supplement academic programs with the widest range of services. The results of these pressures have led to a call for "one-stop," "seamless," coordinated health and social services. In the past ten years, districts from throughout the United States have heeded this call by creating full-service high school programs.

Many high schools and a growing number of middle and elementary schools have established school-based health centers. While almost always controversial, these clinics build on a long tradition of having a school nurse in the building and relate directly to some of the major health-related dangers to healthy adolescent development: pregnancy, venereal disease, AIDS, and substance, tobacco, and alcohol abuse.

In some schools, as many as 40 percent of the students take advantage of health services when they are available, since many of these students have no other form of health care. Clinics also reduce the number of teenage pregnancies in the school (even though the role of the clinic in preventing pregnancies is one of the intervention's greatest controversies). The goals of most programs are to provide for comprehensive, ongoing health care and health education as well as crisis intervention. Clinics are often operated through partnerships between the school and community-based social service agencies and hospitals, which work together to move services closer to the needs of adolescents.

School health clinics are increasingly important because of the continuing scarcity of health care facilities for adolescents. Unfortunately, the Center for Population Options reported in 1991 that there were only 327 such centers in thirty-three states and Puerto Rico. More than half of the users of these clinics reported they had no other health care. While 51 percent of the centers serve high schools, centers serve middle schools and elementary schools as well. In 1988, there were fewer than 100 school-based health centers. By 1998, there were more than 1,000 (37 percent based at high schools). In addition to traditional health services, school health clinics provide physical examinations, treatment, screening, pregnancy tests, and psychological services (C. Tomlinson 1999).

Several recent reports regarding the possible effects on teen behavior are very encouraging. In New York City, students who use the clinics miss fewer days of school. In Kansas City, the clinics reported a significant decline in the number of adolescents who used alcohol or drugs or tobacco (C. Tomlinson 1999). Similar findings are expected as more data become available.

RESEARCH

- The more that is known about the challenges and problems of at-risk children and youth, the more remarkable it is that many of these students even make it to school, let alone experience academic success.
- Schools lack the resources to provide the broad range of social and health services that so many at-risk students need.
- Studies of full-service schools have reported that students miss school less often. School health clinics also have a positive effect on reducing drug, alcohol, and tobacco use.
- With 25 percent or more of our nation's children living in poverty, schools increasingly must assist students beyond their academic needs.

TAKE ACTION

- ☑ **Understand the problems and challenges of youth.** Recognize and identify youth problems with substance abuse, alcohol, tobacco, and sexual behaviors. National data from the National Centers for Disease Control's biennial Youth Risk Behavior Survey provide an excellent means of obtaining insight into the risky behavior of today's youth. The Search Institute's Community Assets Survey (<www.search-institute.org>) provides another powerful source of data focused on the needs and available sources of support to youth in a community.
- ☑ **Seek allies.** Collaborate with social agencies, hospitals, mental health clinics, YMCA/YWCA, Boys and Girls Clubs, law enforcement agencies, and other service providers in identifying resources and needed services for students.
- ☑ **Coordinate school and community resources and services.** Work aggressively with community agencies and organizations to encourage partnerships to provide needed resources and services at the school level.
- ☑ **Engage stakeholders.** Most people in the community have either a direct connection or vested interest in the needs of at-risk students. Find them and solicit their support and assistance.

See the "50 Strategies Suggested Reading" section for a list of resources selected to complement the fifty strategies as you put them to use in your classroom.

SAVING MY STUDENTS, SAVING MY SCHOOL

How can **Strategy #50: Become a Full-Service School** be put to use in your classroom? What can you do to increase awareness and education among your group of colleagues?

_____

_____

_____

_____

_____

_____

_____

_____

_____

_____

Share your thoughts with a colleague or group of colleagues.

PART III

Summon the Will to Leave No Child Behind

15

The Inalienable Right to a Quality Education

It suddenly dawned on me that today a high-quality education is a prerequisite to success in life. As a result, education has become the most basic civil right. It is the birthright of every child born in America. Anything less than a high-quality education denies our children the promises of the American dream.

—Teacher, Wisconsin

WITH LIBERTY AND JUSTICE FOR SOME?

The battleground for the civil rights of our nation's children is the reform-weary world of public education. After decades of civil rights battles for school desegregation, equal opportunity, and affirmative action, a growing national consensus is emerging. The consensus is clearly focused on ensuring that all public school students, regardless of race or socio-economic level, learn effectively and achieve satisfactory academic standards. Whether or not it was ever true, the concept of providing all students an *equal opportunity* to learn is being replaced at the federal and state levels with the mandated expectation that all students will achieve established, acceptable academic standards.

This is not to say that the civil rights movement in the United States will not continue with contentious human rights litigation and legislation as combatants battle over abortion, voting, assisted suicide, gender issues, equal access to jobs, hate crimes, workplace discrimination, and other important issues. Today, there is a growing awareness that high-quality education is a fundamental and inalienable civil right all of the nation's citizens.

THE EMERGENT NATIONAL CONSENSUS: NO CHILD LEFT BEHIND

Our nation's most sacred government documents did not endorse liberty and justice for *some*. After many years, a national consensus is emerging in the United States to educate all students effectively. This has taken shape for a number of reasons (see Figure 15.1 and the discussion that follows).

A National Consensus to Educate Every Student

- Compelling research
- School effectiveness
- Changes in the international marketplace

Figure 15.1

Compelling Research

First, there has been a dramatic increase in educational, neurobiological, and social science research in recent years revealing that teaching is both an art and, for the first time, a science. This new science is growing out of studies that have followed children for decades into adulthood, research on the teaching of reading, and research on effective schools. The nexus of this research has clearly documented that all children can, in fact, learn effectively. Furthermore, it has been documented conclusively that schools can overcome the debilitating effects of poverty and dysfunctional families and help children and youth achieve high levels of academic proficiency. In addition, this research has verified the reality that quality teachers indeed make a critical difference in student achievement.

School Effectiveness

Effective education is no longer a theory; research has documented a growing list of high-performing schools that are effectively educating all students, even those at risk. As more is learned about these schools, our nation has grown confident that public education in the United States can indeed educate all students effectively.

Changes in the International Marketplace

The technological revolution has transformed the world of commerce. The industrial age has given way to a new era of technology, information, and service. Today, everyone must be able to read, acquire high-level cognitive skills, and be technologically literate to access good jobs and a satisfactory income. Today, all students need the education skills that our previous generation provided only for the elite few.

BREAKING FREE FROM IGNORANCE

The world of work known to the adults of the twentieth century has vanished. It has been replaced with the age of the mind: education has become the only door of opportunity in the United States and, increasingly, throughout the world. Hard work, perseverance, and determination are no longer sufficient to realize the American dream. It is education that separates the rich from the poor; the haves from the have-nots; and those who enjoy the life, liberty, and justice of the American dream from those who do not. Today, it is education that creates, sustains, and perpetuates this difference.

To attain equal social, political, and economic rights, a high-quality education is essential. Unfortunately, despite decades of school reform and school improvement, court cases, policy shifts, and legislation, too many students have been left behind. For many, public education in this country continues to represent an educational apartheid no less destructive than the racial apartheid that characterized the early years of our country and, too often, cultures around the world. This educational separation has been practiced and perpetuated throughout our history under a wide variety of insidious political and legal concepts, all resulting in the continued failure of at-risk students. In the past, apartheid was practiced through school segregation and separate-but-equal schools. More recently, separation was perpetuated through attendance boundaries and state educational school funding formulas that allowed for rich schools and poor schools, for high-performing schools and failing schools—what Jonathan Kozol (1991) termed a "savage inequality." Tracking, retention, expulsion, and special education have been used to sort, stigmatize, isolate, and abandon more than 25 percent of our nation's children and youth.

Yet today, for the first time in history, our nation has set a goal of educating all children to acceptable levels of academic achievement. This is easily one of the most significant developments ever to occur in public education, anywhere in the world, at any time. To truly succeed in leaving no child behind, the fifty strategies detailed in this book provide schools and communities with specific direction, methodology, and hope.

THE FIFTY STRATEGIES

Teachers and schools need effective strategies for successfully educating all students, particularly for our most at-risk children and youth. The fifty strategies illustrated in this book, representing decades of research and effective practice, serve as a plan to ensure that all students succeed. When these strategies are used, students can and will achieve to proficiency, and failing educational programs will be transformed into high-performing schools. Each of these strategies works; the evidence is clear. Furthermore, the use of these strategies appears to have a cumulative effect: the more of the strategies that are employed together in schools and classrooms, the greater the power to ensure that all students learn. The racism, class prejudice, and apartheid of ignorance that has divided our nation of learners is currently giving way to a new age, where all children are learning effectively and achieving skills necessary for the good life. It is at last becoming possible to leave no child behind.

Achieving this goal will not come easily. Experienced teachers must learn new and more effective approaches to teaching and learning. Schools must change; they must be restructured to create the essential educational environment for effective education. School boards and legislatures must create new educational policy, and, most important, districts, schools, and teachers must be held accountable. We must move beyond the aesthetics of education—the feel-good world of teaching and learning—and transform our classrooms from offering what teachers enjoy or are comfortable doing to offering what is effective. We must establish high standards for all children and youth; align curriculum, instruction, and assessment with those standards; better prepare preservice teachers; and provide targeted professional development for practicing teachers.

It is particularly encouraging that landmark research begun in the last decades of the twentieth century has continued to identify the necessary components to achieve the goals of proficiency and effective education for all students. Today, this goal has become a reality in a growing number of districts and schools nationwide. Yet the challenge is to hold firm to these goals until they become a reality in the life of every child. We cannot be content with providing freedom and justice for some; the American dream must be fulfilled so that all children, regardless of race or economic status, can achieve their potential and access the life, liberty, and pursuit of happiness that has been the promise to all of our citizens as their birthright. We cannot leave any child behind.

Only the future will tell whether we have the will to fulfill this hope for all our nation's children. We clearly know, as of 2008, how to accomplish the essential challenge to save our students and our schools. Yet the question remains: Do we have the will to make it happen?

50 Strategies
Suggested Reading

Strategy #1:

Barr, R. D., and W. H. Parrett. 2001. *Hope fulfilled for at-risk and violent youth: K–12 programs that work* (2d ed.). Needham Heights, MA: Allyn & Bacon.

Frieman, B. B. 2001. *What teachers need to know about children at risk.* Boston: McGraw-Hill.

Strategy #2:

Benson, P. L., J. Galbraith, and P. Espeland. 1998. *What kids need to succeed.* Minneapolis, MN: Free Spirit.

Strategy #3:

Benard, B. 1991. *Fostering resiliency in kids: Protective factors in the family, school, and community.* Portland, OR: Northwest Regional Educational Laboratory.

Brooks, R., and S. Goldstein. 2001. *Raising resilient children.* Chicago: Contemporary Books.

Brown, J. H., M. D'Emidio-Caston, and B. Benard. 2001. *Resilience education.* Thousand Oaks, CA: Corwin Press.

Krovetz, M. L. 1999. *Fostering resiliency: Expecting all students to use their minds and hearts as well.* Thousand Oaks, CA: Corwin Press.

Strategy #4:

Gurian, M. 2001. *Boys and girls learn differently! A guide for teachers and parents.* San Francisco: Jossey-Bass.

Pipher, M. 1996. *Reviving Ophelia: Saving the selves of adolescent girls.* New York: Random House.

Pollack, W. 1998. *Real boys: Rescuing our sons from the myths of boyhood.* New York: Owl Books.

Pollack, W., and K. Cushman. 2001. *Real boys workbook: Exercises and advice about how to help boys be successful.* New York: Villard.

Pollack, W., and T. Shuster. 2000. *Real boys' voices: Anecdotes written by boys about their lives.* Toronto, ON: Penguin Books.

Strategy #5:

Bempechat, J. 1999. Learning from poor and minority students who succeed in school. *Harvard Education Letter* 15(3): 1–3.

Brendtro, L. K., M. Brokenleg, and S. Van Bockern. 1990. *Reclaiming youth at risk.* Bloomington, IN: National Educational Service.

Comer, J. P. 1980. *School power: Implications of an intervention project.* New York: Free Press.

Comer, J. P., M. Ben-Avie, N. M. Haynes, and E. T. Joyner, eds. 1999. *Child by child: The Comer process for change in education.* New York: Teachers College Press.

Comer, J. P., N. M. Haynes, E. T. Joyner, and M. Ben-Avie, eds. 1996. *Rallying the whole village: The Comer process for reforming education.* New York: Teachers College Press.

Delpit, L. 1995. *Other people's children.* New York: New Press.

Haberman, M. 1991. Pedagogy of poverty versus good teaching. *Phi Delta Kappan* 73(4): 290–294.

Kohl, H. 1994. *I won't learn from you and other thoughts on creative maladjustment.* New York: New Press.

Kuykendall, C. 1992. *From rage to hope.* Bloomington, IN: National Education Service.

Ladson-Billings, G. 1994. *The dreamkeepers: Successful teachers of African-American children.* San Francisco: Jossey-Bass.

McLaughlin, B., and B. McLeod. 1996. *Educating all our students from culturally and linguistically diverse backgrounds,* vol. 1. Santa Cruz, CA: National Center for Research in Cultural Diversity and Second-Language Learning.

Reyes, P., J. D. Scribner, and A. P. Scribner. 1999. *Lessons from high-performing Hispanic schools.* New York: Teachers College Press.

Ryan, M. 2003. *Ask the teacher: A practitioner's guide to teaching and learning in the diverse classroom.* Boston: Allyn & Bacon.

Sanders, M. G., ed. 2000. *Schooling students placed at risk: Research, policy, and practice in the education of poor and minority adolescents.* Mahwah, NJ: Lawrence Erlbaum.

Stringfield, S., and D. Land, eds. 2002. *Educating at-risk students* (Yearbook of National Society for the Study of Education, vol. 101, part 2). Chicago: University of Chicago Press.

Stringfield, S., and D. Land, eds. 2002. The extent and consequence of risk in U.S. education. In *Educating at-risk students* (Yearbook of National Society for the Study of Education, vol. 101, part 2, pp. 1–28), edited by S. Stringfield and D. Land. Chicago: University of Chicago Press.

Strategy #6:

Conrath, J. 1988. A new deal for at-risk students. *NASSP Bulletin* 72(504): 36–40.

Conrath, J. 2001. Changing the odds for young people: Next steps for alternative education. *Phi Delta Kappan* 82(8): 585–587.

Strategy #7:

Books, S., ed. 1998. *Invisible children in the society and its schools.* Mahwah, NJ: Lawrence Erlbaum.

Bracey, G. W. 2002. Raising achievement of at-risk students—or not. *Phi Delta Kappan* 83(6): 431–432.

Bracey, G. W. 2002. What students do in the summer. *Phi Delta Kappan* 83(7): 497–498.

Coleman, J., et al. 1966. *Equality of educational opportunities.* Paper prepared for a Harvard conference on the U.S. Office of Education Report on "Equality of Educational Opportunity," October 21, 1967, Cambridge, MA.

Epstein, J. 2001. *School, family, and community partnerships: Preparing educators and improving schools.* Boulder, CO: Westview.

Jerald, C. D. 2001. *Dispelling the myth revisited: Preliminary findings from a nation-wide analysis of "high-flying" schools.* Washington, DC: Education Trust. (ERIC Document Reproduction Service No. ED462485)

Parnell, D. 1982. *Neglected minority.* Washington, DC: Community College Press.

Sanders, W. L., and J. C. Rivers. 1996. *Cumulative and residual effects of teachers on future student academic achievement.* Research Progress Report. Knoxville, University of Tennessee, Value-Added Research and Assessment Center.

Schorr, L. B., and D. Schorr. 1989. *Within our reach: Breaking the cycle of the disad-vantaged.* New York: Anchor Books.

Teddlie, C., and S. Stringfield. 1993. *Schools make a difference: Lessons learned from a ten-year study of school effects.* New York: Teachers College Press.

Wright, S. P., S. P. Horn, and W. L. Sanders. 1997. Teacher and classroom context effects on student achievement: Implications for teacher evaluation. *Journal of Personnel Evaluation in Education* 11(1): 57–67.

Strategy #8:

Darling-Hammond, L. 1998. Alternatives to grade retention. *The School Administrator* 55(7): 18–21.

Fager, J., and R. Richen. 1999. *When students don't succeed: Shedding light on grade retention.* Portland, OR: Northwest Regional Educational Laboratory.

Haberman, M., and V. Dill. 1993. The knowledge-base on retention vs. teacher ideology: Implication for teacher preparation. *Journal of Teacher Education* 44(5): 352–360.

Kozol, J. 1991. *Savage inequalities: Children in America's schools.* New York: Hayser Perennial.

Oakes, J. 1993. *Last Chance High: How girls and boys drop in and out of alternative schools.* New Haven, CT: Yale University Press.

Wheelock, A. 1992. *Crossing the tracks: How "untracking" can save America's schools.* New York: New Press.

Strategy #9:

Dryfoos, J. G. 1998. *Full-service schools: A revolution in health and social services for children, youth, and families.* San Francisco: Jossey-Bass.

Schargel, F. P., and J. Smink. 2001. *Strategies to help solve our school dropout problem.* Larchmont, NY: Eye on Education.

Strategy #10:

Cawelti, G., and N. Protheroe. 2001. *How six school districts changed into high-performance systems.* Arlington, VA: Educational Research Service.

DuFour, R., and R. Eaker. 1998. *Professional learning communities at work: Best practices for enhancing student achievement.* Bloomington, IN: National Education Service.

Schmoker, M. 1999. *Results: The key to continuous school improvement.* Alexandria, VA: Association for Supervision and Curriculum Development.

Walsh, J. A., and B. D. Sattes. 2000. *Inside school improvement: Creating high-performing learning communities.* Charleston, WV: Appalachian Educational Laboratory.

Strategy #11:

Comprehensive Center. 2001. *Using data for educational decision-making.* Madison: University of Wisconsin.

Holcomb, E. L. 1999. *Getting excited about data: How to combine people, passion, and proof.* Thousand Oaks, CA: Corwin Press.

Peters, T. 1987. *Thriving on chaos.* New York: Alfred Knopf.

Strategy #12:

Deming, W. E. 1986. *Out of the crisis.* Cambridge: Massachusetts Institute of Technology Press.

Northwest Regional Educational Laboratory. 1990. *Effective school practices: A research synthesis 1990 update.* Portland, OR: Author.

Schmoker, M. 2001. *The results handbook.* Alexandria, VA: Association for Supervision and Curriculum Development.

Williams, R. B., and S. Dunn. 1999. *Brain-compatible learning for the block.* Thousand Oaks, CA: Corwin Press.

Strategy #13:

Cromey, A. D. 2001. Data retreats: A conduit for change in schools. *Using Data for Educational Decision-Making: The Newsletter of the Comprehensive Center—Region VI* 6(1): 21–23.

National Commission on Time and Learning. 1994. *Prisoners of time.* Washington, DC: U.S. Government Printing Office.

Raywid, M. A. 1993. Finding time for collaboration. *Educational Leadership* 51(2): 30–34.

Strategy #14:

Collins, J. 2001. *Good to great: Why some companies make the leap—And others don't.* New York: HarperBusiness.

Glickman, C. D. 2002. *Leadership for learning: How to help teachers succeed.* Alexandria, VA: Association for Supervision and Curriculum Development.

Massell, D. 2000. *The district's role in building capacity: Four strategies.* Philadelphia: Consortium for Policy Research in Education.

Shewhart, W. A. 1939. *Statistical method from the viewpoint of quality control.* Washington, DC: Department of Agriculture.

Strategy #15:

Chavkin, N. F. 1989. Debunking the myth about minority parents. *Educational Horizons* 67(4): 119–123.

Epstein, J. L. 1995. School/family/community partnerships: Caring for the children we share. *Phi Delta Kappan* 76(9): 701–712.

Epstein, J. L., M. G. Sanders, B. S. Simon, K. Salinas, J. Clark, N. Rodriquez, and F. L. VanVoorhis. 2002. *School, family, and community partnerships: Your handbook for action* (2d ed.). Thousand Oaks, CA: Corwin Press.

Jackson, B. L., and B. S. Cooper. 1993. Involving parents in urban high schools. *Education Digest* 58(8): 27–31.

Jones, R. 2001. How parents can support learning. *American School Board Journal* 188(9): 18–22.

National PTA. 1998. *National standards for parent/family involvement programs.* Chicago: Author.

Sanders, M. G. 1996. *School-family-community partnerships and the academic achievement of African American, urban adolescents* (Report #7). Baltimore, MD: Center for Research on the Education of Students Placed at Risk. (ERIC Document Reproduction Service No. ED402404)

Yap, K. O., and D. Y. Enoki. 1995. In search of the elusive magic bullet: Parental involvement and student outcomes. *School Community Journal* 5(2): 97–106.

Strategy #16:

Amundson, K. J. 1991. *101 ways parents can help students achieve.* Arlington, VA: American Association of School Administrators.

Center for the Study of Reading. 1988. *Ten ways to help your children become better readers* (An excerpt from *Becoming a Nation of Readers*). Urbana-Champaign: University of Illinois, Center for the Study of Reading. (ERIC Document Reproduction Service No. 347496)

Cotton, K. 2000. *The schooling practices that matter most.* Portland, OR: Northwest Regional Educational Laboratory.

Northwest Regional Educational Laboratory. 1998. *Easy ways for families to help children learn.* Portland, OR: Author.

Strategy #17:

Burke, K. 2000. *What to do with the kid who . . . : Developing cooperation, self-discipline, and responsibility in the classroom.* Thousand Oaks, CA: Corwin Press.

Kohl, H. 1994. *I won't learn from you and other thoughts on creative maladjustment.* New York: New Press.

Northwest Regional Educational Laboratory. 1990. *Effective schooling practices: A research synthesis, 1990 update.* Portland, OR: Author.

Strategy #18:

Levin, H. M. 1989. *Accelerated schools: A new strategy for at-risk students* (Policy Bulletin #6). Bloomington, IN: Consortium for Educational Policy Studies.

National Clearinghouse for Educational Facilities Center for School Change. 2001. *Smaller, safer, saner successful schools.* Minneapolis: Hubert Humphrey Institute of the University of Minnesota.

Senge, P. 2000. *Schools that learn: A Fifth Discipline fieldbook for educators, parents, and everyone who cares about education.* New York: Doubleday/Currency.

Wehlage, G. G., R. A. Rutter, G. A. Smith, N. Lesko, and R. R. Fernandez. 1989. *Reducing the risk: Schools as communities of support.* Philadelphia: Falmer.

Strategy #19:

Barr, R. D., and W. H. Parrett. 1997. *How to create alternative, magnet, and charter schools that work.* Bloomington, IN: National Education Service.

Gamoran, A. 1996. Do magnet schools boost achievement? *Educational Leadership* 54(2): 42–46.

Hardy, L. 2000. Public school choice. *American School Board Journal* 187(2): 22–26.

Maslow, A. 1962. *Toward a psychology of being.* Princeton, NJ: Nostrand Reinhold.

Nathan, J. 1996. *Charter schools: Creating hope and opportunity for American education.* San Francisco: Jossey-Bass.

Smith, G. R., T. B. Gregory, and R. C. Pugh. 1981. Meeting student needs: Evidence of the superiority of alternative schools. *Phi Delta Kappan* 62(8): 561–564.

West, P. 1996. Career academies appear to benefit students and teachers. *Education Week*, June 19, 15.

Strategy #20:

Clinchy, E. 2000. *Creating new schools: How small schools are changing American education.* New York: Teachers College Press.

Jackson, A. W., and G. A. Davis. 2000. *Turning points 2000: Educating adolescents in the 21st century.* New York: Teachers College Press.

National Association of Secondary School Principals. 1996. Breaking ranks: Changing an American institution. A report of the National Association of Secondary School Principals on the high school of the 21st century. *NASSP Bulletin* 80(578): 55–66.

Strategy #21:

Janey, C. B. 2002. Must high school last four years? *Educational Leadership* 59(7): 64–67.

Pianta, R. C., and M. J. Cox 1999. *The transition to kindergarten.* Baltimore, MD: Brookes.

Strategy #22:

Duke, D. L. 2002. *Creating safe schools for all children.* Boston: Allyn & Bacon.

Education Commission of the States. 1996. *Youth violence: A policy maker's guide.* Denver, CO: Author.

U.S. Department of Education. 1998. *Early warning, timely response: A guide to safe schools.* Washington, DC: Author.

Strategy #23:

Banks, R. 1997. *Bullying in schools.* Eric Digest. (Eric Document Reproduction Service No. ED407154)

Beane, A. L. 1999. *The bully-free classroom: Over one hundred tips and strategies for teachers K–8.* Minneapolis, MN: Free Spirit.

Fager, J., and S. Boss. 1998. *Peaceful schools.* Portland, OR: Northwest Regional Educational Laboratory.

Portner, J. 2001. Lost children. *Teacher Magazine* 12(8): 31.

U.S. Department of Education. 1999. *Preventing bullying: A manual for schools and communities.* Washington, DC: Author.

Strategy #24:

Gronson, R. 2001. *At-risk students: Defy the odds.* Lanham, MD: Scarecrow.

Safe Schools and Communities Coalition, Correctional Office of Policy and Management, Juvenile Justice Advisory Committee. 1998, May. *Alternative education: A force for our future.* Washington, DC: Authors.

Strategy #25:

Hootstein, E. 1998. Motivating the unmotivated child. *Teaching PreK–8* 29(3): 58–59.

Levine, E. 2002. *One kid at a time: Big lessons from a small school.* New York: Teachers College Press.

Mendler, A. N. 2000. *Motivating students who don't care.* Bloomington, IN: National Education Service.

Mendler, A. N., and R. L. Carwin. 1998. Seven keys to motivating difficult students. *Reaching Today's Youth* 3(3): 13–15.

Strategy #26:

Campbell, L., and B. Campbell. 1999. *Multiple intelligences and student achievement: Success stories from six schools.* Alexandria, VA: Association for Supervision and Curriculum Development.

Fogarty, R. 1997. *Brain-compatible classrooms.* Thousand Oaks, CA: Corwin Press.

Gardner, H. 1999. *Intelligence reframed: Multiple intelligences for the 21st century.* New York: Basic Books.

Silver, H. F., et al. 2000. *So each may learn: Integrating learning styles and multiple intelligences.* Alexandria, VA: Association for Supervision and Curriculum Development.

Strategy #27:

Bracey, G. W. 1989. Moving around and dropping out. *Phi Delta Kappan* 70(5): 407–410.

Harrington-Lueker, D. 1998. Retention vs. social promotion. *School Administrator* 55(7): 6–12.

National Commission on the High School Senior Year. 2001. *The low opportunity of the senior year: Finding a better way* (Preliminary report, January 2001). Washington, DC: Author.

Strategy #28:

Darling-Hammond, L. 1997. *The right to learn: A blueprint for creating schools that work.* San Francisco: Jossey-Bass.

DuFour, R., and R. Eaker. 1998. *Professional learning communities at work: Best practices for enhancing student achievement.* Bloomington, IN: National Education Service.

Fullan, M. 2000. Revisioning professional development. *Journal of Staff Development* 21(3): 40.

National Board for Professional Teaching Standards. 1999. *What teachers should know and be able to do: The five core propositions.* Available at <www.nbpts .org/the_standards/the_five_core_propositio>

Stronge, J. H. 2002. *Qualities of effective teachers.* Alexandria, VA: Association for Supervision and Curriculum Development.

U.S. Department of Education. 1998. *Promising practices: New ways to improve teacher quality.* Washington, DC: Author.

Strategy #29:

Brandt, R. 2002. Customizing our schools: The case for diversified schooling. *Educational Leadership* 59(7): 12–19.

Gamoran, R. A. 1996. Student achievement in public magnet, public comprehensive, and private city high schools. *Educational Evaluation and Policy Analysis* 18(1): 1–8.

Stern, D., M. Raby, and C. Dayton. 1992. *Career academics: Partnerships for restructuring American high schools.* San Francisco: Jossey-Bass.

Vancouver Public Schools. 2001. *Report to the Community* 12(1): 107. Vancouver, BC, Canada.

Weertz, M. 2002. The benefits of themed schools. *Educational Leadership* 59(7): 68–71.

Strategy #30:

Bracey, G. W. 2002. Raising achievements of at-risk students—or not. *Phi Delta Kappan* 83(6): 431–432.

Fogarty, R. 1999. *How to raise test scores.* Thousand Oaks, CA: Corwin Press.

Gerstner, L. V., Jr. 2002. The tests we know we need. *New York Times.* March 14, Sec. A, p. 7.

Marzano, R. J., D. J. Pickering, and J. E. Pollock. 2001. *Classroom instruction that works: Researched-based strategies for increasing student achievement.* Alexandria, VA: Association for Supervision and Curriculum Development.

Popham, J. W. 2000. *Testing! Testing! What every parent should know about school tests.* Boston: Allyn & Bacon.

Readeance, J. E., T. W. Bean, and R. S. Baldwin. 2000. *Content area literacy: An integrated approach* (7th ed.). Dubuque, IA: Kendall/Hunt.

Strategy #31:

Cole, R. W. 1995. *Educating everybody's children: Diverse teaching strategies for diverse learners.* Alexandria, VA: Association for Supervision and Curriculum Development.

Hilliard, A., III. 1991. Do we have the will to educate all children? *Educational Leadership* 49(1): 31–36.

Schoenbach, R., C. Greenleaf, C. Cziko, and L. Hurwitz. 1999. *Reading for understanding: A guide to improving reading in middle and high school classrooms.* San Francisco: Jossey-Bass.

Slavin, R. E., and H. A. Madden. 1989. What works for students at risk: A research synthesis. *Educational Leadership* 46(5): 4–13.

Wasik, B., and R. E. Slavin. 1993. Preventing early reading failure with one-to-one tutoring: A review of five programs. *Reading Research Quarterly* 29(2): 179–200.

Wheaton, C., and S. Kay. 1999. Every child will learn to read—We guarantee it. *Educational Leadership* 57(2): 52–56.

Strategy #32:

Herman, R., project director. 1999. *An educator's guide to schoolwide reform* (Prepared by the American Institutes for Research). Washington, DC: American Institute for Research.

Manning, M. L., and L. Baruth. 2000. *Teaching learners at risk.* Norwood, MA: Christopher-Gordon.

Pinnell, G. S. 1990. Success for low achievers through Reading Recovery. *Educational Leadership* 48(1): 17–21.

Pinnell, G. S., et al. 1994. Comparing instructional models for the literacy education of high-risk first graders. *Reading Research Quarterly* 29(1): 8–39.

Schoenbach, R., C. Greenleaf, C. Cziko, and J. Hurwitz. 1999. *Reading for understanding: A guide to improving reading in middle and high school classrooms.* San Francisco: Jossey-Bass.

Slavin, R. E. 2000. Letter to the editor: Research overwhelmingly supports success for all. *Phi Delta Kappan* 81(7): 559–560.

Slavin, R. E., and O. S. Fashola. 1998. *Show me the evidence! Proven and promising programs for America's schools.* Thousand Oaks, CA: Corwin Press.

Stone, R. 2002. *Best practices for high school classrooms: What award-winning secondary teachers do.* Thousand Oaks, CA: Corwin Press.

Taylor, B. M., and P. D. Pearson. 2002. *Teaching reading: Effective schools, accomplished readers.* Mahwah, NJ: Lawrence Erlbaum.

Strategy #33:

Adler, J. 1998. The tutor age. *Newsweek,* March 30, 4 pp. 7–57.

Glasser, D. 2002. *High school tutors: Their impact on elementary students' reading fluency through implementing a research-based instructional model.* Doctoral Dissertation, Boise State University, Idaho.

Hermann, B., ed. 1994. *The volunteer tutor's toolbox.* Newark, DE: International Reading Association.

Slavin, R. E., N. L. Karseit, and B. A. Wasik. 1992. Preventing early school failure: What works. *Educational Leadership* 50(4): 10–18.

Slavin, R. E., and N. A. Madden. 1989. What works for students at risk: A research synopsis. *Educational Leadership* 46(5): 4–20.

Winter, S. 1986. Peers as paired reading tutors. *British Journal of Special Education* 13(3): 103–106.

Strategy #34:

Barnett, W. S. 1996. *Lives in the balance: Age 27 benefits cost analysis of the High/Scope Perry Preschool program.* Monographs of the High/Scope Educational Research Foundation, 11. Ypsilanti, MI: High/Scope Press.

ERIC Clearinghouse on Elementary and Early Childhood. 1993. *What should be learned from kindergarten?* Urbana, IL: Author.

Lang, C. N. 1992. *Head Start: New challenges, new champions.* Newton, MA: Education Development Center.

Pianta, R. C., and M. J. Cox. 1999. *The transition to kindergarten.* Baltimore, MD: Brookes.

Ramey, S. L., and C. T. Ramey. 1999. *Going to school: How to help your child succeed—A handbook for parents of children ages 3–8.* New York: Goddard.

Strategy #35:

Rasmussen, J. 1998. Looping—Discovering the benefits of multi-year teaching. *Education Update* 40(2): 1, 3.

Northwest Regional Educational Laboratory. 2001. Reading is thinking: Overcome literacy challenges. In *Using Educational Research and Development to Promote Success: 2001 Annual Report*, pp. 14–15. Portland, OR: Author.

Walser, N. 1998. Multi-age classrooms: An age-old grouping method is still evolving. *Harvard Education Newsletter* 14(1): 1–3.

Strategy #36:

Cotton, K. 2000. *The schooling practices that matter most.* Portland, OR: Northwest Regional Educational Laboratory.

Northwest Regional Educational Laboratory. 2001. Focus on improved reading achievement. In *Using Educational Research and Development to Promote Student Success: 2001 Annual Report* (pp. 16–17). Portland, OR: Author.

Northwest Regional Educational Laboratory. 2001. Unlock the power of data. In *Using Educational Research and Development to Promote Student Success: 2001 Annual Report* (pp. 12–13). Portland, OR: Author.

Strategy #37:

Keefe, J. W., and J. M. Jenkins. 1997. *Instruction and the learning environment.* Larchmont, NY: Eye on Education.

Keefe, J. W., and J. M. Jenkins. 2002. Personalized instruction. *Phi Delta Kappan* 83(6): 440–447.

Newmann, F. M., W. G. Secada, and G. G. Wehlage. 1995. *Guide to authentic instruction and assessment: Vision, standards, and scoring.* Madison: Wisconsin Center for Educational Research, University of Wisconsin.

Strategy #38:

Carr, J. F., and D. E. Harris. 2001. *Succeeding with standards: Linking curriculum, assessments, and action planning.* Alexandria, VA: Association for Supervision and Curriculum Development.

Easton, L. B. 2002. *The other side of curriculum.* Portsmouth, NH: Heinemann.

English, F. W. 1992. *Deciding what to teach and test.* Thousand Oaks, CA: Corwin Press.

Meier, D. 1995. *The power of their ideas: Lessons for America from a small school in Harlem.* Boston: Beacon.

Strategy #39:

Johnson, D. W., and R. T. Johnson. 1999. *Learning together and alone: Cooperative, competitive, and individualistic learning.* Boston: Allyn & Bacon.

Marzano, R. J. 1998. *A theory-based meta-analysis of research on instruction.* Aurora, CO: Mid-continent Research for Education and Learning.

Marzano, R. J., D. J. Pickering, and J. E. Pollock. 2001. *Classroom instruction that works: Research-based strategies for increasing student achievement.* Alexandria, VA: Association for Supervision and Curriculum Development.

Strong, R. W., H. F. Silver, and M. J. Perini. 2001. *Teaching what matters most: Standards and strategies for raising student achievement.* Alexandria, VA: Association for Supervision and Curriculum Development.

Strategy #40:

Cooper, H. 2001. *The battle over homework: An administrator's guide to setting sound and effective policies* (2d ed.). Thousand Oaks, CA: Corwin Press.

Cooper, H., J. C. Valentine, B. Nye, and J. J. Lindsay. 1999. Relationship between five afterschool activities and academic achievement. *Journal of Educational Psychology* 91: 1–10.

Marzano, R. J., J. S. Norford, D. E. Paynter, D. J. Pickering, and B. B. Gaddy. 2001. *A handbook for classroom instruction that works.* Alexandria, VA: Association for Supervision and Curriculum Development.

Muhlenbruck, L., H. Cooper, B. Nye, and J. J. Lindsay. 1999. Homework and achievement: Explaining the different relations at the elementary and secondary level. *Social Psychology of Education* 3(4): 295–317.

Tomlinson, C. 1999. *The differentiated classroom: Responding to the needs of all learners.* Alexandria, VA: Association for Supervision and Curriculum Development.

Strategy #41:

Cushman, K. 1997. Demonstrating student performance in essential schools. *Horace* 14(2): 51.

Kelly, K. 2001. Seeking a cure for senior-year slump. *Harvard Education Letter* 17(4): 1–4.

Mahoney, J. 2002. *Power and portfolios: Best practices for high school classrooms.* Portsmouth, NH: Heinemann.

National Commission on the High School Senior Year. 2001. *The lost opportunity of senior year: Finding a better way* (Preliminary Report, January 2001). Washington, DC: Author.

Osher, C. 2001. *The impact of the senior project.* Greensboro, NC: Regional Educational Laboratory at the SouthEast Regional Vision for Education (SERVE).

Wagner, T. 2002. *Making the grade: Reinventing America's schools.* New York: RoutledgeFalmer.

Weisstein, E. 2001. A high school diploma and more. *Educational Leadership* 58(6): 73–77.

Wisely, S. 1999. *The senior project: A road map to student success.* Medford, OR: Medford School District.

Strategy #42:

Eisenberg, M., and D. Johnson. 1996. *Computer skills for information problem solving: Learning and teaching technology in context.* ERIC Digest. (ERIC Document Reproduction Service No. ED392463)

Gordon, D. 2002. Curriculum access in the digital age. *Harvard Education Letter,* January/February.

Irving, L. C. 1999. *Falling through the Net: A report on the telecommunications and information technology gap in America.* Washington, DC: U.S. Department of Commerce, National Telecommunications and Information Administration.

Koetke, C. 1999. One size doesn't fit all. *Technos Quarterly* 8(2).

Peck, C., L. Cuban, L., and H. Kirkpatrick. 2002. Techno-promoter dreams, student realities: The effect of increased technology access on the high school experience. *Phi Delta Kappan* 83(6): 472–480.

Thorsen, C. 2003. *Tech Tactics: Instructional models for educational computing.* Boston: Allyn & Bacon.

Strategy #43

Black, P., and D. William. 1998. Inside the black box: Raising standards through classroom assessment. *Phi Delta Kappan* 79(8): 139–148.

Earl, L. M. 2002. Assessment as learning. In *The keys to effective schools* (pp. 65–73), edited by W. D. Hawley, with D. L. Rollie. Thousand Oaks, CA: Corwin Press.

Hawley, W. D., ed. (with D. L. Rollie). 2002. *The keys to effective schools: Educational reform as continuous improvement.* Thousand Oaks, CA: Corwin Press.

Nathan, J., and N. Johnson. 2000. *What should we do? A practical guide to assessment and accountability in schools.* Minneapolis, MN: Hubert Humphrey Institute of Public Affairs, University of Minnesota.

Stiggins, R. L. 1999. Teams. *Journal of Staff Development* 20(3): 17–19.

Stiggins, R. L. 2001. *Student-involved classroom assessment.* Upper Saddle River, NJ: Prentice Hall.

Veale, J. R., R. E. Morley, C. L. Erickson, and J. Dryfoos. 2001. *Practical evaluation for collaborative services: Goals, processes, tools and reporting-systems for school-based programs.* Thousand Oaks, CA: Corwin Press.

Strategy #44:

Elias, M. J., J. E. Zins, R. P. Weissberg, K. S. Frey, M. T. Greenberg, N. M. Haynes, R. Kessler, M. E. Schwab-Stone, and T. P. Shriver. 1997. *Promoting social and emotional learning: Guidelines for educators.* Alexandria, VA: Association for Superior Curriculum Development.

Flaxman, E., C. Ascher, and C. Harrington. 1988. *Youth mentoring: Programs and practices* (Urban Diversity Series No. 97). New York: Columbia University, Teachers College Press. (ERIC Document Reproduction Service No. ED308257)

Integrated Research Services. 2002. Mentoring issue. *Prevention Researcher* 9(1).

National Dropout Prevention Center. 1990. *Mentoring programs for at-risk youth.* Clemson, SC: Clemson University Press.

Strategy #45:

Billig, S. H. 2000. Research on K–12 school-based service learning: The evidence builds. *Phi Delta Kappan* 81(9): 658–663.

Duckenfield, M., and J. Wright, eds. 1995. *Pocket guide to service learning.* Clemson, SC: National Dropout Prevention Center.

Gomez, B. 1999. *Service learning: Every child a citizen* (Issue Paper). Denver, CO: Education Commission of the States.

Kielsmeier, J. C. 2000. A time to serve, a time to learn: Service learning and the promise of democracy. *Phi Delta Kappan* 81(9): 652–657.

Strategy #46:

American Academy of Child and Adolescent Psychiatry. 2002. *Children and TV violence.* Facts for families. Washington, D.C.: Author. Available at <www.aacap.org/publications/factsfam/violence.htm>

Rogers, M. 1994. *Resolving conflict through peer mediation. A series of solutions and strategies,* no. 9. Clemson, SC: National Dropout Prevention Center, Clemson University.

Wampler, F. W., and S. A. Hess. 1992. *Conflict mediation for a new generation—Training manual.* Harrisonburg, VA: Community Mediation Center.

Strategy #47:

Berman, S. 1997. *Children's social consciousness and the development of social responsibility.* Albany: State University of New York Press.

Robelen, E. W. 1998. Re-engaging young people. In *ASCD Info Brief: Education for Democratic Life*, no. 13. Alexandria, VA: Association for Supervision and Curriculum Development.

Wood, G. H. 1993. *Schools that work: America's most innovative public education programs*. New York: Plume.

Strategy #48:

Dewey, J. 1916. *Democracy and education*. New York: MacMillan.

Foxfire approach: Core practices. 1993. *Hands-On: A Journal for Teachers* 47: 2–3.

Herman, R., project director. 1999. *An educator's guide to school-wide reform* (Prepared by the American Institutes for Research). Washington, DC: Educational Research Service.

Ulichny, P. 2000. *Academic achievement in two expeditionary learning Outward Bound demonstration schools*. Available at <www.elschools.org/results/success/ulichny.html>

Strategy #49:

Carnegie Council on Adolescent Development, Task Force on Youth Development and Community Programs. 1992. *A matter of time: Risk and opportunity in the nonschool hours*. Washington, DC: Carnegie Council on Adolescent Development.

Fashola, O. S. 2002. *Building effective afterschool programs*. Thousand Oaks, CA: Corwin Press.

Hodgkinson, H. L. 1991. *Beyond the schools: How schools and communities must collaborate to solve the problem facing American youth*. Arlington, VA: American Association of School Administrators.

Strategy #50:

Schorr, L. B., and D. Schorr. 1989. *Within our reach: Breaking the cycle of the disadvantaged*. New York: Anchor Books.

For General Reading:

Adler, J. 1998. The tutor age. *Newsweek*, March 30, pp. 47–57.

Amundson, K. J. 1991. *101 ways parents can help students achieve*. Arlington, VA: American Association of School Administrators.

Aronson, R. 2001. *At-risk students defy the odds: Overcoming barriers to educational success*. Lanham, MD: Scarecrow.

Banks, R. 1997. *Bullying in schools*. ERIC Digest. (ERIC Document Reproduction Service No. ED407154)

Barr, R. D. 1999. *Final report: Governor's task force on safe schools*. Boise, ID: Center for School Improvement.

Barr, R. D., and W. H. Parrett. 1997. *How to create alternative, magnet, and charter schools that work.* Bloomington, IN: National Education Service.

Bempechat, J. 1999. Learning from poor and minority students who succeed in school. *Harvard Education Letter* 15(3): 1–3.

Benson, P. L., J. Galbraith, and P. Espeland. 1998. *What kids need to succeed: Proven practical ways to raise good kids.* Minneapolis, MN: Free Spirit.

Berman, S. 1997. *Children's social consciousness and the development of social responsibility.* Albany: State University of New York Press.

Black, P., and D. William. 1998. Inside the black box: Raising standards through classroom assessment. *Phi Delta Kappan* 79(8): 139–148.

Books, S., ed. 2006. *Invisible children in the society and its schools* (3d ed.). Mahwah, NJ: Lawrence Erlbaum.

Bracey, G. W. 2002. What students do in the summer. *Phi Delta Kappan* 83(7): 497–498.

Brandt, R. 2002. Customizing our schools: The case for diversified schooling. *Educational Leadership* 59(7): 12–19.

Brendtro, L. K., M. Brokenleg, and S. Van Bockern. 1990. *Reclaiming youth at risk.* Bloomington, IN: National Educational Service.

Brooks, R., and S. Goldstein. 2001. *Raising resilient children.* Chicago: Contemporary Books.

Brown, J. H., M. D'Emidio-Caston, and B. Benard. 2001. *Resilience education.* Thousand Oaks, CA: Corwin Press.

Campbell, L., and B. Campbell. 1999. *Multiple intelligences and student achievement: Success stories from six schools.* Alexandria, VA: Association for Supervision and Curriculum Development.

Carnegie Council on Adolescent Development, Task Force on Youth Development and Community Programs. 1992. *A matter of time: Risk and opportunity in the nonschool hours.* Washington, DC: Carnegie Council on Adolescent Development.

Carr, J. F., and D. E. Harris. 2001. *Succeeding with standards: Linking curriculum, assessments, and action planning.* Alexandria, VA: Association for Supervision and Curriculum Development.

Cawelti, G., and N. Protheroe. 2001. *How six school districts changed into high-performance systems.* Arlington, VA: Educational Resource Service.

Center for the Study of Reading. 1988. Ten ways to help your children become better readers (An excerpt from *Becoming a Nation of Readers*). Urbana-Champaign: University of Illinois, Center for the Study of Reading, Reading Research and Education. (ERIC Document Reproduction Service No. ED347496)

Chavkin, N. F. 1989. Debunking the myth about minority parents. *Educational Horizons* 67(4): 119–123.

Children's Defense Fund. 1998. *The state of America's children: Yearbook 1998.* Washington, DC: Author.

Clinchy, E. 2000. *Creating new schools: How small schools are changing American education.* New York: Teachers College Press.

Cole, R. W. 1995. *Educating everybody's children: Diverse teaching strategies for diverse learners.* Alexandria, VA: Association for Supervision and Curriculum Development.

Collins, J. 2001. *Good to great: Why some companies make the leap—And others don't.* New York: HarperBusiness.

Colorado Foundation for Families and Children. 1995. *School expulsions: Across system problem.* Denver, CO: Author.

Comer, J. P. 1980. *School power: Implications of an intervention project.* New York: Free Press.

Comprehensive Center. 2001. *Using data for educational decision-making.* Madison: University of Wisconsin.

Conrath, J. 1988. A new deal for at-risk students. *NASSP Bulletin* 72(504): 36–40.

Cooper, H. 2001. *The battle over homework: An administrator's guide to setting sound and effective and effective policies* (2d ed.). Thousand Oaks, CA: Corwin Press.

Cooper, H., J. C. Valentine, B. Nye, and J. J. Lindsay. 1999. Relationship between five afterschool activities and academic achievement. *Journal of Educational Psychology* 91:1–10.

Cushman, K. 1997. Demonstrating student performance in essential schools. *Horace* 14(2): 51. Available at Coalition of Essential Schools Web site: <www.essentialschools.org/cs/resources/view/ces_res/73>

Darling-Hammond, L. 1998. Alternatives to grade retention. *School Administrator* 55(7): 18–21.

Duckenfield, M., and J. Wright, eds. 1995. *Pocket guide to service learning.* Clemson, SC: National Dropout Prevention Center.

Duke, D. L. 2002. *Creating safe schools for all children.* Boston: Allyn & Bacon.

Easton, L. B. 2002. *The other side of curriculum.* Portsmouth, NH: Heinemann.

Education Commission of the States. 1996. *Youth violence: A policy maker's guide.* Denver, CO: Author.

Eisenberg, M., and Berkowitz. 2001. *Comparison of information skills process models.* Available at <www.big6.com/showarticle.php?id=87>

Elias, M. J., J. E. Zins, R. P. Weissberg, K. S. Frey, M. T. Greenberg, N. M. Haynes et al. 1997. *Promoting social and emotional learning: Guidelines for educators.* Alexandria, VA: Association for Superior Curriculum Development.

Fager, J., and S. Boss. 1998. *Peaceful schools.* Portland, OR: Northwest Regional Educational Laboratory.

Flaxman, E., C. Ascher, and C. Harrington. 1988. *Youth mentoring: Programs and practices* (Urban Diversity Series No. 97). New York: Columbia University, Teachers College. (ERIC Document Reproduction Service No. ED308257)

Fogarty, R. 1997. *Brain-compatible classrooms.* Thousands Oaks, CA: Corwin Press.

Fogarty, R. 1997. *Problem-based learning and other curriculum models for the multiple intelligences classroom.* Thousands Oaks, CA: Corwin Press.

Foxfire approach: Core practices. 1993. *Hands-On: A Journal for Teachers* 47: 2–3.

Frieman, B. B. 2001. *What teachers need to know about children at risk.* Boston: McGraw-Hill.

Fullan, M. 2000. Revisioning professional development. *Journal of Staff Development* 21(3): 40.

Gamoran, A. 1996. Do magnet schools boost achievement? *Educational Leadership* 54(2) 42–46.

Gerstner, L. V., Jr. 2002. The tests we know we need. *New York Times,* March 14, Sec. A, p. 7.

Gomez, B. 1999. *Service learning: Every child a citizen* (Issue paper). Denver, CO: Education Commission of the States.

Gordon, D. 2002. Curriculum access in the digital age. *Harvard Education Letter,* January/February.

Gronson, R. 2001. *At-risk students: Defy the odds.* Lanham, MD: Scarecrow.

Haberman, M. 1991. Pedagogy of poverty versus good teaching. *Phi Delta Kappan* 73(4): 290–294.

Hardy, L. 2000. Public school choice. *American School Board Journal* 187(2): 22–26.

Harrington-Lueker, D. 1998. Retention vs. social promotion. *School Administrator* 55(7): 6–12.

Hawley, W. D. 2002. *The keys to effective schools: Educational reform as continuous improvement.* Thousand Oaks, CA: Corwin Press.

Hermann, B., ed. 1994. *The volunteer tutor's toolbox.* Newark, DE: International Reading Association.

Hodgkinson, H. L. 1991. *Beyond the schools: How schools and communities must collaborate to solve the problem facing American youth.* (Part I by Harold Hodgkinson; Part II containing joint recommendations by American Association of School Administrators and National School Boards Association.) Arlington, VA: American Association of School Administrators.

Holcomb, E. L. 2004. *Getting excited about data: How to combine people, passion, and proof* (2d ed.). Thousand Oaks, CA: Corwin Press.

Integrated Research Services. 2002. Mentoring issue. *Prevention Researcher* 9(1).

Irving, L. C. 1999. *Falling through the Net: A report on the telecommunications and information technology gap in America.* Washington, DC: U.S. Department of Commerce National Telecommunications and Information Administration.

Jackson, A. W., and G. A. Davis. 2000. *Turning points 2000: Educating adolescents in the 21st century.* New York: Teachers College Press.

Jackson, B. L., and B. S. Cooper. 1993. Involving parents in urban high schools. *Education Digest* 58(8): 27–31.

Janey, C. B. 2002. Must high school last four years? *Educational Leadership* 59(7): 64–67.

Jones, R. 2001. How parents can support learning. *American School Board Journal* 188(9): 18–22.

Kann, L., S. A. Kinchen, B. I. Williams, J. G. Ross, R. Lowry, J. A. Grunbaum, and L. J. Kolbe. 2000. *Youth risk behavior surveillance, United States 1999.* National Centers for Disease Control Surveillance Summaries: MMWR 49(SS05). Washington, DC: U.S. Government Printing Office. Available at <www.cdc.gov/mmwr/preview/mmwrhtml/ss4905a1.htm>

Katz, L. G. 1994. *What should be learned in kindergarten?* Rockville, MD: ACCESS ERIC.

Keefe, J. W., and J. M. Jenkins. 1997. *Instruction and the learning environment*. Larchmont, NY: Eye on Education.

Kelly, K. 2001. Seeking a cure for senior-year slump. *Harvard Education Letter* 17(4): 1–4.

Kielsmeier, J. C. 2000. A time to serve, A time to learn: Service learning and the promise of democracy. *Phi Delta Kappan* 81(9): 652–657.

Koetke, C. 1999. One size doesn't fit all. *Technos Quarterly 8(2)*.

Lang, C. N. 1992. *Head start: New challenges, New champions*. Newton, MA: Education Development Center.

Levin, H. M. 1989. *Accelerated schools: A new strategy for at-risk students* (Policy Bulletin #6). Bloomington, IN: Consortium for Educational Policy Studies.

Levine, E. 2002. *One kid at a time: Big lessons from a small school*. New York: Teachers College Press.

Mahoney, J. 2002. *Power and portfolios: Best practices for high school classrooms*. Portsmouth, NH: Heinemann.

Making Afterschool Count. n.d. Periodic newsletter of the Charles Stewart Mott Foundation, no longer published. Archives available at <http://www.mott.org/publications.aspx>

Manning, M. L., and L. Baruth. 1997. *Teaching learners at risk*. Norwood, MA: Christopher-Gordon.

Marzano, R. J., J. S. Norford, D. E. Paynter, D. J. Pickering, and B. B. Gaddy. 2001. *A handbook for classroom instruction that works*. Alexandria, VA: Association for Supervision and Curriculum Development.

Maslow, A. 1967. *Toward a psychology of being*. Hoboken, NJ: Wiley.

Maslow, A. 1987. *Motivation and personality* (3d ed.). New York: Harper.

Meier, D. 1995. *The power of their ideas: Lessons for America from a small school in Harlem*. Boston: Beacon.

Mendler, A. N. 2000. *Motivating students who don't care*. Bloomington, IN: National Education Service.

Mendler, A. N., and R. L. Curwin. 1998. Seven keys to motivating difficult students. *Reaching Today's Youth* 3(3): 13–15.

Monroe, L. 1997. *Nothing's impossible: Leadership lessons from inside and outside the classroom*. New York: Times Books.

Muhlenbruck, L., H. Cooper, B. Nye, and J. J. Lindsay. 1999. Homework and achievement: Explaining the different strength of relation at the elementary and secondary level. *Social Psychology of Education* 3(4): 295–317.

Nathan, J. 1996. *Charter schools: Creating hope and opportunity for American education*. San Francisco: Jossey-Bass.

Nathan, J., and N. Johnson. 2000. *What should we do? A practical guide to assessment and accountability in schools*. Minneapolis: Hubert Humphrey Institute of Public Affairs, University of Minnesota.

National Association of Secondary School Principals. 1996. Breaking ranks: Changing an American institution. A report of the National Association of Secondary School Principals on the high school of the 21st century. *NASSP Bulletin* 80(578): 55–66.

National Board for Professional Teaching Standards. 1999. *What teachers should know and be able to do: Five core propositions.* Available at <www.nbpts.org/the_standards/the_five_core_propositio>

National Commission on Teaching and America's Future. 1996. *What matters most: Teaching for America's future* (Summary report). New York: Author.

National Commission on Time and Learning. 1994. *Prisoners of time.* Washington, DC: U.S. Government Printing Office.

National Institute of Child Health and Human Development. 2001. Bullying behaviors among U.S. Youth: Prevalence and association with psychosocial adjustment. *Journal of the American Medical Association, 285,* 2094–2100.

Newmann, F. M., W. G. Secada, and G. G. Wehlage. 1995. *Guide to authentic instruction and assessment: Vision, standards, and scoring.* Madison: Wisconsin Center for Educational Research, University of Wisconsin.

Northwest Regional Educational Laboratory. 1990. *Effective school practices: A research synthesis 1990 update.* Portland, OR: Author.

Northwest Regional Educational Laboratory. 1998. *Easy ways for families to help children learn.* Portland, OR: Author.

Northwest Regional Educational Laboratory. 2001. Focus on improved reading achievement. In *Using Educational Research and Development to Promote Student Success: 2001 Annual Report* (pp. 16–17). Portland, OR: Author.

Northwest Regional Educational Laboratory. 2001. Reading is thinking: Overcome literacy challenges. In *Using Educational Research and Development to Promote Success: 2001 Annual Report* (pp. 14–15). Portland, OR: Author.

Northwest Regional Educational Laboratory. 2001. Unlock the power of data. In *Using Educational Research and Development to Promote Student Success: 2001 Annual Report* (pp. 12–13). Portland, OR: Author.

Oakes, J. 1993. *Last chance high: How girls and boys drop in and out of alternative schools.* New Haven, CT: Yale University Press.

Parnell, D. 1982. *Neglected minority.* Washington DC: Community College Press.

Payne, R. K. 2001. *A framework for understanding poverty.* Highland, TX: Aha! Process.

Peck, C., L. Cuban, and H. Kirkpatrick. 2002. Techno-promoter dreams, student realities: The effect of increased technology access on the high school experience. *Phi Delta Kappan* 83(6): 472–480.

Peters, T. 1987. *Thriving on chaos.* New York: Alfred Knopf: 486.

Pipher, M. 1996. *Reviving Ophelia: Saving the selves of adolescent girls.* New York: Random House.

Pollack, W. 1998. *Real boys: Rescuing our sons from the myths of boyhood.* New York: Owl Books.

Pollack, W., and K. Cushman. 2001. *Real boys workbook: Exercises and advice about how to help boys be successful.* New York: Villard.

Pollack, W., and T. Shuster. 2000. *Real boys' voices: Anecdotes written by boys about their lives.* Toronto, Canada: Penguin Books.

Popham, W. J. 2000. *Testing! Testing! What every parent should know about school tests.* Boston: Allyn & Bacon.

Portner, J. 2001. Lost children. *Teacher Magazine* 12(8): 31.

Ramey, S. L., and C. T. Ramey. 1999. *Going to school: How to help your child succeed—A handbook for parents of children ages 3–8.* New York: Goddard.

Rasmussen, J. 1998. Looping—Discovering the benefits of multi-year teaching. *Education Update* 40(2): 1,3.

Readeance, J. E., T. W. Bean, and R. S. Baldwin. 2000. *Content area literacy: An integrated approach* (7th ed.). Dubuque, IA: Kendall/Hunt.

Reyes, P., J. D. Scribner, and A. P. Scribner. 1999. *Lessons from high-performing Hispanic schools.* New York: Teachers College Press.

Robelen, E. W. 1998. Re-engaging young people. In *ASCD Info Brief: Education for Democratic Life,* no. 13. Alexandria, VA: Association for Supervision and Curriculum Development.

Ryan, M. 2003. *Ask the teacher: A practitioner's guide to teaching and learning in the diverse classroom.* Boston: Allyn & Bacon.

Safe Schools and Communities Coalition, Correctional Office of Policy and Management, Juvenile Justice Advisory Committee. 1998. *Alternative education: A force for our future.* Washington, DC: Authors.

Sanders, M. G. ed. 2000. *Schooling students placed at risk: Research, policy, and practice in the education of poor and minority adolescents.* Mahwah, NJ: Lawrence Erlbaum.

Schmoker, M. 2001. *The results handbook.* Alexandria, VA: Association for Supervision and Curriculum Development.

Schneider, B., and Y. Lee. 1990. A model for academic success: The school and home environment of East Asian students. *Anthropology and Education Quarterly* 21(4): 358–77.

Schoenbach, R., C. Greenleaf, C. Cziko, and L. Hurwitz. 1999. *Reading for understanding: A guide to improving reading in middle and high school classrooms.* San Francisco: Jossey-Bass.

Senge, P. 2000. *Schools that learn: A Fifth Discipline fieldbook for educators, parents, and everyone who cares about education.* New York: Doubleday/Currency.

Silver, H. F., R. W. Strong, and M. J. Perini. 2000. *So each may learn: Integrating learning styles and multiple intelligences.* Alexandria, VA: Association for Supervision and Curriculum Development.

Slavin, R. E. 2000. Letter to the editor: Research overwhelmingly supports success for all. *Phi Delta Kappan* 81(7): 559–560.

Slavin, R. E., N. L. Karseit, and B. A. Wasik. 1992. Preventing early school failure: What works. *Educational Leadership* 50(4): 10–18.

Slavin, R. E., and N. A. Madden. 1989. What works for students at risk: A research synthesis. *Educational Leadership* 46(5): 4–13.

Slavin, R. E. and N. A. Madden. 2000. Research on achievement outcomes of success for all: A summary and response to critics. *Phi Delta Kappan* 82(1): 38–40, 59–66.

Stern, D., M. Raby, and C. Dayton. 1992. *Career academics: Partnerships for restructuring American high schools.* San Francisco: Jossey-Bass.

Stiggins, R. L. 1999. Teams. *Journal of Staff Development* 20(3): 17–19.

Stiggins, R. L. 2001. *Student-involved classroom assessment.* Upper Saddle River, NJ: Prentice Hall.

Stone, R. 2002. *Best practices for high school classrooms: What award-winning secondary teachers do.* Thousand Oaks, CA: Corwin Press.

Stringfield, S., and D. Land, eds. 2002. *Educating at-risk students* (Yearbook of National Society for the Study of Education, vol. 101, part 2). Chicago: University of Chicago Press.

Springfield, S. and D. Land, eds. 2002. The extent and consequence of risk in US education. In *Educating at-risk students* (Yearbook of National Society for the Study of Education, vol. 101, part 2, pp. 1–28), edited by S. Stringfield and D. Land. Chicago: University of Chicago Press.

Strong, R. W., H. F. Silver, and M. J. Perini. 2001. *Teaching what matters most: Standards and strategies for raising student achievement.* Alexandria, VA: Association for Supervision and Curriculum Development.

Stronge, J. H. 2002. *Qualities of effective teachers.* Alexandria, VA: Association for Supervision and Curriculum Development.

Sylwester, R., ed. 1998. *Student brains, school issues: A collection of articles.* Thousand Oaks, CA: Corwin Press.

Taylor, B. M., and P. D. Pearson. 2002. *Teaching reading: Effective schools, accomplished readers.* Mahwah, NJ: Lawrence Erlbaum.

Tomlinson, J. 1999. A changing panorama. *Infobrief,* Issue 17. Alexandria, VA: Association for Supervision and Curriculum Development.

U.S. Department of Education. 1999. *Preventing bullying: A manual for schools and communities.* Washington, DC: Author.

Vancouver Public Schools. 2001. *Report to the community* 12(1): 107. (Vancouver, B.C., Canada)

Veale, J. R., R. E. Morley, C. L. Erickson, and J. Dryfoos. 2001. *Practical evaluation for collaborative services: Goals, processes, tools, and reporting-systems for school-based programs.* Thousand Oaks, CA: Corwin Press.

Walser, N. 1998. Multi-age classrooms: An age-old grouping method is still evolving. *Harvard Education Newsletter* 14(1): 1–3.

Walsh, J. A., and B. D. Sattes. 2000. *Inside school improvement: Creating high-performing learning communities.* Charleston, WV: Appalachian Educational Laboratory.

Wampler, F. W., and S. A. Hess. 1992. *Conflict mediation for a new generation—Training manual.* Harrisonburg, VA: Community Mediation Center.

Weertz, M. 2002. The benefits of themed schools. *Educational Leadership* 59(7): 68–71.

Weisstein, E. 2001. A high school diploma . . . and more. *Educational Leadership* 58(6): 73–77.

West, P. 1996. Career academies appear to benefit students and teachers. *Education Week,* June 19, p. 15.

Wheaton, C., and S. Kay. 1999. Every child will learn to read—We guarantee it. *Educational Leadership* 57(2):52–56.

Wheelock, A. 1992. *Crossing the tracks: How "untracking" can save America's schools.* New York: New Press.

Wisely, S. 1999. *The senior project: A roadmap to student success.* Medford, OR: Medford School District.

Wood, G. H. 1993. *Schools that work: America's most innovative public education programs.* New York: Plume.

Yap, K. O., and D. Y. Enoki. 1995. In search of the elusive magic bullet: Parental involvement and student outcomes. *School Community Journal* 5(2): 97–106.

References

American Academy of Child and Adolescent Psychiatry. 2002. *Children and TV violence. Facts for families.* Washington, DC: Author. Available at <www.aacap.org/publications/factsfam/violence.htm>

August, D., and K. Hakuta, eds. 1998. *Educating language-minority children.* Washington, DC: National Academy press.

Barnett, W. S. 1996. Lives in the balance: Age 27 benefit cost-analysis of the High/Scope Perry Preschool program. *Monographs of the High/Scope Educational Research Foundation, 11.* Ypsilanti, MI: High/Scope Press.

Barr R. D., and W. H. Parrett. 2001. *Hope fulfilled for at-risk and violent youth: K–12 programs that work* (2d ed.). Needham Heights, MA: Allyn & Bacon.

Barr R. D., and W. H. Parrett. 2007. *The kids left behind: Catching up the underachieving children of poverty.* Bloomington, IN: Solution Tree.

Barth, P., K. Haycock, H. Jackson, K. Mora, P. Ruiz. S. Robinson, and A. Wilkins. 1999. *Dispelling the myth: High-poverty schools exceeding expectations.* Washington, DC: Education Trust. (ERIC Document Reproduction Service No. ED445140)

Beane, A. L. 2005. *The bully-free classroom: Over 100 tips and strategies for teachers K–8.* Minneapolis, MN: Free Spirit.

Benard, B. 1991. *Fostering resiliency in kids: Protective factors in the family, school, and community.* Portland, OR: Northwest Regional Educational Laboratory.

Billig, S. H. 2000. Research on K–12 school-based service learning: The evidence builds. *Phi Delta Kappan* 81(9): 658–664.

Boykin, A. W., ed. 2000. *CESPAR findings 1994–1999.* Mahwah, NJ: Lawrence Erlbaum.

Bracey, G. W. 1989. Moving around and dropping out. *Phi Delta Kappan* 70(5): 407–410.

Bracey, G. W. 2002. Raising achievement of at-risk students—or not. *Phi Delta Kappan* 83(6): 431–432.

Bransford, J. D., ed. 1999. *How people learn.* Washington, DC: National Academy Press.

Burke, K. 2000. *What to do with the kid who . . . : Developing cooperation, self-discipline, and responsibility in the classroom.* Thousand Oaks, CA: Corwin Press.

Burke, N. 1998. *Teachers are special: A tribute to those who educate, encourage, and inspire.* New York: Random House.

Carnegie Council on Adolescent Development. 1989. *Turning points: Preparing American youth for the 21st century.* Report of the task force on education of youth adolescents. Washington, DC: Author.

Coleman, J., et al. 1966. *Equality of educational opportunities.* Paper prepared for a Harvard conference on the U.S. Office of Education Report on "Equality of Educational Opportunity," October 21, 1967, Cambridge, MA.

Comer, J. P., M. Ben-Avie, N. M. Haynes, and E. T. Joyner, eds. 1999. *Child by child: The Comer process for change in education.* New York: Teachers College Press.

Comer, J. P., N. M. Haynes, E. T. Joyner, and M. Ben-Avie, eds. 1996. *Rallying the whole village: The Comer process for reforming education.* New York: Teachers College Press.

Comprehensive School Reform Quality Center. 2006 October. *CSRQ Center report on middle and high school comprehensive school reform models.* Washington, DC: American Institutes for Research.

Comprehensive School Reform Quality Center 2006 November. *CSRQ Center report on middle and high school comprehensive school reform models.* Washington, DC: American Institutes for Research.

Conrath, J. 2001. Changing the odds for young people: Next steps for alternative education. *Phi Delta Kappan* 82(8): 585–587.

Cooke, G. 2007. *Keys to success for urban school principals* (2d ed.). Thousand Oaks, CA: Corwin Press.

Cotton, K. 2000. *The schooling practices that matter most.* Portland, OR: Northwest Regional Educational Laboratory.

Cromey, A. D. 2001. Data retreats: A conduit for change in schools. *Using Data for Educational Decision-Making: The Newsletter of the Comprehensive Center— Region VI* 6(1): 21–23.

Darling-Hammond, L. 1997. *The right to learn: A blueprint for creating schools that work.* San Francisco: Jossey-Bass.

Decker, L. E., et al. 1994. *Getting parents involved in their children's education.* Arlington, VA: National Association of School Administrators.

Delpit, L. 1995. *Other people's children.* New York: New Press.

Deming, W. E. 1986. *Out of the crisis.* Cambridge: Massachusetts Institute of Technology Press.

Dewey, J. 1916. *Democracy and education.* New York: Macmillan.

Dryfoos, J. G. 1998. *Full-service schools: A revolution in health and social services for children, youth, and families.* San Francisco: Jossey-Bass.

DuFour, R., and R. Eaker. 1998. *Professional learning communities at work: Best practices for enhancing student achievement.* Bloomington, IN: National Education Service.

Earl, L. M. 2002. Assessment as learning. In *The keys to effective schools* (pp. 65–73), edited by W. D. Hawley, with D. L. Rollie. Thousand Oaks, CA: Corwin Press.

Eaton, D. K., L., Kann, S. A. Kinchen, J. G. Ross, J. Hawkins, W. A. Harris, et al. 2006. *Youth risk behavior surveillance—United States 2005.* National Centers for Disease Control Surveillance Summaries: MMWR 55(SS05). Washington,

DC: U.S. Government Printing Office. Available at <www.cdc.gov/mmwr/preview/mmwrhtml/ss5505a1.htm.>

Education Trust. 2002. *Dispelling the myth over time.* Washington, DC: Author.

Eisenberg, M., and D. Johnson. 2000. *Computer skills for information problem solving: Learning and teaching technology in contest.* ERIC Digest. (ERIC Document Reproduction Service No. ED392463)

English, F. W. 1992. *Deciding what to teach and test* (Millennium ed.). Thousand Oaks, CA: Corwin Press.

Epstein, J. L. 1995. School/family/community partnerships: Caring for the children we share. *Phi Delta Kappan* 76(9): 701–712.

Epstein, J. L. 2001. *School, family, and community partnerships: Preparing educators and improving schools.* Boulder, CO: Westview.

Epstein, J. L., M. G. Sanders, B. S. Simon, K. Salinas, J. Clark, N. Rodriquez, et al. 2002. *School, family, and community partnerships: Your handbook for action* (2d ed.). Thousand Oaks, CA: Corwin Press.

ERIC Clearinghouse on Elementary and Early Childhood.1993. *What should be learned from kindergarten?* Urbana, IL: Author.

Fager, J., and R. Richen. 1999. *When students don't succeed: Shedding light on grade retention.* Portland, OR: Northwest Regional Educational Laboratory.

Fashola, O. S. 2002. *Building effective afterschool programs.* Thousand Oaks, CA: Corwin Press.

Federal Interagency on Child Family Statistics. 1997. *America's children: Key national indicators of well-being.* Washington, DC: National Center for Educational Statistics.

Fogarty, R. 1999. *How to raise test scores.* Thousand Oaks, CA: Corwin Press.

Frymier, J., L. Barber, R. Carriedo, W. Denton, B. Gansneder, S. Johnson-Lewis, et al. 1992. *Growing up is risky business and schools are not to blame: Final Report, Phi Delta Kappa Study of Students at Risk, vol. 1.* Bloomington, IN: Phi Delta Kappa.

Gamoran, A. 1996. Student achievement in public magnet, public comprehensive, and private city high schools. *Educational Evaluation and Policy Analysis* 18(1): 1–18.

Gardner, H. 1983. *Frames of mind: The theory of multiple intelligences.* New York: Basic Books.

Gardner, H. 1999. *Intelligence reframed: Multiple intelligences for the 21st century.* New York: Basic Books.

Glasser, D. 2002. *High school tutors: Their impact on elementary students' reading fluency through implementing a research-based instructional model.* Doctoral dissertation, Boise State University, Idaho.

Glickman, C. D. 2002. *Leadership for learning: How to help teachers succeed.* Alexandria, VA: Association for Supervision and Curriculum Development.

Godfrey, R. J. 1980. *Outward Bound: Schools of the possible.* Garden City, NY: Anchor Books.

Good, T. L., and J. E. Brophy. 2002. *Looking in classrooms* (9th ed.). Upper Saddle River, NJ: Pearson Education.

Grunbaum, J. A., L. Kann, L., S. A. Kinchen, J. G. Ross, J. Hawkins, R. Lowry, et al. 2004. *Youth risk behavior surveillance—United States 2003.* National Centers for Disease Control Surveillance Summaries: MMWR 53(SS02). Washington, DC: U.S. Government Printing Office. Available at <www.cdc.gov/mmwr/ preview/mmwrhtml/ss5302a1.htm>

Gurian, M. 2001. *Boys and girls learn differently! A guide for teachers and parents.* San Francisco: Jossey-Bass.

Haberman, M., and V. Dill. 1993. The knowledge-base on retention vs. teacher ideology: Implication for teacher preparation. *Journal of Teacher Education* 44(5): 352–360.

Harlow, C. 2003 January. *Bureau of Justice Statistics special report: Education and correctional populations.* Washington, DC: U.S. Department of Justice, Office of Justice Programs. Available at <www.ojp.usdoj.gov/bjs/pub/pdf/ecp.pdf>

Haycock, K. 2006. *Teaching inequality: How poor and minority students are short-changed on teacher quality.* Washington, DC: Education Trust.

Head Start. 2007. *Head Start Program fact sheet, fiscal year 2007.* Available at <http://www.acf.hhs.gov/programs/hsb/about/fy2007.html>

Herman, R., project director. 1999. *An educator's guide to schoolwide reform* (Prepared by the American Institutes for Research). Arlington, VA: Educational Research Service.

Hilliard, A., III. 1991. Do we have the will to educate all children? *Educational Leadership* 49(1): 31–36.

Hootstein, E. 1998. Motivating the unmotivated child. *Teaching PreK-8,* 29(3): 58–59.

Howley, C., and R. Bickel. 2002. The influence of scale: Small schools make a big difference for children from poor families. *American School Board Journal* 189(3): 28–30.

Jagers, R. J., and G. Carroll. 2002. Issues in educating African American children and youth. In *Educating at-risk students* (Yearbook of National Society for the Study of Education, vol. 101, part 2, pp. 49–65), edited by S. Stringfield and D. Land. Chicago: University of Chicago Press.

Jensen, E. 1998. *Teaching with the brain in mind.* Alexandria, VA: Association for Supervision and Curriculum Development.

Jerald, C. D. 2001. *Dispelling the myth revisited: Preliminary findings from a nation-wide analysis of "high-flying" schools.* Washington, DC: Education Trust. (ERIC Document Reproduction Service No. ED445140)

Johnson, D. W., and R. T. Johnson. 1999. *Learning together and alone: Cooperative, competitive, and individualistic learning.* Boston: Allyn & Bacon.

Karoly, L. A., P. W. Greenwood, S. S. Everingham, J. Hoube, M. R. Kilburn, C. P. Rydell, et al. 1998. *Investing in our children: What we can learn and don't know about the cost and benefits of early childhood education.* Santa Monica, CA: RAND.

Keefe, J. W., and J. M. Jenkins. 2002. Personalized instruction. *Phi Delta Kappan* 83(6): 440–447.

Kohl, H. 1994. *I won't learn from you and other thoughts on creative maladjustment.* New York: New Press.

Kozol, J. 1991. *Savage inequalities: Children in America's schools.* New York: Hayser Perennial.

Krovetz, M. L. 1999. *Fostering resiliency: Expecting all students to use their minds and hearts as well.* Thousand Oaks, CA: Corwin Press.

Kuykendall, C. 1992. *From rage to hope.* Bloomington, IN: National Education Service

Ladson-Billings, G. 1994. *The dreamkeepers: Successful teachers of African-American children.* San Francisco: Jossey-Bass.

Land, D. and N. Legters. 2002. The extent and consequences of risk in U.S. education. *Educating at-risk students* (pp. 1–28), edited by S. Stringfield and D. Land. Chicago: National Society for the Study of Education.

Loveless, T. V. 1998. *The tracking and ability grouping debate.* Washington, DC: Thomas B. Fordham Foundation.

Marzano, R. J. 1998. *A theory-based meta-analysis of research on instruction.* Aurora, CO: Mid-continent Research for Education and Learning.

Marzano, R. J., D. J. Pickering, and J. E. Pollock. 2001. *Classroom instruction that works: Research-based strategies for increasing student achievement.* Alexandria, VA: Association for Supervision and Curriculum Development.

Massell, D. 2000. *The district's role in building capacity: Four strategies.* Philadelphia: Consortium for Policy Research in Education.

McLaughlin, B., and B. McLeod. 1996. *Educating all our students from culturally and linguistically diverse backgrounds,* vol. 1. Santa Cruz, CA: National Center for Research in Cultural Diversity and Second-Language Learning.

National Association of Attorneys General. 2000. *Bruised inside: What our children say about youth violence, what causes it, and what we need to do about it.* Olympia, WA: Author.

National Association of Secondary School Principals. 2004. *Breaking ranks II: Strategies for leading high school reform. A report of the National Association of Secondary School Principals on the high school of the 21st century.* Reston, VA: Author.

National Clearinghouse for Educational Facilities Center for School Change. 2001. *Smaller, safer, saner successful schools.* Minneapolis: Hubert Humphrey Institute of the University of Minnesota.

National Commission on the High School Senior Year. 2001. *The lost opportunity of senior year: Finding a better way* (Preliminary report, January 2001). Washington, DC: Author.

National Dropout Prevention Center. 1990. *Mentoring programs for at-risk youth.* Clemson, SC: Clemson University.

National PTA. 1998. *National standards for parent/family involvement programs.* Chicago, IL: Author. Available at <www.pta.org/archive_article_details_1118251710359.html>

Osher, C. 2001. *The impact of the senior project.* Greensboro, NC: Regional Educational Laboratory at the SouthEast Regional Vision for Education (SERVE) University of Georgia.

Padron, Y. N., H. C. Waxman, and H. H. Rivera. 2002. Issues in educating Hispanic students. In *Educating at-risk students* (Yearbook of National Society for the Study of Education, vol. 101, part 2, pp. 66–88), edited by S. Stringfield and D. Land. Chicago: University of Chicago Press.

Parents Resource Institute on Drug Education (PRIDE). n.d. *Pride questionnaire report.* Available at <www.pridesurveys.com/Reports/index.html>

Peregoy, S. F., and O. F. Boyle. 2000. *Reading, writing, and learning in ESL: A resource book for K–12 teachers.* Upper Saddle River, NJ: Pearson Education.

Perie, M., R. Moran, and A. D. Lutkus. 2004. *Trends in academic progress: Three decades of student performance in reading and mathematics.* Washington, DC: National Assessment for Educational Progress.

Pianta, R. C., and M. J. Cox. 1999. *The transition to kindergarten.* Baltimore, MD: Brookes.

Pinnell, G. S. 1990. Success for low achievers through Reading Recovery. *Educational Leadership* 48(1): 17–21.

Pinnell, G. S., et al. 1994. Comparing instructional models for the literacy education of high-risk first graders. *Reading Research Quarterly* 29(1): 8–39.

Public Agenda. 2002 March 2. *Where's the backlash? Students say they don't fret standardized tests.* Available at <www.publicagenda.org/press/press_release_detail.cfm?list=44]>

Raywid, M. A. 1993. Finding time for collaboration. *Education Leadership* 51(2): 30–34.

Roderick, M. 1995. Grade retention and school dropout: Policy debate and research questions. *Phi Delta Kappan* 15(12): 1–6.

Rogers, M. 1994. *Resolving conflict through peer mediation. A series of solutions and strategies,* no. 9. Clemson, SC: National Dropout Prevention Center, Clemson University.

Sanders, M. G. 1996. *School-family-community partnerships and the academic achievement of African American urban adolescents* (Report #7). Baltimore, MD: Center for Research on the Education of Students Placed at Risk. (ERIC Document Reproduction Service No. ED402404)

Sanders, W. L., and J. C. Rivers. 1996. *Cumulative and residual effects of teachers on future student academic achievement.* Research Progress Report. Knoxville: University of Tennessee, Value-Added Research and Assessment Center.

Schargel, F. P., and J. Smink. 2001. *Strategies to help solve our school dropout problem.* Larchmont, NY: Eye on Education.

Schmoker, M. 1999. *Results: The key to continuous school improvement* (2d ed.). Alexandria, VA: Association for Supervision and Curriculum Development.

Schorr, L. B., and D. Schorr. 1989. *Within our reach: Breaking the cycle of the disadvantaged.* New York: Anchor Books.

Search Institute. 1997. *The 40 developmental assets for adolescents.* Available at <www.search-institute.org/assets/>

Shaywitz, B. A., and S. E. Shaywitz. 1990. Prevalence of reading disability in boys and girls: Results of the Connecticut Longitudinal Study. *Journal of American Medical Association* 264(8): 998–1002.

Shewhart, W. A. 1939. *Statistical method from the viewpoint of quality control.* Washington, DC: Department of Agriculture.

Slavin, R. E., and O. S. Fashola. 1998. *Show me the evidence! Proven and promising programs for America's schools.* Thousand Oaks, CA: Corwin Press.

Smith, G. R., T. B. Gregory, and R. C. Pugh. 1981. Meeting student needs: Evidence of the superiority of alternative schools. *Phi Delta Kappan* 62(8): 561–564.

Sylwester, R. 1998. *A celebration of neurons: An educator's guide to the human brain.* Alexandria, VA: Association for Supervision and Curriculum Development.

Teddlie, C., and S. Stringfield. 1993. *Schools make a difference: Lessons learned from a ten-year study of school effects.* New York: Teachers College Press.

Thorsen, C. 2003. *TechTactics: Instructional models for educational computing.* Boston: Allyn & Bacon.

Tomlinson, C. 1999. *The differentiated classroom: Responding to the needs of all learners.* Alexandria, VA: Association for Supervision and Curriculum Development.

Toole, P. 1999. *Essential elements of service learning.* St. Paul, MN: National Youth Leadership Council.

Ulichny, P. 2000. *Academic achievement in two Expeditionary Learning/Outward Bound demonstration schools.* Available at <www.elschools.org/results/success/ulichny.html>

U.S. Bureau of the Census. 2004. *Income, poverty, and health insurance coverage in the United States: 2004* (Report P60, n. 229, Table B-2, pp. 52–57). Available at <www.census.gov/prod/2004pubs/p60–226.pdf>

U.S. Department of Education. 1998a. *Early warning, timely response: A guide to safe schools.* Washington, DC: Author.

U.S. Department of Education. 1998b. *Promising practices: New ways to improve teacher quality.* Washington, DC: Author.

Wagner, T. 2002. *Making the grade: Reinventing America's schools.* New York: RoutledgeFalmer.

Walsh, M. 1997. Court strengthens protections for districts from civil rights suits. *Education Week* (16, May 7): 7.

Wasik, B., and R. E. Slavin. 1993. Preventing early reading failure with one-to-one tutoring: A review of five programs. *Reading Research Quarterly* 29(2): 179–200.

Wehlage, G. G., R. A. Rutter, G. A. Smith, N. Lesko, and R. R. Fernandez. 1989. *Reducing the risk: Schools as communities of support.* Philadelphia: Falmer.

Williams, R. B., and S. Dunn. 1999. *Brain-compatible learning for the block.* Thousand Oaks, CA: Corwin Press.

Winter, S. 1986. Peers as paired reading tutors. *British Journal of Special Education* 13(3): 103–106.

Wolfe, P. 2001. *Brain matters: Translating research into classroom practice.* Alexandria, VA: Association for Supervision and Curriculum Development.

Wright, S. P., S. P. Horn, and W. L. Sanders. 1997. Teacher and classroom context effects on student achievement: Implications for teacher evaluation. *Journal of Personnel Evaluation in Education* 11(1): 57–67.

Index